Education in Religion and the Emotions

Language and Christian Belief (Macmillan 1958)
Language and the Pursuit of Truth (C.U.P. 1960)
Reason and Morals (C.U.P. 1961)
Public Schools and Private Practice (Allen & Unwin 1962)
Philosophy and Religion (O.U.P. 1965)
Logic and Sexual Morality (Penguin 1965)
Thinking with Concepts (C.U.P. 1966)
Equality (Hutchinson 1966)
Education and the Concept of MentalHealth (Routledge 1968)
Introduction to Moral Education (Penguin 1968)
Philosophy (Heinemann 1969)
Moral Thinking (Heinemann 1970)

JOHN WILSON

Director, Farmington Trust Research Unit

Education in Religion
and the Emotions

HEINEMANN

LONDON

Heinemann Educational Books Ltd

LONDON · EDINBURGH · MELBOURNE
SINGAPORE · JOHANNESBURG · IBADAN
HONG KONG · TORONTO · AUCKLAND
NAIROBI · NEW DELHI

I SBN 0 435 80926 I
© Farmington Trust, Oxford 1971

First published 1971

Published by Heinemann Educational Books Ltd
48 Charles Street, London W1X 8AH

Printed in Great Britain by
C. Tinling & Co Ltd, London and Prescot

Contents

Acknowledgements

The Author and Publisher wish to thank the following for per-
mission to reproduce extracts from copyright material: The
Farmington Trust and Penguin Books Ltd for *Introduction to Moral
Education*; Edwin Cox and Routledge & Kegan Paul for *Changing
Aims in Religious Education*; A. J. P. Kenny and Routledge & Kegan
Paul for *Action, Emotion and Will*; G. E. M. Anscombe and Basil
Blackwell for *Intention*.

The Farmington Trust

The Trust is administered by a Council, the Chairman of which is A. D. C. Peterson, M.A., O.B.E., Director of the Department of Educational Studies at Oxford University. The Research Unit in Moral Education was set up under the Trust in October 1965, with Research Fellows in the fields of philosophy, psychology and sociology. The Unit is housed at 4 Park Town, Oxford (telephone Oxford 57456 and 56357); it is directed by John Wilson, and has the assistance of an academic steering committee.

Publications of the Trust that are particularly relevant to this book are given in the bibliography. Other publications include:

JOHN WILSON, *Approach to Moral Education:* pamphlet (Farmington Trust 1968)

JOHN WILSON, NORMAN WILLIAMS and BARRY SUGARMAN, *Problems of Research in Moral Education:* pamphlet (Farmington Trust 1968)

JOHN WILSON, *Approach to Religious Education:* a much simplified (pamphlet) version of some of the main points made in this book (Farmington Trust 1969)

JOHN WILSON, *Moral Thinking* (Heinemann 1969)

JOHN WILSON, *Testing and Assessment in Moral Education: conceptual notes* (Farmington Trust working paper 1969)

Moral Education: a journal (Pergamon Press, Oxford)

Preface

In the first publication of the Farmington Trust[1] we set out to give some shape and coherence to the subject of our research as enshrined in the phrase 'moral education'. This introductory work inevitably left a number of loose ends. In particular, the phrase led us (I think justifiably) to concentrate on one typical, perhaps central, aspect of morality: that is, on interpersonal morality, which we there described as being logically related to other people's interests and to certain other formal criteria and rules of procedure. This concentration involved a much less adequate treatment of other topics: in particular of religious and metaphysical ideals and outlooks, and the education of the emotions.

If it were possible to claim that these wider topics can be separated from the topic of morality and moral education without loss, the present work would not be strictly relevant to our task. But, as we said in the introductory volume, it is not possible: and indeed we there tried briefly to show their importance for and relevance to moral education.[2] The chief purpose of this book is to pursue them further.

This task has a severely practical aspect. The authorities of almost all nations set out to give their young people some kind of teaching in this area, under such titles as 'Christian values', 'socialist principles', 'national ideals', and so forth. Thus the title 'religious education' represents a going concern, both in this country and many others: and a lot of money and man-hours are spent on whatever this title is taken to represent. It would be strange if a great deal of what is practised under such titles as these were not relevant to what is or could be practised under the heading of 'moral education'. At the same time, a good deal of work, often informal or untitled, is going on which may be roughly described as 'education of the emotions'; and this is also highly relevant to moral education.

[1] JOHN WILSON *et al. Introduction to Moral Education* (Penguin Books 1968): henceforth referred to as *I.M.E.*

[2] *I.M.E.*, pp. 94–7, 176–83. See also Appendix VII.

It is a major part of the thesis of this book that these two topics are indivisible: in particular, that it is not possible to reach any coherent or satisfactory conclusions about religious education without placing it in a wider context. This cannot be done, of course, without trying to expose something of the logical foundations of religion and of the education of the emotions. The book is intended for educators, and I cannot hope to have produced as full, detailed and precise an account as some professional philosophers might wish. However, it may be that, even (perhaps particularly) for the pure philosopher, to face some such general question as 'What can we reasonably teach our children?' is a useful starting-point from which to approach the vast and intractable mass of material that goes under the headings of 'philosophy of religion' and 'the emotions'. So it may be that at least those philosophers who are interested in education will find something useful here. Meanwhile, those responsible in the world of practical affairs for religious education and the education of the emotions – whether for teaching, the education of students and student-teachers, for general policy-making, for the direction of research, or for any other such function – stand much in need of a clear, coherent account of the subject. I hope this will do the job.

Readers whose interest in these topics is not primarily academic or research-orientated – those who have syllabuses to make up, student-teachers to instruct, children to teach, and so forth – may find some of this book rather heavy going (just as some philosophers may find it rather light). I have done my best to help them by putting some of the less central points in Appendices, to which the reader need turn only if he wishes; I have tried to be as brief and lucid as possible throughout; and in Part III I have taken a few tentative steps off the conceptual platform into the area of practical teaching and practical politics. But I think it only fair to state my belief that it is impossible for philosophers simply to give 'conclusions', which educators can grasp without to some extent appreciating the reasons for them. Philosophy does not have 'conclusions': or if it does, they are not worth much by themselves.

I should like to express my thanks to the Council and Steering Committee of the Farmington Trust, especially to Alec Peterson, Harold Loukes, Professor R. M. Hare and Professor R. S. Peters; also to Professor Basil Mitchell, Alan Montefiore, Philippa Foot,

Derek Parfit, Tim Beardsworth, and many other critics; and in particular I am grateful to Mr J. R. Bambrough for letting me see the manuscript of his *Reason, Truth and God* before publication.

J. B. W. 1970

BIBLIOGRAPHICAL NOTE

Where bibliographical footnotes give only the author's name and the title of the work, fuller references may be found in the bibliography.

Abbreviations: P.A.S.: *Proceedings of the Aristotelian Society*

I.M.E.: *Introduction to Moral Education*, by JOHN WILSON *et al.* (Penguin Books 1968)

1. Statement of the problem

A. What 'Religious Education' Means

There is one use of the term 'education' whereby it cannot properly refer to just *any* way of operating on human beings: whereby we distinguish it from training, conditioning, indoctrinating, curing, brain-washing and other processes. In this use, 'education' involves initiating people into various forms of thought and activity in such a way that they are helped to become better informed, more understanding and more reasonable. 'Education' in religion cannot (logically) be a matter of inculcating or persuading people into a particular religious faith, or into the religious attitude generally. It must, rather, be a matter of helping them to become more reasonable in the sphere of religion. Similarly, the 'education of the emotions', whatever else we may mean by that phrase, cannot simply be a matter of conditioning people or inculcating certain emotions in them. It must rather be a matter of helping them to become more reasonable in the sphere of the emotions.

I shall not here argue that this is the only, or even the 'normal', use of the term 'education': those that wish to pursue this linguistic topic in depth may do so elsewhere.[1] But when I speak of education, I shall be using the term in a way which does distinguish it from other ways of dealing with human beings, on the lines described above. Those who are not concerned with education in this sense – not concerned, that is, with helping people to be reasonable (sane, sensible, rational, unprejudiced, etc.) in these areas – may still find certain parts of this book relevant: perhaps in particular Chapter 7, where I shall argue that most objectives associated with education in *any* sense of the word cannot, logically, be achieved by other than educational (in my sense) methods. But such people—I hope few – should be warned that my prime concern is with education as I have (roughly) defined it.

Any person interested in religious education, in this sense, would be inclined to pursue the problem along the lines suggested by

[1] See in particular R. S. Peters, *Ethics and Education*, Part I.

Professor Hirst for knowledge and education in general.[1] He would
first seek clarity about what 'form of thought' or 'form of knowledge'
religion is or can be reduced to; just as, if he were worried about
'historical education' or 'education in mathematics', he would first
try to get a clear idea about what 'history' or 'mathematics' were as
disciplines or subjects, what their logic was, how a person per-
formed well or badly in these forms, and hence how we could
educate people in them. It goes without saying that he would find
great difficulty in trying to clarify his ideas about religion in this
way: compared with history, or mathematics, or science, religion is
obviously a tough nut to crack. He might well feel, as he proceeded,
that there were difficulties in speaking of religion as a 'form of
thought' at all: that this model fitted mathematics and perhaps some
other disciplines well, but did not fit religion. But this would not
make him abandon his prime task, which would be to find out *what
sort of thing religion was*; what sort of activities were specifically
religious; and hence, what sort of education was appropriate to this
particular area. He would approach it, in other words, very much
as we approached moral education in an earlier work:[2] that is, he
would first try to make logical sense of it as a subject or topic; if not
exactly as a 'form of thought', at least as a coherent area of human
activity and hence of education.

Achieving this kind of clarity is a philosophical matter. It needs
to be said that there are many men and women, taking what may be
important educational or social decisions, who seem quite unaware
of the very existence of philosophical work that is highly relevant
to those decisions. Thus almost every day bishops and politicians,
headmasters and H.M.I.s (not to mention the members of innumerable conferences and the writers of innumerable reports, books and
pamphlets), discuss religious education, and may be reasonably
supposed to exercise some influence upon educational practice in
this respect. The same is true of the more nebulous areas labelled
'the education of the emotions' or 'mental health'. If one listed
some of the outstanding philosophers whose work has shed light
on the topic – Wittgenstein, Wisdom, MacIntyre, Flew, Bambrough, Hare, Mitchell, Braithwaite, Kenny, Williams, Peters,
and others – it would be interesting to know how many educationalists (a) knew that these writers had done some very important

[1] See his essay in R. Archambault's *Philosophical Analysis and Education*.
[2] *I.M.E.*, Part I

work on the topic, (b) had read them, (c) had understood them. If the results of such an enquiry were as depressing as I should expect, this would not imply that educationalists should remain silent on the whole topic of religious education, still less that they should shelve all decisions until all the philosophers' cows had come home (they never do). It would imply only that communications were very poor. But this is quite bad enough, and part of the purpose of this book is to do something towards remedying it.

It is important to see this philosophical task as having a necessary *priority*. Briefly, if we are not yet clear about what religion and religious education are, then other enquiries are logically premature and may be worthless. Until we know what aims we are trying to achieve under such headings as 'R.E.', 'moral education', the education of the emotions', and so on, we shall, necessarily, be at a loss to know what practical teaching-methods, what sort of syllabus, or even what general approach will meet those aims. Certainly we may, by accident as it were, hit on kinds of teaching which are popular, or seem to interest the children or to do them some kind of good. But we shall not know how to assess their merits, and we shall not even have a clear idea of their point or purpose. For the notions of 'assessment', 'merits', 'point' and 'purpose' all relate to goals and objectives, and these in turn relate to our own conception of the nature and logic of the form of discourse or activity.

For similar reasons, psychological and sociological research into 'religious belief' or 'religious education', however interesting in itself, can give no clear guidance to educational practice. For empirical findings are useful only if we are clear about, and agreed upon, our ends: as for instance in medicine, where we know what counts as 'health' and agree that we should make children healthy. But if we don't know what counts as 'being religious', and (consequently) don't know whether or in what sense we want to teach children to 'be religious', then we do not know *what* empirical findings are relevant.[1] The same applies to those who attempt to

[1] This is the trouble with, for instance, Ronald Goldman's *Religious Thinking from Childhood to Adolescence* (Routledge 1964) and other works; and it is regrettable, in view of the other merits and the influence of such works, that Goldman and his followers show little or no appreciation of the conceptual difficulties, or of the way in which these affect the status of such research. I mention this author only for the sake of example: the same point applies to most educational writers and research workers in empirical disciplines.

discover the attitude of parents, teachers, children and others to 'religious education', 'religious knowledge', and so forth: unless it is clear what these phrases *mean*, sociological enquiry is premature.

SOME POPULAR EVASIONS

The task, as I have described it, is obviously a very difficult one; and it is not surprising that many people try to evade it. Some do so deliberately, by claiming (in effect) that it is impossible or unnecessary. Impossible, some people say, because religion is 'not a rational matter', or 'not within the scope of reason', so that we could not in principle make the kind of educational sense of it that we want to make; unnecessary, other people say, because religion is so obviously unreasonable (childish, stupid, obsolete) that there is no educational sense to be made of it at all – to investigate its place in education would be like investigating the place of astrology or alchemy. We shall briefly consider each of these.

1. '*Religion not within the scope of reason*'[1]

Consideration of the criteria of rationality – of what it means to be reasonable – in the area of religion is apt to evoke the reaction expressed by such remarks as 'religion isn't a rational matter', or 'religion is a matter of faith, not reason'. Important points may emerge from such remarks: but, of the various uses to which we may put them, there is one which none of us (so at least I believe and hope) would on reflection wish to adopt. I refer to that use which consists of denying the merits – not the possibility – of any process which might be called *defending* religious belief, *justifying* it, or *giving good grounds* for it. To deny the possibility of doing this is, indeed, a respectable and widely held (though I think a mistaken) view. But to deny the merits of doing it, if it is possible, is to advocate a kind of anti-rationalism which in the last resort may be incoherent, and which is certainly not characteristic of the vast majority of religious believers.

It is true enough that a good deal of Christian and other religious apologetics creates the impression of being *ad hoc* and *post eventum*. *Ad hoc*, in that it often seems designed to meet fashionable or topical objections, the objections that arise in a particular generation, class, culture or historical period: and *post eventum*, in that the event of the author's arrival at belief comes first, and his apologetics after-

[1] See John Wisdom, *Paradox and Discovery*, Chapter 1.

wards. Hence such apologetics seem of little use to anyone who wants to start from scratch: to the adolescent or adult who is genuinely open-minded. For the crucial steps are always the first ones: as with many other activities, it is the way one starts that is both difficult and interesting. Many believers may indeed interpret the phrases I have used above ('defending', 'justifying', 'giving good grounds for') as a demand for apologetics in this sense only – that is, as a demand to make their position, which has not and perhaps could not be rationally arrived at, look as plausible as possible. This may be all that they feel they can do. But it is not, surely, all they feel they ought to do.

For the notions of rationality and reasonableness extend beyond these phrases. They are conceptually linked to words which all believers use about their beliefs: words like 'true', 'right', or 'appropriate'. None of these is comprehensible without bringing in the notion of *reasons* or *criteria*. Even if (which few believers would want to maintain, even in the modern religious climate) religion in no sense involves factual beliefs or assertions, but simply certain attitudes, feelings or commitments, there is nevertheless still a question of *justifying* these. Words like 'right' and 'appropriate', even if not 'true', are still applicable. A man may no doubt *have* a religious belief, or at least 'be religious' (whatever this may mean), whilst refusing to consider whether it is reasonable, appropriate, or right; and no doubt such a man may even try to persuade (in some loose sense of the word) others into adopting his religion. But such a man cannot deal with such questions as 'Why *ought* I to believe?' or 'Do I have any *right* to claim that what I believe is *worthy* of belief?' or even, perhaps, 'In what sense is what I have actually a *belief*?'[1] Such a man is reduced in effect to saying, 'Well, I utter certain words and have certain attitudes and feelings: but I have no reason to suppose that these words are true or important, or these attitudes appropriate – even for myself, let alone for other people'. If there are believers who are not only willing to say this, but can say it without any feeling of unease or dissatisfaction, this book is not for them. (And they had better not try to *educate* anybody.)

The importance of this remains the same, even though various religious believers might wish to describe the nature of their belief in terms somewhat different from those mentioned above. For

[1] See Chapter 2.

instance, the notion of religion as a *commitment* has been stressed in the last few decades. There are of course various kinds of commitment: commitment to an authority-figure, to a particular Church, to certain sacred writings, to some concept of 'conscience', or more generally to some picture of the universe in terms of which the person sees himself as a created and dependent being. But whatever the commitment – and very much more could of course be written about this particular concept – the same crucial questions arise, both for the individual believer and the educator: 'Is it a *reasonable* commitment?' '*Ought* people to commit themselves in this way, or to this sort of thing?' 'How would we *educate* people to make (or refrain from making) such commitments?' For, as even the most ardently 'committed' person must agree, it is plainly possible to make an unreasonable (false, dangerous, prejudiced, insane) commitment – to Baal-worship, the Nazi party, and so on. However we describe the concept of religion (and there is a sense in which religion 'means different things' to different people), these are the questions which the educator – and indeed any objective and unprejudiced person – is bound to face: and these are the questions we shall try to answer in this book.

2. 'Religion can be written off'
Some people are convinced that religion is so *obviously* silly that we need not waste our time taking it seriously as an educational topic. But this is, of course, to assume that we are already clear about what religion is: an assumption which I hope the reader may already see reason to doubt. In practice, many of those who hold this view are reacting sharply (and it may be, justifiably) either against one particular type of religion in itself, or against the indoctrination of children in a particular religion or the religious outlook generally. They would, for instance, be likely to be against compulsory R.E. in schools, on the grounds that R.E. is, necessarily, a form of indoctrination which serves the interests only of a particular church or group of believers. However, as we have seen, genuine 'religious education' cannot mean 'indoctrination in a particular religion' or anything like it.[1]

It is a point worth making, certainly, that religion as a form of

---

[1] Of course some teachers who are supposed to be doing R.E. may be indoctrinating, and this is regrettable. But what this shows is, not that R.E. is bad, but that they are not doing anything one could seriously call R.E.

activity or thought differs in some important respects from other activities such as mathematics, science, history, and even morality. One difference is this: whereas everybody is inevitably engaged in these latter activities, by no means everybody has a religion. It would be hard to see how human beings, living any sort of normal life, could avoid having to deal in some way or other with numbers, the natural world, the past, and relationships with other men: so that mathematics, science, history and morality seem inescapable. But it is simply not correct to say that religion is inescapable in the same way. This permits one to go on to say, if that is what one thinks, that religion is not only not necessary, but a positive waste of time, pernicious, a symptom of insecurity, or whatever. Indeed one could say this even if everybody did have a religion: the point is that religion is not inescapable for men.

Nevertheless (and we shall expand this in Chapter 5) it is much more implausible to maintain that any human being could be totally immune from those feelings, doubts, questions, and other phenomena which enter into religion, and for which religious belief purports to provide *one* sort of 'answer'. Even in our society, which may in some sense be, as sociologists of religion constantly tell us, now largely secular, what we may call 'metaphysical'[1] (as opposed to religious) belief still retains a hold. It is interesting, from the psychological and sociological standpoint at least – and perhaps for the philosopher as well – that there is one kind of metaphysical discourse in particular that seems to die hard. This is the discourse that includes these 'ultimate' questions and answers – questions like: 'What is everything for?' 'What is man's destiny?' 'What is the meaning of life?' 'Why does everything exist?' 'What is ultimate reality?' and so on, and answers like: 'God made everything', 'Life is meaningless', 'The universe is rationally planned', 'Reality is spiritual', and so forth.

Of course there are problems about what these 'ultimate questions' could conceivably mean.[2] A man who (rightly) does not wish to take such questions and answers at their face value, so to speak, may hold various opinions about them. He may think (with Freud) that to ask questions of this sort is a sign of mental illness, or (with some Christian psychologists) of mental health: that whatever feelings make people want to talk in this way can and

[1] See Chapter 5.
[2] On this see Appendix I.

should be grown out of, or can and should be grown into. But he cannot reasonably hold that the occurrence of such talk, even if it is only a symptom, is *unimportant* or cannot be taken seriously. The questions and answers do have a grip on our minds. It is plausible to maintain that in certain societies religion is dying out; it is infinitely less plausible to maintain that metaphysics is.

There is, therefore, a powerful pragmatic argument against those who simply wish to drop the whole business of religious education in our schools on the grounds that religion is not worth having. The argument is not only that it is far from clear whether religion is worth having or not, since it is far from clear what religion *is*: it is also that, whether it is worth having or not, people *have* it – and if what they have cannot always be called religion, it can certainly be called metaphysics. Nor is it certain, as some have claimed, that such belief is something which children do not naturally acquire, and only exists because it is imposed on them by adults. We have, then, to deal with the situation in some way. We cannot write off religion in the way that we might write off astrology, as something obviously unreasonable: nor in the way that we might write off bed-wetting, as something which most children grow out of naturally.

We turn now to two other evasions, which may be dealt with even more briefly.

3. *Education not in but about religion*

One might argue that children should know about the Bible because of its important effect on literature, that they should know about Christianity because of its contemporary social effects, that they should know about the Church because of its historical importance in our culture, and so forth. But this is to teach the history, or the literature, or the sociology *of* religion: it is not to teach religion. We may, if we like, make the child do some rigorous and hard-headed theology, in an endeavour to prevent the subject from becoming 'mushy'. But do we know whether there is any *point* in doing theology? Perhaps it is just another autistic academic game. What any intelligent person, even an intelligent child, will want to know is whether religion is true: or, if that word is inappropriate, whether it is *worth having*. He will want to know what are the criteria of success for religion – whether it is worth while playing the religious game at all, and if so, in what form. Failure to face up to this is merely to sidestep the whole problem.[1]

[1] *I.M.E.*, p. 182.

These are strong words. But it is important to recognize that such studies in themselves, though no doubt useful and valuable, are not central to education *in* religion: any more than, for instance, the history of mathematics is central to education *in* mathematics. They would more properly come under the headings of history, literature, etc. than under the domain 'religion' (just as the study of the architecture of Catholic cathedrals comes under architecture rather than under religion or Catholicism). These and other forms of discourse must be understood and taught separately, if 'religious education' is not to stand for a mere rag-bag of various disciplines and subjects taught (probably badly) in periods labelled 'religious education', 'R.I.', or 'R.K.' or 'scripture' or 'divinity'. The core of religious education does not lie here.

Nor, for the same reasons, is it sufficient to teach the child

about different creeds, usually under some such title as 'comparative religion', in the hope that we shall avoid forcing him to become Christian. Such a notion is not so much dangerous as inadequate. It amounts to a form of window-shopping, in which the child can buy whatever happens to appeal to him: and it indicates the bankruptcy of our thinking about morality and religion. What we are failing to provide is a set of standards, or a set of criteria of rationality, which are appropriate to the subject and which we can help the child to apply. If we do not do this – and in the case of religion we have notoriously failed to do it – we cannot be said in any serious sense to be educating the child: we are merely amusing him with a number of different pictures, which he cannot evaluate intelligently because neither he nor we know how.[1]

(This is like being content to confine moral education to teaching children about the various norms and *mores* of various cultures, together with any relevant sociology, psychology and history, without offering them any criteria or principles by which to evaluate these norms and *mores*.)

4. *Teaching a publicly acceptable religion*
In the prevailing pluralism and chaos about religious belief, valiant but misconceived efforts have been made to establish 'common ground' for religious education shared by different sects of Christianity, by Christians and humanists, and (for all I know) by all the religions, metaphysics and 'philosophies' of the world. We need

[1] *I.M.E.*, p. 214.

not repeat here arguments already deployed against the parallel attempt to find common ground in morality:[1] the basic objections are (a) that beliefs may be politically or publicly acceptable at a particular time in a particular society but still be false and possibly dangerous; (b) that in any case it is not the job of the educator to sell any particular or partisan set of beliefs, whether publicly acceptable or not.

I hope there is no need to argue these points at length here. What is important is that establishing 'common ground', in any useful sense, cannot be done simply by taking the highest common factor (so to speak) of all prevailing religious or other creeds: or by reaching some kind of political agreement or compromise about what values or beliefs to put across to our children. Education is not a matter of politics or fashion. Common ground can only be established by first getting clear about what sort of thing religion is.

5. Teaching 'a religious outlook'

Another move is very popular nowadays, and requires a somewhat longer treatment. Many writers have appreciated that points 3 and 4 above are evasions, and have tried to put religion on the map as a subject in its own right by extending the concept of religion (and hence the concept of R.E.) in a way that will be less doctrinaire or less offensive to modern tastes. Unfortunately this approach does not do the job either.

I take as an example passages from a book which (I must say at once) seems to me extremely well written and interesting. The author is considering the possible aims of religious education.[2] He first considers three possible aims, and regards them as not wholly adequate (teaching the Bible, teaching morals, and converting to Christianity). In discussing the last of these, he very properly writes:[3] '. . . to look on religious education as aiming at conversion –

---

[1] *I.M.E.*, pp. 23–8.
[2] *Changing Aims in Religious Education*, by Edwin Cox, p. 53 ff. The fact that I use this book as an example of the difficulties mentioned below does not mean that it is not also an example of how a very clear and sensible book may be written without these difficulties being resolved. Indeed, I have chosen it partly for this reason: for its very clarity shows the gap that requires to be filled more obviously than books of a more confused and turbulent kind. I ought also perhaps to say that I am in general agreement with the author's practical conclusions.
[3] op. cit., p. 63.

or, to use an emotionally less respectable term, indoctrination – is to put it out of line with present educational theory'; later, 'To regard religious education as aiming at conversion is . . . to base it on ecclesiastical rather than educational principles': and again, 'But while it may be permissible to give guidance on how to behave to children . . . is it educationally sound, or even possible, to tell them what they are to think or believe?'[1]

Short of an extensive philosophical account, one could hardly hope for a clearer understanding of the differences between education and indoctrination. But the difficulties appear when the author considers a fourth possible aim, which he takes to be the main aim of religious education: 'to help pupils have a religious view of life and to make up their own minds on religious questions'. The author explains:

> By 'a religious view of life' is meant these attitudes: that man is one part of the whole complex of creation, the most highly developed and sensitive part, but none the less bound in a close relationship with the other parts which are to be respected and not ruthlessly exploited for the pleasure either of the individual or the species; that the individual has to live among his fellows, who have to be accorded the same consideration that he gives himself; that the whole has some overall purpose which has to be sought, even if it can only be partially understood; that apprehension of that purpose will give a clue to practical decisions and lead to the adoption of a moral code; and that aesthetic experience, as well as rational thought, can give awareness of that purpose, so that natural beauty and the arts are to be revered and cultivated as one of the roads to truth.

The author continues,

> It will be pointed out that this is the aim of education in general. What then is the specific aim of religious education? It will be to help cultivate these attitudes and, in particular, to help children to appreciate the questions that such attitudes raise, and consciously to seek the answers for themselves. These questions are of the type: 'Is creation adequately explained as a series of connected and mechanically caused events?'; 'Is there some spiritual reality of which the created world is but an outward manifestation?'; 'If so, does that spiritual reality reside in some single personal source which men have called "God"?'; 'Has an individual's life significance in its own right, or is it important only as part of some greater process?'; 'Is it possible for us to have any knowledge of what that significance is?'

[1] op. cit., p. 64.

I have quoted this passage in full, because it illustrates the crux so well. *For the only specifically religious (or metaphysical) features of this programme are precisely those features which we ought to have doubts about.* Few rational people object to teaching children to respect and consider their fellows, or to appreciate natural beauty and the arts. But plenty object to teaching children that 'the whole has some overall purpose', or that 'apprehension of that purpose will give a clue to practical decisions'. They would object to any mode of teaching which implied that children *ought* to ask, and try to answer, the kind of questions mentioned above: what the author, in common with many other people, calls 'ultimate questions'. The objection is not to this or that specific 'religious answer' to 'religious questions', but to the whole business of persuading or even 'helping' children to ask and answer questions of this sort: not to indoctrination in this or that particular religious view, but to indoctrination in the religious or 'metaphysical' outlook generally.

Those with what might be described as 'left-wing', tough-minded, positivist, anti-indoctrination temperaments may therefore fairly make the point that this programme is still a form of indoctrination, though a highly generalized one. Children are being encouraged to be, if not specifically religious, at least 'metaphysical'. Granted (as we observed in 2 above), this may be a widespread human tendency: but it is not one to be encouraged – or at least its desirability has to be shown. Of course it sounds high-minded, and may by its vagueness avoid offending those people who would have been offended by any insistence on the inculcation of specific religious doctrines: but it is no real improvement.

Those with different, more 'right-wing' or traditionalist leanings, may also fairly make a criticism. They could point out that authors of this kind are simply using the aegis and title of 'religion' or 'R.E.' to advance types of teaching, and general values, which they think appropriate to pupils in this day and age, and which are not 'out of line with present educational theory'. Their values are liberal, 'child-centred', 'open-ended', and so on: no doubt other liberals would agree with them, and of course they are borne onwards by a rising tide of fashion. But other authors, who think that religion has more to do with the acceptance of authority, obedience, etc., may fairly advocate different aims, and different methods. These may be unfashionable, but who is to say that they are wrong?

Thus atheists and agnostics will object that what the liberal authors offer as a necessary part of the child's diet is in fact either a dangerous drug, or a mere sop, a placebo, like a baby's dummy: authoritarian believers will agree that it is necessary, but claim that the diet does not contain enough calories, that the meat is not strong enough.

Both these criticisms are fair, but there are two others which seem to me far more important. First, it is not clear that such authors are discussing anything that might reasonably and speci- fically be called *religion* or *religious* belief. What we are being offered is something that looks more like a political compromise than a genuine solution; and for that very reason, it seems remote, abstract, airy-fairy, and a long way from what the word 'religion' means to most ordinary people. For fear that we may be inculcating one particular version of religious belief, which some of us may regard as old-fashioned or partisan, we so water down the concept of religion that it is barely recognizable as religion at all. To talk of 'spiritual reality' or 'ultimate concern' may offend fewer people than talk about Jehovah and Jesus, but it may also inspire fewer people; and it is in any case not clear that it will inspire them in a specifically *religious* way.

Second, and more important, this retreat from what is specifically religious to what I have called 'metaphysics' – the area of 'general ideals', 'ultimate values', 'ultimate concern', and so forth – does nothing in itself to solve our problem. For problems about the nature of this sort of 'metaphysics' are just as hard as (in fact harder than) problems about the nature of religion. We still need to know just what this area (not now religion but 'metaphysics') is, how one performs well or badly in it, what counts as being reasonable in it, and what educational objectives it incorporates for the teaching of children. No advance has been made on any of these central questions.

This is partly because it is easy to be philosophically naïve about this kind of talk. It is still generally supposed that the significant gulf is between those who give one sort of 'answer', the religious answer, to these questions, and those who give another sort. Thus Bishop Sansbury in a letter to the *Observer*: 'The gulf between those who believe they see the glory of God in the face of Jesus Christ and those who believe in a closed and self-explanatory universe . . .'. Again, Mr Cox, in the last words of his book, says that religious education is 'a search based on the belief that life has been given us with point and purpose by a personal power greater than man, and is therefore not "a tale told by an idiot, full of sound and fury, signifying nothing".' But why should we believe *either* of these? What would it *mean* to believe either? These are the important questions: and the important gulf for our purposes is between those to whom these questions appear sufficiently straightforward and unworrying for them to feel happy about answering them without ado, and those to whom the *sense, meaning* or *use* of the questions seems thoroughly problematic.

B. THE RELEVANCE OF THE EMOTIONS

The conjunction of religious belief with the emotions may seem strange to some, or mistaken to others. I have conjoined them because I believe that the same conceptual problems underlie both. Some connection between the two has, of course, been widely acknowledged, particularly by the psychoanalytic school of writers: but such acknowledgement has been chiefly of an empirical connection between the psychic states of individuals and the kind of religion those individuals have. Our concern will be rather with the conceptual connection between the two: that is, between the criteria whereby we should judge the truth or correctness of religious beliefs, and the criteria whereby we should make judgements about the emotions. This connection has generally remained unacknowledged. A good deal of the first part of this book will be devoted to demonstrating the connection, and we shall not pursue it here at length; but it is worth trying to show briefly why we are inevitably led on from the one topic to the other – and why, in consequence, it would be unsatisfactory to try to deal with the topic of religious education without conjoining it to some consideration of the education of the emotions.

Many religious believers themselves speak in a way which implies the kind of connection we shall later try to establish. It will be worth our while here to consider some (fragmentary) quotations from an interesting article by Colin Alves.[1]

> The purpose of religious education is to help our pupils build up *a worthwhile sense of direction in life, to help them achieve a valid perspective on the whole business of living.* To deny them the religious

[1] *The Times Educational Supplement*, 24 March 1967: my italics throughout.

element in education, at any stage, is to imply that all attempts to achieve a sense of direction are pointless and not worth bothering with.

Again,

> Religious education is fundamentally concerned with the *education of attitudes*, not with the study of cultures, nor with the assessment of systems of belief (though, of course, both the latter play their part in the former). It is concerned with the pupil's development of *a faith in which to travel through life*.

As with many other such statements, one is here in doubt about which way the author would jump on a number of crucial issues; in particular about how far he is interested in anything one could strictly call *religion*. Our problem is to know what would count as a child's having developed 'a faith', 'a sense of direction', 'a valid perspective', etc. The possibilities are:

- (i) Some particular religious faith (thus Christianity might count, but Buddhism and Islam not);
- (ii) Any religious faith (Christianity and perhaps Buddhism would count, but Marxism not);
- (iii) The right sort of religious faith (Christianity, perhaps Buddhism, but not Baal-worship);
- (iv) The right sort of faith, not necessarily religious (perhaps existentialism or humanism might count, but Marxism or materialism not);
- (v) Any sort of overall creed or metaphysic;
- (vi) Simply the right sort of attitudes, a 'healthy' outlook on life, etc.

No doubt the author regards some of these as unreal choices: as a Christian he may think, for instance, that in practice the Christian faith (i) *is* the only one that will give a child the right perspective or a 'healthy' outlook (vi). But the truth of this, and of any other such particular propositions, has to be shown. Conceptually (i)–(vi) are all different; and if we are setting out a statement of aims, we have to decide between them. Only (vi), in fact, is wholly unexceptionable to any rational person: for all the others assume the merits of a particular faith, or of a particular type of faith, or of the notion 'having a (any) faith'. As we have seen earlier, this cannot be assumed.

The distinction between (v) and (vi) – between anything that we could reasonably call a *faith* and just a healthy outlook – is very blurred: and the terms used by the author ('sense of direction', 'valid perspective') do nothing to sharpen it. It is a commonplace of psychological writings that the mentally healthy person will not live purely for the moment, but will have a number of long-term aims: that he will incorporate a number of different aspects of his life within these aims: that he will have 'a sense of proportion', approach life with confidence and happiness, and so forth. Psychologists with a preference for a metaphysical diction may express some of these truisms by saying that such a person's life will be 'meaningful', or that he will be 'sustained by his faith in life', or 'find value in human existence' (a phrase also used by Alves in the same article). If this is all that is meant by 'a faith to live by', then we can make no objection: for all that these phrases point to are criteria of rationality or 'mental health'. But if it is meant that the rational or 'mentally healthy' individual must assent to a number of propositions about 'the meaning', or 'the purpose' of life, and about 'the supernatural': and in particular if it is meant that he should regard himself as in some way *placed* in the world by some external superbeing, Nature, Life-Force or whatever, whose purposes and intentions he is bound to accede to; then, so far from being truistic, such a view seems highly dubious.

What is plain from all this is that those who – like the author, and in my opinion rightly – regard religious education as 'fundamentally concerned with the education of attitudes', whatever else it may be concerned with, cannot avoid making some attempt to clarify what the aims of such education *in general* should be. Attitudes involve emotions: and whether or not there are any specifically religious emotions, it is plain that religion offers us at least an arena in which all the most important emotions are considered and dealt with in one way or another. Most modern religions – and one may include quasi-religions, such as extreme forms of Marxism or hero-worship – make some attempt to deal with the whole range of human emotions. Thus in the New Testament and equally in the Koran, Buddhist writings, Communist handbooks and elsewhere, we read not only of awe, reverence and worship, but also of pity, forgiveness, anger, hatred, lust, guilt and so on. These and other emotions are catered for by various religions and other outlooks: they are considered, criticized, assigned to certain objects deemed to be appropriate, and so forth.

To put it briefly, science may have taken over any claims religion might have made to deal with empirical facts: but, despite the rise of such neutral approaches as psychoanalysis, religion is still very much concerned with the emotions in general: with their education and proper direction. In turning to the emotions and the education of the emotions, therefore, we shall not, in an important sense, have abandoned the topic of religion. The non-partisan educator (if this is not indeed a tautological phrase) will therefore be concerned to discover the general criteria of rationality involved in the education of the emotions, and to devise educational methods whereby his pupils can be helped to become more reasonable in their emotional lives. And these are likely to be very much the same criteria as those by which we should assess religious and metaphysical ideals and outlooks.

The difficulty of this task has been partly obscured, because in the past many have claimed to *know*, by some easy and certain way, just what emotions and attitudes people should have towards what objects and on what occasions. This is comparable to the claim to easy and certain knowledge about what is morally right and wrong or about what religious beliefs we ought to have. Such claims cannot be justified, and are in any case insufficient for the educator, who has to help children learn such things for themselves. As soon as we face this problem squarely, we can see how enormously complex and difficult the topic is. In what sense can emotions be said to be 'reasonable' or 'unreasonable'?[1] In what kinds of ways can a person fail to be 'emotionally educated'? How much can education, as opposed to other methods of dealing with people, help in such matters? These are some of the questions that face us; and we cannot have a clear and detailed grasp of the aims of religious education, and of the education of the emotions in other areas, until we have made some attempt to answer them.

I am not saying, of course, that religious education is the *same thing* as education of the emotions: though I hope to show that the

---

[1] Some people, misled by a popular antithesis between 'reason' and 'emotion' which is valid for some contexts but not for others, claim to find the notion of 'reasonable or unreasonable emotions' a strange one. Yet no doubt such people, like everyone else, say such things as 'He's unreasonably jealous', 'He had good reason to be angry', and so forth. The chief trouble here is the failure to realize that (to put it quickly) *beliefs are part of emotions*, not in some way additional to them. It is very unfortunate that this failure has also afflicted nearly all psychological research into emotions and attitudes. For a fuller account, see Chapter 7.

most important part of the former is coextensive with part of the latter, each will naturally have areas and aspects not shared by the other. In Part III of this book[1] the relationship is stated more fully: here it may be useful to give a simple sketch, so that the reader may see as clearly as possible why the two topics have to be treated conjointly:

Religious
Education

Education of the
Emotions

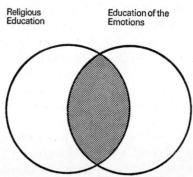

I have used the phrase 'education of the emotions': and there is indeed some (though not much) good philosophical literature on this topic. The vast bulk of current non-philosophical (mostly psychological or pseudo-psychological) literature, however, usually hangs itself on the peg labelled 'mental health'. This latter phrase is, I think, misleading for many, because it carries an air of false expertise: it suggests that there are experts who know what is 'mentally healthy', just as the existence of a curricular subject called 'religious knowledge' suggests that there are experts who know what sort of knowledge this is – and this suggestion, also, the reader may already see reason to doubt. However, some people are conditioned to respond more readily to the phrase 'mental health' than to 'the education of the emotions': and it is worth saying here that I hope they too will find parts of the text relevant to their problems, to which I have also devoted an Appendix[2].

In Part I of this book, then, (Chapters 2–4) we shall be dealing specifically with religion, relating the religious outlook towards the end of the part to the wider context of metaphysical outlooks and ideals in general, and their connections with the emotions (Chapter 5). In Part II we shall deal with the important problems of method-

[1] pp. 161–6.
[2] Appendix V.

ology which this presents (Chapter 6), and then go on to consider the education of the emotions in its own right (Chapters 7–10). Part III (Chapters 11 and 12) contains a brief account of some of the practical implications of our thesis for teaching and government; but we thought it more satisfactory to include psychological material, and suggestions for the detailed practical guidance of teachers and others, in separate volumes to be published later.

PART ONE

Religion

2. What is to count as religion?

Much that has been written about religion is vitiated by a partisan approach. This fact is obvious at some levels; less so at others. It is obvious when the author's intention is primarily apologetic – to attack or defend some particular creed, or to reinterpret and reinforce some particular religion. It is less obvious when the author makes no explicit attempt to consider the concept of religion, but tacitly employs some one element or elements of this concept in a culture-bound view: thus many appear to mean by 'religion' either some form of Christianity, or one of the 'higher' religions.[1] It is not obvious at all when philosophical writers investigate some particular phenomenon or concept under the general aegis of religion: thus there will be talk about 'sense of the contingent', or 'the existence of God', without it being at all clear whether these are either necessary or sufficient criteria for identifying religion.

This problem of classification will occupy us in this chapter. It may be approached by considering the reactions of an uncommitted neutral – perhaps a Martian. Such a person, let us assume, will have identified various forms of discourse and forms of life in our culture, and seen their point and purpose. He encounters the religious form (whatever that is) merely as an area of obscurity. He observes people talking in certain ways, attending certain institutions, and going through certain motions, and he wishes to grasp what is going on. He would naturally hope to identify something *distinctive* about religion. He will ask such questions as 'What is it that religion does that other forms of life do not?', 'What is the general *point* or *purpose* of having a religion?' In particular, if he meets those who

---

[1] Thus Paul Hirst ('Logical and Psychological Aspects of Teaching', in R. S. Peters' collection *The Concept of Education*, p. 51): 'In religious discourse you cannot use the term God in any old way. He is not an object or being in space and time, he has no extension or colour. He does not act as a human being acts.' Hirst is talking of *one example* of 'religious discourse', namely a kind of sophisticated monotheism. Other gods (e.g. Zeus) do not keep these rules.

try to persuade him to adopt a religion, he will want to know why he should be persuaded. In this he would be doing no more than express the general lack of understanding shared by most adolescents, and perhaps most adults, in our own culture. He would probably express it more clearly, since his status as an entirely uncommitted and totally ignorant neutral would free him from the temptation to make a premature and partisan misidentification of religion: a temptation to which even the most atheistic of people in a religious or post-religious culture like our own almost inevitably yield.

Of course the Martian may not get any answer which identifies something distinctive about religion, for there may be no such thing. But he would hope for it. This hope, and its corresponding fear, lie behind much religious writing, and may be briefly expressed as follows. Suppose we list other forms of life with their purposes, including science, moral discourse, the creation and enjoyment of art, the sustaining and inspiring of individuals and communities by means of myths, psychotherapy, poetry, the institutional forms of social solidarity, and so forth. We now ask, 'What does religion do that is worth doing, and that these other things don't?' This is precisely parallel to (indeed essentially the same as) the problem about the role of priests in the modern world. We list roles on the criteria of various expertises (doctor, teacher, psycho-analyst, social worker, father-figure, ritual functionary, and so forth); and then we ask, 'What do priests know or do which isn't reducible to some combination of these?'

Since much of the language that is obscure to our Martian appears in the form of indicative sentences ('God is love', 'Christ died for our sins', and so on), it would be natural for him to ask a rather more specific question, namely: 'What is it that religious people *believe* that others don't?' He might certainly be led (or misled) to ask this question by the existence of various institutions and phrases: for instance, by the various professorships of theology, by phrases like 'religious *knowledge*', by common terms like 'believer' and 'unbeliever' and 'agnostic'. He would be told, rightly, by both religious and non-religious people, that religious language and religious practices include far more than belief; but this would not prevent him (rightly again) from trying to answer his question. It is here that our enquiry begins.

A. IDENTIFYING RELIGIOUS BELIEFS

A convenient starting-point is Renford Bambrough's discussion,[1] in which he makes use of what he calls 'examples of ancient Greek theology' to throw light on problems about religious belief today. About Homer's belief in Poseidon, Bambrough says:

> It is a matter of empirical, contingent fact that the moods of the sea are not the moods of a superhuman spirit, Poseidon. There might have been sufficient evidence for the existence of Poseidon instead of sufficient evidence against it. It might have been true that a super-human spirit did control the winds and waves in the way that Homer thought Poseidon controlled them.

and earlier,

> Homer has expectations that we lack. Even if he does not expect that he himself will under certain circumstances see the god Poseidon appearing in person, on earth or on the surface of the waves, he has expectations that we do not have in the sense that he believes in the *existence* of such a being as Poseidon, independently of the waves that are his manifestations.

The first problem that strikes one here is the problem of verifying exactly what it is that Homer believes. It may seem to be clear, to Bambrough and the rest of us, that Homer's belief is as he describes it, 'a matter of empirical, contingent fact'. But consider what might happen if we cross-questioned Homer. We might ask him, 'Do you believe that there is a being, shaped more or less like us only larger, whom in principle you could catch with a fishing-net, who controls the winds and waves?' And in order to make it clear that we were trying to persuade him to commit himself to an ordinary empirical belief, we could add questions such as: 'What does he eat?' 'Does he control the winds and waves by flapping his arms, or how? Does he breathe air or water?' and so on. In the same way we could try to elucidate the status of the belief that there are gods on Olympus by asking 'Could you photograph them?' or 'Do they throw snowballs?'

What would Homer say to this? Quite possibly he would begin by doing what a believer might call 'refusing to accept the trap', and a non-believer might describe as cheating or dithering. He might say in effect 'It is an empirical fact that the gods are there,

[1] *The Listener*, 20 April, 7 May and 14 May, 1964.

but you mustn't ask empirical questions about them.' Of course this won't do; and if we pin him down he might, indeed (though I doubt it), react as Bambrough seems to be suggesting – that is, he might commit himself to a straightforward factual belief about a god Poseidon who is like us only bigger and more powerful. Then we send trawlers and skin-divers into the Aegean Sea who find nothing, and he says 'Sorry, I was wrong, the evidence is against it.' The implausibility of this sort of move being made by religious believers in general is obvious, and has been pointed out by many other writers.

In any case, if Homer did take this line, it would be sufficient to convince us that the belief we had asked him about was not a *religious* belief at all, not part of 'ancient Greek theology': it looks like (we should have to say) part of ancient Greek marine biology. Bambrough would be right in saying that the belief was factually false, but wrong in implying that it was a religious belief. So perhaps Homer takes another line, which removes his belief from the realm of 'empirical, contingent fact'. Various lines are offered by Bonhoeffer, Bultmann, Tillich, Braithwaite, the Bishop of Woolwich and others. Bambrough implies fairly strongly that these lines do not lead to anything that we might properly call religious *belief*: 'theology is a branch of *knowledge*'. If Homer took any of these lines, then, he would no longer believe what Bambrough takes him to have believed before we started our cross-questioning.

It is a striking fact that whichever way Homer jumps, we fail (and Homer fails) to identify what we assumed to have existed as the object of our enquiry, namely Homer's original religious belief. This opens up the possibility that the very process of cross-questioning has (we might say) destroyed the original belief. For in so far as the cross-questioning succeeds, and Homer grasps the point of it, this happens only because we have introduced Homer to certain distinctions and criteria that (let us assume) were not current in his society, or at least were not applied to certain areas of belief. By making clear to Homer the difference between a scientific belief – part of marine biology – and other uses of language, we induce him to draw a distinction, and hence to plump for one or the other side of it. No doubt he will do so with reluctance, though not necessarily with more reluctance than some modern theologians show. But if he does it at all, it seems that the original religious belief perishes.

This has led some writers to suggest that religious belief is only possible as a form of belief which is – as it appears to us in the twentieth-century – an incoherent mixture of other beliefs, perhaps with the addition of certain (moral or non-moral) attitudes. Religious belief, we might say, is only at home in a society where scientific procedure is not properly understood or not widely practised. Speaking of the belief of the Azande – that the performance of certain rites is necessary for their welfare, but that the occasional ineffectiveness of these rites is always due to the evil thoughts of a participant – A.C. MacIntyre says:[1] 'It seems to me that one could only hold the belief of the Azande rationally *in the absence of* any practice of science and technology in which criteria of effectiveness, ineffectiveness and kindred notions had been built up'; and he goes on to compare the case of Christianity: 'Understanding Christianity is incompatible with believing in it, not because Christianity is vulnerable to sceptical objections, but because its peculiar invulnerability belongs to it as a form of belief which has lost the social context which once made it comprehensible.'[2]

As sociological comment on the conditions under which religious belief seems comprehensible or incomprehensible, these passages and the essay as a whole are illuminating. But they leave our problem unsolved. For it is not to be supposed that, if we were to persuade the Azande to adopt distinctions in the same way as we have persuaded Homer, our persuasion is an unjustified imposition of twentieth-century conceptual apparatus on an innocent primitive people. The distinctions are real ones: just as the distinctions between the areas which we separate under such titles as 'morality', 'law', 'convention', and 'custom' are real ones, even though primitive peoples may not recognize them. Our cross-questioning educates them, rather than indoctrinates; and if it educates them out of religious belief, so much the worse for religious belief. But again, how can it do this if they had something which we could truly call a religious belief in the first place? It is not that the Azande have a perfectly coherent and comprehensible religious belief which they then lose. It is rather that they never had one, but only come to realize this when they learn to look more closely at what they mean, via the conceptual apparatus and distinctions with which we supply them. It is not that 'one could only hold the belief of the

---

[1] *Faith and the Philosophers* (ed. J. Hick), p. 121.
[2] ibid., p. 132.

Azande rationally *in the absence of* any practice of science', etc.; it is rather that one cannot hold it rationally at all. One might seem to oneself and to others to 'hold a belief' and even to hold it rationally: and this appearance may well correlate with certain social conditions. But in order to actually hold a belief, and to hold it rationally, more is required: and the absence of what is required is precisely what cross-questioning would reveal.

One of the things that is required for belief, in the usual sense of the word, is that what you believe shall be intelligible. There must be, as it were, some meaningful proposition for you *to* believe. This is necessary in order to preserve a distinction between simply *uttering* words and *meaning* them. You can utter nonsense, but not mean it. Thus I might constantly assert something which was contradictory or meaningless, and I might also behave in ways causally connected with my assertions: but this would not be enough to say that I *believed* the words. Our considerations so far, therefore, suggest there is no such thing as religious belief in the normal sense of 'belief'.

This suggestion is strengthened rather than weakened by the kind of replies that philosophers are apt to get from religious believers. Commenting on MacIntyre's essay, Norris Clarke says[1] that 'conceptual thinking' in the religious beliefs of primitive peoples is not really conceptual at all, but 'symbolic': 'The aim of such thought and language is not to analyse, assert or explain anything in a literal way, but rather to express in a dramatic manner the speaker's existential communion with nature and the forces behind it.' The Eskimo 'belief' in a 'great woman who lives at the bottom of the sea and sends them up their food from her bounty . . . is less a causal explanation of the source of their food supply than a dramatic restatement of the actual facts of their daily life. . . .' In other words, one is tempted to say, they don't really *believe* it at all. Clarke further claims that 'the living core of Christian belief . . . is not at all, as any competent Christian theologian will explicitly admit, intellectual acceptance of a set of propositions held as true on exclusively intellectual grounds. It is rather first and foremost an existential, global and unconditional commitment. . . .' And this again suggests that religious belief is not primarily propositional belief at all.[2]

[1] J. Hick, op. cit., p. 137.
[2] See also Bernard Williams' essay in *New Essays in Philosophical Theology* (ed. A. Flew and A. C. MacIntyre), and L. Wittgenstein, *Lectures and Conversations*.

If we adopt this suggestion, we may then proceed to develop it and argue about the exact role played by what seemed (before our enquiry) to be propositional religious beliefs: and many able writers have done this. But it is not clear that the suggestion is correct; and there are still some difficulties about how we would ever know whether it was correct or not. The method advocated by Bambrough[1] – that of taking 'cases of propositions which are definitely theological and which are also either definitely known to be true or definitely known to be false' – is hence (to say the least) not as simple as it sounds. For in such cases we have first to be sure (a) that they really are propositions, as opposed to just having the grammatical form of propositions; and, more importantly, (b) that they are *theological* propositions. As we have seen, our chief difficulty may be said to consist precisely of being able to *identify* a 'theological proposition', or a religious belief. This difficulty is not, or not only, the result of our ignorance of what Homer, or the Azande, or any other people who *prima facie* qualify as religious believers would actually *say* when cross-questioned.

B. Problems of Taxonomy

This difficulty of the identification of religious beliefs is crucial. Such injunctions as 'We have not only to give the rules for the use of the relevant expressions, but to show what the point could be of following such rules'[2] are a considerable advance on talk about 'the meaning' or 'the use' of religious language (as if one could find out what religious believers were doing by just glaring at what they said): but they still jump the gun, for our difficulty consists precisely in determining what *are* 'the relevant expressions'. The overwhelming objection to many 'analyses', 'accounts' or 'interpretations' of religious belief is their failure to face up to the problem of taxonomy; and this objection applies as much to those who use the methods of philosophical or conceptual analysis as to those whose orientation is primarily sociological. Predictably, most of such writers put religious belief into a category with which we are already familiar: it operates as stories designed to reinforce a morality or way of life, as a pseudo-scientific type of explanation which can flourish only in a non-scientific society, and so on.

[1] op. cit., *The Listener*, 30 April 1964, p. 709.
[2] A. C. MacIntyre, *Faith and the Philosophers* (ed. J. Hick), p. 123.

The importance of taxonomy is not peculiar to religious belief. Writers on 'the language of morals', 'moral beliefs', 'moral principles' and so on have often jumped the gun in a similar way, by assuming that it was already clear what counted as a moral belief and what did not.[1] Often this hardly mattered: for such writers usually had in the back of their minds, and indeed often clarified, certain kinds of human *activity* – evaluating, commending, recommending, prescribing, committing oneself, etc. – which could justifiably be categorized as at least part of what we would normally mean by 'morality'. At worst, they painted a one-sided view of morality by including some activities and excluding others. Again, the recent philosophy of history has been, at least tacitly, an attempt to identify some activity which the historian engages in and other experts (scientists, sociologists, and so on) do not: i.e. the nature of historical explanation; and this activity would certainly be part of what we normally mean by 'history'.

What we have to do, then, is to separate out various activities and label them: we distinguish between (say) 'following a social code', 'obeying an authority', 'freely commending something and committing oneself to a rule'. As Austin says,[2] 'this clarification is as much a creative act as a discovery or description. It is as much a matter of making clear distinctions as of making already existent distinctions clear'. It comes then to this, that what we must distinguish is different *possible* types of activity. If we put these activities under different titles such as 'morality', 'history', 'religion', etc., we must of course ensure that the activities are at least to some degree co-extensive with what, in our language, is normally understood by these titles: otherwise there would be no reason to put them under *these* titles rather than others. But the task of distinguishing the different activities is not the same as the task of determining the way in which the title-words are used in various social groups.[3]

We might also hope that the activities thus logically distinguished were activities which had, in fact and in social practice, actually been carried on independently of each other. But this need not be so. Some past societies, for instance, may have drawn no distinctions, either in their own minds or in their social practice, between

[1] See G. J. Warnock, *Contemporary Moral Philosophy*, pp. 75-76.
[2] J. L. Austin, *How to Do Things with Words* (O.U.P. 1954), p. 72.
[3] See Appendix VII.

what *we* might want to distinguish under the titles of 'convention', 'tradition', 'law', 'custom' and 'morality'; and similarly many societies may put under the general heading of 'religion' activities which we may wish to separate logically under such titles as 'magic', 'morality', 'scientific explanation', 'social ritual', and so forth. Nevertheless, our distinctions may still be helpful: for the point of such taxonomy is not just to be intellectually clearer about these possible types, but thereby to be able to see what the use and purpose of these types is. This may have various results. An astrologer who gets clearer about the activity we distinguish as 'science' will then, perhaps, abandon astrology altogether (if what he has been wanting to do was science); or perhaps he may continue it as a kind of game or pastime to amuse himself and his friends. But at least he will then know what he is doing, and hence have some chance of making a rational decision about whether he wants to do it or not.

Thus the multifarious activities which people, in the past and present, have thought to be 'religious' need to be sorted out, with the general intention or hope of trying to find activities (and beliefs) which are *sui generis*. These need not correspond either with the self-descriptions of past believers, or with the self-descriptions of present believers:[1] and we need not expect that past or present believers distinguished, either in their own minds or in social practice, between these specific activities or beliefs and others.

In trying to sketch out a *sui generis* activity which has a fair claim to be called 'religious', we may reasonably start by considering how 'religious' is normally used in contemporary society. There is sufficient consensus about this to delimit quite severely the extent to which we may call certain activities 'religious' or 'non-religious' without being arbitrary. A man who said that scientific explanation was a religious activity, or that worshipping was not, would not have a firm grasp on the meaning of the word. At the same time, we have to remember that current religious beliefs may have narrowed the limits of the concept unduly, and we must be willing to inspect beliefs which are either on the borderline (such as Buddhism, or an extreme Marxist metaphysic) or which would not normally count as religious at all except perhaps in a metaphorical sense: as when

[1] And they certainly need not correspond with past or contemporary *interpretations* of religious belief.

we say that a man 'makes a religion' out of something, or 'worships' his mother. We have rather to use those activities which we *recognize* as religious as a starting-point for a consideration of the nature not only of these but of similar activities that we might not recognize; and here we have to appreciate that our recognition may be surreptitiously governed by our approval or our cultural style of religious (and anti-religious) thought, rather than by taxonomic interests. Thus we may be tempted to dismiss what for our purposes ought to count as religious beliefs under the title of 'superstition'; just as a man might dismiss a moral belief of which he disapproved as something which was not a moral belief at all, instead of classifying it as a false moral belief. This may well mislead us. We have to allow ourselves to say that there are bad, or false, or mistaken religions (rather than dismissing them as superstitions): and we also have to allow ourselves to grant the possibility of religions lacking some features that we tacitly but perhaps wrongly assume to be necessary for a concept of religion that will be usefully *sui generis*.

The word 'religion' and its adjective 'religious' embrace a wide variety of categories. Many writers have singled out three categories for particular mention: (a) a mode of behaviour, (b) a system of intellectual beliefs, and (c) certain feelings and emotions. In the English language, we can refer to these by attaching the adjective 'religious' – as (a) 'religious observances', (b) 'religious belief', (c) 'religious experience' or 'religious awe'. There are words which refer only within one or another category: thus we talk (a) of a 'churchman', (b) of a 'believer', (c) of a 'mystic', but these words tend often to be culture-bound or in other ways too specific and misleading for the general purposes of definition. In other languages the concepts are more clearly distinguished: thus classical Greek has (a) *latreia* (the practical worship or service of the gods), (b) *nomizein* (to believe in the gods), and (c) *sebas* (a feeling of awe, wonder or reverence).

We have already seen the difficulties of attempting to define religion by reference to the second of these categories, the category of belief. The first category, the category of social action or 'religious observance', is hard to use for much the same reason: namely, that it seems impossible to identify something as a specifically *religious* observance or social practice, just as it seems impossible to identify something as a specifically *religious* belief. For how would we know whether a piece of behaviour was religious, without knowing (to put it briefly) what went on in the minds of those who thus behaved? We should be unable to distinguish, for instance, those who attended church and went through the motions of a religious observance out of a sense of social duty or a desire for respectability, from those who behaved overtly in the same way but were 'genuinely religious' (whatever this may mean). Or, again, we see a man bowing down, kneeling, and striking his head on the floor in a large building: but this of itself does not tell us whether he is engaged in a religious ritual in a church, or going through physical exercises in a gymnasium. And if we cannot rely on him to give us a clear answer, as in the case of religion it seems we cannot, what alternative line of enquiry can we pursue?

There is in fact another line of enquiry, which seems to me more promising for the kind of taxonomy we require, and which is connected with the third category mentioned above, (c) – to consider what kind of emotions, feelings, postures, attitudes and natural signs or expressions of these are involved in a particular activity. The relationships between this approach and an approach conceived in terms of identifying particular 'language-games', 'forms of life', or 'social practices' are complex, and would repay study. But if we cannot rely either on his own explanation or on a bald description of physical movements, at least one sort of clue to the question 'What is he doing?' may be afforded by noticing the man's facial expression, bodily posture, and other symptoms which might enable us to say (for instance) that he was expressing sorrow, or anger, or obedience. Indeed it seems to me that without some prior awareness of the various categories of emotion and of the natural signs of emotion our understanding would hardly be able to get a grip at all upon a great many human activities.

Be this as it may, I shall proceed by listing a number of such phenomena which would normally be regarded as characteristically 'religious'. Amongst these are: praying, revering, worshipping, being in awe, adoring, praising, glorifying, repenting, confessing, sacrificing, bowing down before, obeying. I shall want to argue an ancient but often mis-stated thesis: that any concept of religion as a *sui generis* activity ought to rest primarily upon a central emotion, the emotion of awe; and upon a central activity, the activity of worship. This approach will be developed in what follows. But first we must dispose of some popular approaches which seem to me misconceived.

C. WHAT RELIGION IS NOT

In looking at the very mixed bag of *prima facie* 'religious' activities mentioned at the end of the last section (worshipping, glorifying, etc.), the reader will remember that our intention is to discover, if possible, something peculiar to religion, or at least some *sui generis* activity to which the word 'religion' can be most usefully applied. This is a different task from trying to produce a *definition* of 'religion' or of 'a religion'. If that were our objective, I suppose one might proceed by listing a large number of religions and trying to detect something that they all had in common: or, if there was nothing in common, trying to detect and map out ways in which different religions or different types of religion all had a 'family resemblance'.[1] But our concern does not lie here.

To elucidate this activity, we need first to go through a number of other activities which have, historically, often formed part of particular religions, and have been associated with the activity in which we are interested: but which are conceptually distinct from it, and seem to have no particular claim to be called peculiarly *religious*. It should hardly surprise us that these other activities have been associated with particular religions, just as it should not surprise us that what we now identify as 'morality' has often been associated with law, custom, tradition, taboo, etc., or that what we now identify as 'science' has, historically, grown up along with alchemy and astrology. But unless we can elucidate something *sui generis*, there will be no permanent place, no *locus standi*, for religion: for there will be nothing that religion is uniquely concerned with that (to put it crudely) is not done better by science, or morality, or psychiatry, or some other and more readily intelligible activity. It is this sort of criterion that the reader should bear in mind during the following discussion.

1. First, our bag of *prima facie* activities does not, fairly obviously, include anything we would normally count as 'science'. Activities like explaining, predicting, framing hypotheses, experimenting, and so forth, are not in place here. To use 'religion' as the name for some kind of pseudo-science or pseudo-technology (like rain-making) is to be bewitched by forms of activity which have often been, and perhaps still are, connected with the social practice of

[1] See J. R. Bambrough's article in *P.A.S.* 1960–61, and the reference to Wittgenstein therein.

religion, but which are not of its essence.[1] It is, in any case, perfectly possible for a person to engage in our religious activities – so that we should certainly have to say that the man 'had a religion' – and *not* thereby to engage in any activity remotely resembling science.

Nor is it clear that such activities as worshipping or adoring necessarily involve anything that we might (roughly) call 'empirical expectations' at all. We can know that Dante adored Beatrice without knowing that he expected anything of her: and a savage can worship the sun without expecting the sun to behave in any particular way. It *need* not even be true that the worshipper or adorer has any conscious *beliefs* that arise from or are connected with his worship or adoration: A and B may share exactly the same beliefs about a girl, but A may adore her while B does not. Worshipping, praying, adoring, and so on are connected primarily with psychological *postures*. If we want to describe what the man does (in a wider sense of 'does'), we have to use very general descriptions. We might say that he 'finds it marvellous', 'is impressed by', 'feels humble when confronted with', and so on. Nor, *a fortiori*, must we maintain that the question of whether a person is *right* to adopt these postures must be answered only by reference to whether his empirical expectations are correct.

It is thus a mistake to insist that gods or other objects of religious belief must, if they are to count as such, perform magically in the empirical world. The very proper objection currently made to using the concept of 'god' as some form of scientific or quasi-scientific explanation illustrates only one aspect of this error. What needs to be attacked is the more general view that religious belief necessarily involves belief in the empirical or physical powers of its object. Not all cultures and belief patterns can be readily assimilated to the model case of Elijah and the prophets of Baal, where the ability, and/or the willingness, to send down fire from heaven is counted as an essential attribute of divinity.

The concepts that describe our religious emotions, attitudes and activities are close, though not very close, to those related to works of art: they are somewhat like 'admiring', 'appreciating', or 'being moved by'. They are closer still to those related to what we some-

[1] These are perhaps best described under the title of 'magic'. Some of the differences between magic and religion are well brought out by J. G. Frazer in *Magic and Religion* (London 1902), Chapter IV, though his definition of religion seems unsatisfactory.

times call (in a mood of post-eighteenth-century arrogance) 'appreciating' nature: here we may be overwhelmed, enraptured, terrified, in awe, and so on. And they are closest of all to those related to people, where 'in awe', 'adore', 'placate', 'worship' and similar terms are very much in place.

Nevertheless an object of religious worship need not be personal. Our short list of 'religious activities' included (a) worshipping, revering, being in awe, adoring, praising, (b) praying, confessing, sacrificing. It is natural to take at least some of these – certainly those in (b) – as intelligible only if coupled with a belief in some person or person-like entity: one must, it may be thought, pray, sacrifice and confess to some*body*. It is also natural to assume that two other beliefs or kinds of belief must be coupled with these activities – the belief that this person or person-like entity can affect one's life in some significant way, and the belief that one's prayers, sacrifices, or confessions can affect the attitude of the entity. For what is the *point* of (say) praying, unless the entity will grant one's wishes? And the possibility of this happening depends, first, on the fact that the entity can grant them and, second, on the fact that it may be moved by one's prayers to do so.

This is perhaps the most common view of religion that sophisticated people take today. It amounts to regarding religion as a crude and pre-scientific way of attempting to control the empirical world via a personal god, and religious beliefs as failed or failing scientific beliefs. The view is natural, because religious believers (like everyone else) want to control the empirical world, and (again like everyone else) have nearly always been prepared to use any methods that might seem to offer some hope of doing so. We may compare the use made of astrology, 'health cures', clairvoyance, witchcraft, and many other such. A great deal of energy has been expended, perhaps justifiably, on attacking orthodox traditional religious bodies (such as the Christian Church) that have evidently misused their beliefs in just this way: and it is certainly not worth the while of any honest Christian either to attempt any defence or to claim that there is nothing to attack.

But the most that can be gained by such observations – and even this may be too much – would be to show that what we had done in the past should not properly be called *religion* at all, but bad science: just as it might be said that the science of the Middle Ages was not science at all but just alchemy. The reason why it may be too much to say this is that we can hardly be certain that *everything* that went on under the heading of religion in the past was contaminated by this false use: indeed, it seems very reasonable to maintain that this is untrue. We could only be certain of this if it were a conceptual, not just an empirical, truth that the notion of religion is tied to this kind of attempted control over the empirical world.

It is not a conceptual truth, because we can think of cases where a man's attitude and beliefs would certainly be most naturally described as 'religious', but where he does not hold the beliefs claimed as necessary. I can worship, praise, adore, and stand in awe of something, and believe that it is a worthy recipient of these feelings and activities, without believing that I can influence it or that it will affect my life empirically. This can still be true even though what I worship and praise is not a person. For example, I may adopt an attitude of devotion, awe, reverence, worship, and so forth to natural phenomena (the sea, the stars, mountains, a dead body, crocodiles). To use a much-worked word, they are to me *numinous*. Trying to influence these things by sacrifice or prayer represents an additional move which I may or may not make.

There is indeed a sense in which the notions of empirical control and exploitation of the world, so far from being central to our concept of religion, are directly opposed to it. Central to the religious attitude is the feeling of there being something 'greater' or 'more important than' oneself. Somewhat different (whether in kind or degree), but still closely associated with this, is the attitude of being 'open' to the world and its contents, of a passive willingness to learn from them and to experience them, as against an active desire to fasten on them as means of fulfilling preconceived ends of one's own. This openness characterizes in one way or another the appreciation of works of art, a *rapport* with nature, and a sympathetic understanding of other human beings. Some have said, not implausibly, that one may gain an idea of the religious attitude by (as it were) screwing up the concepts that go with 'openness' in these fields to the point where we would want to use such words as 'reverence', 'awe' and 'worship'.

2. It also seems clear that our activities are not like anything that we usually describe as 'morals' or even 'ways of life'. We should misdescribe them by saying that worshippers and adorers *placed a moral value* on the objects of their worship and adoration. Words

D

and phrases like 'commending', 'praising', 'thinking good', misdescribe what happens. It is not so much that such phrases are too
weak – one may be very vehement in morality – but rather that they
are too pedestrian. What Professor Hare (following Professor
Braithwaite) calls the 'springs of action', which includes 'desires,
and purposes, and principles',[1] does not cover the relevant ground
at all. For someone who worships, there is no question of desiring
or purposing, much less of framing principles. It is more a matter
of the man's *being impressed by* some part of the world, in a much
more passive sense.

Only certain types of societies, whose religious emotions centre
on certain types of object, make a close connection here between
worship and morality. It is easy for a member of our society to
argue as follows: 'Worshipping God, or Baal, or Hitler, involves
doing his will: hence one of the most important criteria for whether
we should worship somebody or not must be a moral criterion: we
must ask whether the will of God, or Baal, or Hitler is something
which it is morally justifiable to follow.' But this line of thought
becomes less natural (1) if we inhabit a society whose members,
like certain of the ancient Greeks, do not regard their gods as
worshipful for any *moral* reasons (but rather because the gods are
potent, awesome, impressive); and/or (2) if the objects of worship
are not (or do not masquerade as) *people*, and hence are not conceived as having wills at all.

The post-Kantian obsession with morality in the sense of overt,
will-directed, rule-following behaviour tends to blind us to the
proper objections to the worship of inappropriate gods. 'Hitler-
worshippers killed Jews, and Baal-worshippers sacrificed small
children: these are odious acts, grossly immoral, and hence they
argue a mistaken religion.' This is not so much false as superficial
and misleading. The implication is that we should (as it were) stand
before Hitler, or the priests of Baal, balanced, rational and uncommitted, and ask them about their moral intentions. If we approve
of killing Jews and sacrificing children, we then decide that they are
to be worshipped: if not, not. Or again, when Jesus said 'Follow
me', the disciples should have cross-questioned him about his
morality: and then, if satisfied, joined his party and worshipped
him.

This is grotesque, not so much because those who worshipped

[1] *Faith and Logic* (ed. Basil Mitchell), p. 181.

Hitler or Baal or Jesus did not behave like this at all, but because even if they had there would *pro tanto* still be no room for the concept of *worship* – only for the concept of moral approval, partisan adherence, or the warm appreciation of moral wisdom. Men of a particular cast of mind may, as perhaps Kant did, not only appreciate moral wisdom but bow down before it: yet, in general, the critical approval of Hitler's, Baal's or Jesus' morality is very much to be contrasted with the attitude of *worshipping* Hitler, Baal or Jesus.

The same applies, to a lesser extent, to notions like following, serving, obeying, submitting and imitating. The extent is lesser, in so much as these notions are closer to worship than the notions of moral assessment or moral appreciation. As we move further away from the notion of moral assessment or moral appreciation, we do indeed get closer to the notion of worship: this can be seen in the concepts of following, serving, obeying, and so on. Just because they are closer to worship, they are to that extent further from post-Kantian autonomous morality. Yet even these notions are not conceptually tied to worship: we can worship an object without regarding it as any kind of *authority* or *ideal*. If most believers have so regarded their gods, this is at best a contingent fact, not a conceptual one.

3. Another more obvious mistake, and also one which is more topical, is to identify religious belief as being 'concerned with whether one can speak of *ultimate* reality at all and with what character this reality has'.[1] Whether or not these phrases and questions can under analysis yield enough sense for us to wish to go on using them (and this is doubtful), it is plain that religious belief can exist without any such questions cropping up at all: indeed it is plain that religious belief *has* often existed without this. What seems to have happened here is that the progressive dissatisfaction with particular objects of religious belief – first with stocks and stones, then with the Old-Testament Jehovah, and finally with the Christian but still transcendental God – has finally

---

[1] John A. T. Robinson, *The Honest to God Debate* (SCM Press 1963), p. 230. On the same page: 'The question of God is the question whether, for instance, Jesus' relationship to the reality he could only address as "Abba! Father!" is veridical or not. Is the constitution of the universe such that it justifies the trust, "Father, into thy hands I commend my spirit"? Is reality ultimately gracious . . .?'

abolished all such objects. In their place we are offered a non-object, 'ultimate reality', which saves us from what is thought to be the barbarous crudity of actually worshipping something, but only at the price of vacuity. This progression, including its final move, is a commonplace in the history of religion.

Various other writers, particularly over the last decade or so, have spoken of religion in this kind of way. They have used concepts like 'ultimate concern', 'absolute dedication', 'total dependence' or 'commitment', 'relationship with the ground of being', and so forth. It would take many books to criticize such ideas in detail: here we must be brief, though I have added an Appendix[1] for those readers who find themselves attracted by it. First, this is certainly not characteristic of religion in general: it is characteristic chiefly of certain twentieth-century religious apologetics. This sort of language would simply have no place in enquiries about (say) Greek or Roman polytheism, or the worship of the Norse gods. Secondly, it is not clear that there is anything specifically religious about being ultimately 'concerned', 'committed' or 'dedicated': people can be ultimately concerned, committed or dedicated to ways of life that are not normally called religious. Everyone, perhaps, has some 'ultimate concern' but not everyone has a religion – unless, of course, 'religion' is being preemptively defined. Thirdly, even if we can understand phrases like 'the ground of being', and have a 'relationship' with whatever such phrases stand for, it is not clear that this relationship would be a religious one – unless, again, 'religion' has already been defined, by some *fiat*, in this way. All this makes one suspect that what is being talked about here is not what we normally mean by 'religion', but something else, perhaps the sort of feeling I refer to in Appendix I under the heading of 'making sense of the world'. Of course this feeling may result in, or be incorporated into, a religion, and it may in any case be a very important thing to discuss: but it should not be discussed under an improper title.

4. It would be possible, and perhaps enlightening for those who feel tempted in certain particular directions, to extend the list of things that religion is not. For instance, some will wish to say something like 'The Christian religion is a *historical* religion: it is founded on historical facts about the birth, crucifixion and resurrection of Jesus', and so forth. But here again we must remember

[1] Appendix I.

that this may be true of Christianity but not of other religions, and that even if similar statements were true of other religions, they would not give us the *sui generis* activity we are looking for. What is or is not thought to be historically the case may help to generate, destroy or alter a particular set of religious beliefs: but it cannot be what makes them specifically religious. In fact, we recognize a sharp difference between historical statements that connect in some way with religious beliefs, such as 'A man called Jesus was born in such and such a place and was crucified under Pontius Pilate', and other statements which are nearer the essence of religion, and which for that very reason present problems of meaning and verification, such as 'The Son of God came down to earth, was born as a man on earth and saved mankind by his precious blood'.

I shall not here attempt any comprehensive list of all the other activities which religion is not. I shall claim rather that no *sui generis* activity which could reasonably be called 'religion' can be elucidated on any of the lines mentioned above: and that we should look for such an activity rather in the notions of awe and worship. I shall claim further that there is no peculiar difficulty about the intelligibility of religious awe and worship, and that there is no *logical* limit to what a man may, in practice, be in awe of and worship (though this is not to say that a man may not more characteristically and more reasonably be in awe of and worship some things rather than others). I shall try to amplify these points, and to sketch out the concept of religion that seems most appropriate for our purposes, in the following chapter.

3. Awe, worship, and 'having a religion'

It is hard but not impossible to distinguish a particular attitude, which it is fair to call 'religious', from other attitudes. A great part of the difficulty arises from our lack of a clear general taxonomy: it is easy to talk of 'the aesthetic attitude' but very hard to say in what it consists. Moreover, the same *words* – 'admiration' and 'praise', for example – are often used to describe our attitudes to art, nature and human beings. But the notions of awe, worship, and reverence are perhaps *particularly* characteristic of the religious attitude. It is partly for this reason that a belief in fairies or gnomes, for instance, would not naturally be called a religious belief, and that a belief in ghosts or demons may at least border upon it: for the former usually inspire wonder, but not awe. We have to remember that it is not the type of *object*, but the type of *attitude*, which defines the activity we want to call 'religion'. Thus one may view the Great Pyramid with aesthetic pleasure or 'religious' awe: and there are, of course, a great many cases in between. (One might say 'Think of that king lying there all those years'; 'Coo, isn't it huge?'; 'Isn't it mysterious, standing all by itself in the desert?' and so on. One may be awed by the length of time, size, grandeur, strangeness, etc.). Pascal was terrified by the eternal silence of infinite space: most of us today may find it interesting, but not terrifying.

It is important, I think, to see that there is nothing profoundly *unintelligible* or logically mysterious about this attitude. The fact that we are thoroughly familiar with the phenomena of revering, obeying, sacrificing, and so on in non-religious contexts (for instance, obeying men rather than omens, or sacrificing a pawn rather than a fatted calf) should not mislead us into supposing that these concepts become unintelligible (in any ordinary sense of that word) when used in religious contexts: any more than our understanding of the sadness of death should lead us to claim total incomprehension of the sadness of music. Nor is it correct to say that the activities of religion are *like* these ordinary activities: they *are* these activities. What seems odd (to the unbeliever, at least) is the particular *context* of the activity.

Thus we might be tempted to say 'I know well enough what is meant by being in awe of one's father, but what is meant by being in awe of God?' Just what is our difficulty here? It is *not* over the concept of 'being in awe'. We may substitute for 'God' some perfectly intelligible word: one can be in awe of a totem pole, a mountain, a statue, a dark wood. In *Lord of the Flies*[1] the boys were in awe of the dead parachutist. There is no difficulty about intelligibility here. What the unbeliever fails to understand is not what is *meant by saying* that X is in awe of Mount Sinai, or that Y adores a golden calf, but why in the world X and Y should ever attach or direct their awe and adoration *to these objects*.

In much the same way, a person who totally failed to appreciate music might be baffled when a music-lover said that he found a symphony poignant, or tragic, or gay. But he would not be baffled about what was *meant*, either by 'a symphony' or by 'poignant', 'tragic' or 'gay'. He would be baffled about the use of these words *in connection with* symphonies.

Of course there are degrees of bafflement. Few of us, perhaps, would find it utterly curious for a man to be in awe of an earthquake or worship the sun; but we would find it odder for a man to be in awe of the number 9, or to worship human hair. Yet we have only to think of the Pythagoreans, and of hair fetishists, to find it less odd than we thought. Here we have to fill in the background – in terms of the man's individual psychology as well as of his society – and we can begin to sympathize, to feel (however faintly) what it would be like to have such targets for one's emotions.

We sometimes incline to think along these lines: 'A person can't really worship stocks and stones, trees, and so on. So isn't there something else he worships or thinks he worships? Yes, of course, this person has a religious belief: it is really the god or nymph or whatever it is that he thinks lives inside the tree, or which the stone symbolizes. But what is his religious belief, what does it mean to say that he "worships a god"? What does he mean by "a god"?' This is like saying 'an elderly business tycoon can't really adore or feel in awe of a silly girl of 16. So isn't it something else he adores and feels in awe of? Yes, of course, he must have some crazy or

[1] By William Golding (Faber 1954).

mistaken belief about her – perhaps he thinks she's the Queen of Sheba in disguise.' Of course it's often true (perhaps in religion nearly always true) that worshippers *do* have a special sort of belief about the objects they worship. It's often true that elderly tycoons in love have special beliefs about their love-objects. But it doesn't *have* to be true. The tycoon might say, 'Yes, I know exactly what she is, and I still adore her and stand in awe of her.'

It is *logically* possible for any object to be an object of awe and worship: though of course some *descriptions* of objects may be such as to contradict this possibility, and other descriptions may carry with them a conceptual implication for the appropriateness of awe and worship. Thus 'water-sprite' or 'poltergeist' may be thought to imply the inappropriateness of awe or worship, whereas 'god' or titles like 'the Most High' may be thought to imply it. Yet we must be careful. Homeric characters often ask 'Are you a god or a mortal?' ('*theos nu toi, ē brotos essi?*'), as if (one might think) the former meant 'worthy of worship' and the latter 'unworthy of worship'. But also in Homer, people are worshipped '*theos hōs*', 'like a god', or 'as if they were gods' and, conversely, one may think some gods not worth worshipping. Again, some might have thought that descriptions such as 'condemned criminal', 'servant', 'poor', 'powerless', and 'suffering', were conceptually incompatible with any object of worship. Yet Christ satisfied these descriptions. It might be paradoxical, or psychologically or culturally odd, for an object described in a certain way to be asserted to be worthy of worship, but it would rarely be nonsensical or incomprehensible – the worshipper will always have his reasons. There is an autonomy in what may be worshipped, in general parallel to the autonomy in what may be wanted or morally valued.[1]

We can worship 'non-existent' objects, if by 'non-existent' is only meant 'non-material'. We do not have to worship statues or stocks or stones. To worship the memory (revere the memory) of somebody does not mean *either* that we worship and remember them, *or* that we are not worshipping at all: we worship our picture, our memory of them. Again, I can worship Lycurgus (assuming that there was no such person) or Siegfried or James Bond: 'hero-worship' can apply to fictitious heroes as well as real ones, to Bond as well as to Baden-Powell. If we ask 'Just *what* is he worshipping here?' we answer, perhaps, 'a fictitious person'. But this doesn't

[1] See Chapter 6.

mean he isn't worshipping: statues are (in a sense) fictitious people, yet we can worship them. All these things exist *as* fictions, not as real people. Whether the worshipper is *aware* of the logical status of what he worships is another matter.

But can we still talk about the *object* of a man's worship or religious attitudes, if his god is just a concept, a set of attributes or qualities stuck together? Yes. Since 'object' here doesn't mean 'material object', there is no real difficulty. 'Reason' is, if you like, 'just a concept': but you can worship Reason and erect temples to it. It would be possible, and according to some desirable, to have a Religion of Humanity. It is true that such objects of worship tend not to have retained the devotion of their worshippers; but the reasons for this are psychological, not conceptual. We can worship the geographical entity England, by making a sacred object of it (we bow down, kiss the earth, pour libations on the soil), or we can worship some idea or picture of England. Pythagoreans are alleged to have worshipped numbers. There is nothing in the words 'ferret', 'number', 'statue', or 'reason', which exempts such things from being worship-objects.

Again, it is central to the notion of worship that the object of worship should be conceived as, in some sense, 'greater', 'higher', or more important than the human individual or any number of such individuals. This is inherent in the concept of worship, as it is not inherent in the concepts of appreciation, approval, or admiration. But it is not required that the object of worship should be a natural object, like a tree or a mountain. Like objects of wonder – what Herodotus called *thaumata* – they may be artificial: pyramids will do as well as floods. Man-made things can be seen as 'greater than' man, in the sense required.

The inclination to object to this comes from anthropomorphic tendencies. We feel tempted to say: 'But if man makes them, then they can't be 'greater' than man in at least one important sense. We must have something to worship that is capable of doing all the things that man can do, only more': and then we are on the way to a man-type God, preferably a creator, with a will of his own, and much more power than we possess. But this will only be an appropriate object of worship if we regress to the view that power in the empirical or physical world is a necessary feature of any god worth worshipping. Such regression is understandable, but not necessary. We can worship man-made things.

Equally, it is clear that the religious object need not be regarded as *unique* or *supreme*. You can worship more than one god, and there need be no question of one or indeed any of the gods you worship exercising some ultimate control over affairs. We know that the Greeks had a religion, without first having to decide whether they believed Zeus to be in this sense supreme. Indeed we have already shown that being in control of empirical affairs, whether or not this control is supreme, is not a necessary condition for something being an object of religious worship.

However, the concept of awe would not be intelligible if there were not certain things of which men were characteristically in awe, certain characteristic symptoms of awe, and certain behaviour which characteristically followed or accompanied the feeling. And so of course there are. Men are characteristically in awe of large, powerful and mysterious things (the planets, thunderstorms, giants, pyramids); when they are in awe they display such symptoms as being open-mouthed or wide-eyed; and they may then do things like worshipping, abasing themselves, adoring, praising, and so forth.

Here again we need to distinguish awe from other concepts that have commonly been confused with it, and mistaken for necessary features of religious attitudes.

1. Awe does not necessarily imply fear, even though in practice it may often have an admixture of fear. One need not be *frightened* of what is large, powerful and mysterious; if one is wide-eyed and open-mouthed, this may be with something more approximating to delight than to terror; and one's worship of that of which one is in awe need not be placatory or in any way designed to avert wrath or danger. We may find thunderstorms awesome even if we have a good lightning conductor. Conversely and obviously, one may fear without being in awe.

2. Being in awe of something does not include, nor is it included by, *wondering* or *marvelling* at it. We may wonder or marvel at the movement of the planets, or a piece of contrapuntal music, without being in awe: it might be the intricacy or cunning to which our attention is directed. We can wonder at the works of a watch, or the Lord's Prayer engraved in miniature on a cherry-stone. Conversely, we may be in awe without wondering or marvelling in this sense.

3. Awe does not include, nor is it included by, *respect*. 'Respect', like wonder, implies a certain detachment, even if (on some occasions, but not all) it also involves self-subordination. One respects another man's judgement, rank, wisdom, or power (which may be greater than or equal to one's own): to stand in awe of his power is different.

Nevertheless, the words 'fear', 'wonder' and 'respect', and other words such as 'admire', and especially 'revere', are closely connected with awe: and some phrases, such as 'dread' or 'reverential fear', may be made up especially to provide something like a synonym for 'awe'. In other languages there may be more or less drawing of these fine distinctions: *sebas* in Homer, for instance, is often used indifferently for most of the terms above. Religious awe may certainly exist apart from any of the particular conditions that we normally assume for these other terms. But we may arrive at some understanding of awe by (so to speak) screwing up the emotional force which is suggested by 'admire', 'respect', 'marvel' and so on. To be in awe, one might say, is like these only more so.

Thus the concept of reverence is not so *strong* as that of awe. One may, for example, revere one's father, a sage, or the memory of one's ancestors, without being in awe of them. One treats and regards them as somehow important, deserving of respect, even perhaps as sacred: but not as *overwhelmingly impressive*. Awe is best understood, perhaps, as the very opposite of detachment: though it is not, as Otto sometimes seems to suggest, necessarily connected with anything we could properly call a feeling of *dependence*. The notions of passivity and receptivity are in place here: the man in awe feels the awesome object to be in some way 'greater', 'higher', or 'mightier' than himself: hence he adopts such characteristic attitudes and postures as self-abasement, prostration, kneeling, or bowing the head. To feel in awe, again, is to feel humble before something, to feel it as powerful. But it is *not* necessarily to ascribe powers to it, in the sense of believing that (or even acting as if) it could exercise control over one's ordinary empirical existence, for instance by hurling thunderbolts. (One may be in awe of a cathedral, the starry heavens above or the super-ego within, without any such belief.) Similarly one may be tempted to say that the awed man sees the awesome object as *important* or even *valuable*: but 'valuable' at least suggests that he freely chooses to value it, which is misleading – it would be better to say that it is for him in the highest degree *significant*.

So too with some other concepts, such as *praising* and *adoring*. These may be used in a way which is not conceptually tied to worship. Thus one may worship a deity which one does not consider admirable (morally or otherwise) and which one fears: and here one could not be said to praise or adore that deity, in the normal sense of those words. Worship may be said, if we like to say it, to involve attributing *worth* to the object, but it is not any particular *kind* of worth (moral worth, aesthetic merit, or whatever): rather, it is an overall importance, impressiveness or tremendousness. The piling-up of terms in phrases like 'Worship and honour, glory and power be unto thee . . .', 'Might, majesty, dominion and power', and the repeated 'Holy, holy, holy', is an attempt to catch this *non-specific* (though not necessarily uncritical) attribution of worth, an attribution which is better understood in terms of awe than by other concepts.

Awe is an emotion: and like other emotions, it may be felt unconsciously and unwillingly. That is, a man may be in awe without his knowing it, against his will, and even though he rejects or denies it. The same is true of worship, but only in one sense of the word. A man who feels awe characteristically *does* certain things: he bows his head, trembles, or kneels, says certain words about or to the object of awe, and so forth. If we interpret 'does' weakly, so as not to include any notion of conscious intention or deliberate purpose, what he does may be regarded as symptoms rather than as consciously intentional actions. (This may even be true of his linguistic behaviour.) Hence a man may, in a sense, be said to 'worship' an object without doing so deliberately or even knowingly. But if, as is perhaps more usual, we interpret action-words like 'worship' more strongly, we shall not say that a man really worships unless his behaviour is deliberate. A man who worships in the full sense, therefore, not only feels awe but gives it deliberate expression in the activity we call worship.

Worship is the most natural or characteristic expresion of awe: though this is not to say, of course, that a man will worship in all or even in most cases where he feels awe. Worship (in the full sense) occurs when a man freely expresses his awe in his deliberate behaviour: and for this to happen, the man must to some degree accept or *endorse* his feeling of awe. He must think it right or appropriate in some way to give behavioural form to his feeling. This contrasts with the case where a man may find himself impressed, overwhelmed, awed, etc. but hold out against these feelings: just as a man may be, in the ordinary sense, frightened, but not cower or run away. There may be various reasons why a man does not worship when he feels awe: he may be physically constrained, or frightened of what the neighbours will think, or uncertain about what sort of behaviour is appropriate. The only important point in this context is that the man may deliberately reject his own feelings.

If this does not happen, however, and the man worships freely and in the full sense, then he is at least on the way towards having a religion. We here approach the borderline of the concept, and it is probably necessary to add certain conditions. The worship must be formalized, at least to some degree: there must be, so to speak, certain standardized patterns of ritual or formal behaviour which he characteristically uses for his worship. It would not be sufficient for the concept of religion if he merely expressed his awe, however freely and deliberately, in a number of different ways. Certainly the most *usual* feature of such formal patterns is that they are institutionalized or socially shared (e.g. in communal acts of church worship): but it seems at least doubtful that religion must, conceptually, be a social practice. There seems nothing contradictory in supposing that a person could devise his own rituals of worship, and still count as 'having a religion'.

We might put this another way, by saying that the person must accept or endorse his feeling of awe in a very strong and full sense. He must think it to a high degree important for him, not only that he should feel awe, but that he should express this feeling, not just occasionally and in informal ways, but often and in some form or vehicle of worship which did sufficient justice to this importance. Since he thinks his awe appropriate to the object, his worship will involve what we might call some *celebration* of the object: and this will include linguistic behaviour, as well as (for instance) singing, dancing, and ritualistic movements. This linguistic behaviour will itself include the formulation and expression of religious beliefs (we can say this even though we still do not know just what a religious belief is): one function, at least, of these will be to contribute to the believers' endorsement of their awe, or to express their sense of the importance of celebrating their feelings for the religious object.

It is not, of course, necessary for our concept of religion that a man should feel awe for some object all the time, or even that he should feel it very often. One might ask whether it is necessary that he should *ever* feel it. It would no doubt be necessary that he should think that he *ought* to feel it, and that he should go through the motions of that form of worship which is designed to celebrate and express it: but does he ever actually have to *feel* it? We may consider the case of a man who counts himself as a believer, goes to church, kneels down, prays, sings the psalms and hymns, recites the creed and so forth. He does this quite seriously; that is, he is not simply pretending or going through the motions in order (say) to conform to his social group or for fear of what the neighbours may think. Does such a man have a religion?

I think we are bound to say that he has. He has accepted an object as worthy of worship, and he worships it: and he can do this even if he does not feel awe for the object, and indeed even if he is quite unacquainted with the object. He may take it on trust that the object is awesome and worthy of worship, or he may believe that it is on the basis of what he has heard about it. This is indeed a commonplace with highly organized religions that have a long tradition: they may survive as religions even though few, if any, of their adherents actually feel awe. There is a wide gulf, certainly, between the state of mind of the awed centurion who exclaimed 'Truly this was the son of God', and the modern believer who may never have felt in *awe* of Christ at all: but so long as the modern believer thinks that such awe is appropriate – as opposed merely to thinking that Christ was a great teacher, worthy to be followed as a moral ideal, ethically admirable, etc. – then he has a religion.

Nevertheless this case is in an important sense parasitic upon awe. All religions, in practice at least, begin with awe, and are usually sustained by feelings of awe on the part of various believers throughout their history. It might, indeed, be conceptually possible to establish a religion without any such actual feelings: we might all say: 'There is an object X that we all ought to be in awe of, and it's of immense importance that it is an awesome object, and that we should worship it. True, none of us is actually in awe of it: yet we may gain a great deal by worshipping it, by behaving as if we actually felt the awe which it is appropriate to feel'. If we then all did this whole-heartedly, we should have a religion. Yet this would still be parasitic, at least upon the concept of awe and the appropriateness of awe. For without at least the concept, we would have no reason to describe it as a religion.

That this is so can be seen by again contrasting cases that are not cases of religion. Thus (1) we may believe that the universe as we know it is the creation of an immensely powerful super-being from some unimaginable 'fourth dimension', who made us and controls our destinies: but without the concepts of awe and worship of the being, this is no more than an unusually important bit of cosmology; (2) we may talk of 'the absolute' or 'the ground of being' or 'ultimate reality', but this is *pro tanto* only metaphysics, not religion; (3) we may have a strongly-held and well-defined moral or political ideal, such as Buddhism or Marxism, but these will only count as religious if there is some tendency to be in awe of or to worship this ideal, or certain of its features (perhaps the Buddha himself, or Lenin's tomb).

It is thus, in my view, a mistake to suppose that questions of whether a person really has a religion, or believes in a god, turn wholly on whether he has some empirical belief in the existence of some entity. They turn rather on whether the person's attitude, emotions and activities are of a certain kind. Thus it is one question whether Euripides believed in the existence of Aphrodite and Artemis in one way or in another (that is, whether these names stand for real super-beings in the empirical world, or for psychological forces): but quite another question whether he believed that whatever the names referred to were appropriate objects of awe and worship. So too with modern theology. The important question is whether theologians think that there is something of which we should be in awe and which we should worship, or whether the misty talk of 'ultimate reality', 'the ground of being', etc. is just woolly metaphysics or bad psychology.

Worship and awe, as we have described them, are not indeed often directly connected with *choice*, still less with moral choice in particular. They are more concerned with recognition, or awareness of a particular kind of symbolic power which certain objects or phenomena have for us. The linguistic fact (if it is a fact), that there is *one* use of 'worship' in twentieth-century English, by virtue of which we cannot talk of 'worshipping' an object without implying thereby that the worshipper gives some sort of moral approval to that object, is here misleading: and, of course, even in our culture we may talk of being in awe of an object without expressing approval of any kind.

Europides' *Hippolytus* is instructive here. Hippolytus came to grief because he did not worship Aphrodite (sexual passion), but only Artemis (chastity). Relevant points are (1) that it is not suggested that he should have worshipped Aphrodite *rather than* Artemis, but rather that he should have worshipped both, i.e. acknowledged the force of passion as well as the ideal of chastity; (2) nevertheless to worship Aphrodite it was not sufficient for him merely to acknowledge her existence, to 'salute her from afar':[1] what was needed was that he should in some sense *feel her power*; (3) it is not suggested that, had he worshipped Aphrodite, he would have given *moral approval* to her will or to Phaedra's sexual demands: only that he would have understood them and perhaps anticipated them. Worship in this sense, then, (1) does not entail the unqualified acceptance of one supreme god or object of worship as against other gods or objects, (2) nevertheless entails more than intellectual acknowledgement or mere respect, (3) does not entail moral approval.

The activity of worship, and the feeling of awe when directed towards certain objects, do not involve a surrender of autonomy of judgement; any more than to feel and express admiration, wonder or reverence for a work of art, or to feel and express sensual pleasures (for instance the pleasure of eating), implies such surrender. Autonomy is surrendered only if we refuse to raise either the question 'Is this an appropriate feeling?' or the question 'In the light of this feeling, how should we behave?' Thus Hippolytus should have raised the questions (a) 'Is Aphrodite powerful?'; that is, 'Should I feel awe, etc. at the force of sexual passion?': and (b), even if the answer to this is 'Yes', 'How, in the light of this, should I behave towards Phaedra?'

Whether something should properly be called a religion or not, then, I take to be connected with the kind of emotion and attitude involved. This is also true of arguments about whether certain *things* are 'religious': it may be useful to quote one instance of this. When people argue about whether this or that piece of music is 'religious', they are not arguing merely about whether it is used in church, or is a setting of the words of the Mass. They argue about whether it has qualities which are like, or which remind us of,

[1] Euripides, *Hippolytus*, 102 (Oxford Classical Text).

the qualities that we ascribe to religious objects. These arguments show (1) that there is a large no-man's-land between 'religious' and 'non-religious' (secular), but (2) that nevertheless there are cases which can be firmly placed in one territory or the other. Thus (1) we may differ about whether Verdi's *Requiem*, or Wagner's *Tannhäuser*, should count as 'religious', but (2) we should probably agree that Bach's *B Minor Mass* was, and that a Strauss waltz was not.

Suppose now that a certain tribe, one of whose priests had perhaps once been on a holiday in Vienna, constantly used the exact music of *The Blue Danube* waltz in religious ceremonies. Or suppose, conversely, that the well-marked three-time of the tune commonly used in Anglican churches for the hymn 'The day Thou gavest, Lord, is ended' were also used in the dance halls. Wouldn't we have to reverse our decision in each case? And doesn't this show that in fact it's the associations – the words that go with the music, or the context in which it's played – that settle the question of whether it's religious or not?

No. In both these cases it is the attitude of the hearers, rather than the associations or the context, which might at first influence us. If the tribe listened to the Strauss tune with every indication of awe, wonder, seriousness[1] and devotion, we should begin to think that we had missed something: perhaps Strauss had more in him than we thought: perhaps we had misappreciated the music, perhaps we were misled by always hearing it in cafés. And conversely, if all the dancers listened to the waltz of 'The day Thou gavest' without showing any seriousness at all, we might suppose that we had been 'conned' into regarding it as religious – it was just the words and the church atmosphere that had misled us.

But this would not settle the question. Even if the tribe is serious and the dancers are light-hearted, we might still think that both had *misjudged* the music. If the tribe is serious in a certain way about the Strauss waltz, then indeed (we might say) it is for them 'religious

---

[1] I have argued that religious objects are, centrally at least, objects of *awe*. They evoke an attitude of *worship*. This is consistent with some feelings (e.g. perhaps a kind of holy joy or ecstasy) but not with others (e.g. light-hearted gaiety). Hence there is a tolerably clear concept of 'religious music' (even though its borders are not rigid), which is different from the (much easier) concept of what music is or has been used in Anglican churches, Catholic fiestas, etc. Whether music is *suitable for worship* is a perfectly intelligible question, though in practice often very hard to answer.

E

music'. But we might still think that it wasn't *really* religious. Similarly the dancers' waltz is not seen by them as religious. But nevertheless it might really be so. We might regard the tribe as semi-idolatrous, and the dancers as semi-blasphemous. Only semi-, because music is not normally (so far as I am aware) an *object* of religious emotion: but (perhaps) designed to evoke the emotion itself, or to imitate its object.

Arguments about the borderline cases (the Verdi *Requiem* and *Tannhäuser* and many others) are, initially, arguments about musical style. But they are also arguments about what are proper and improper concomitants of religious emotions, attitudes and activities. We have first to agree on the adjectives with which we would describe these works. I may call the *Requiem* 'melodramatic', 'cheap', 'showy', and (in a derogatory sense) 'operatic': you may call it 'dramatic', 'powerful', 'grim'. It reminds me of the scenes with nuns and monks, which you may agree to be only pseudo-religious, in *Il Trovatore* and *La Forza del Destino*: it reminds you of the poems of William Dunbar and the Lyke-Wake Dirge, which I may agree to express truly religious sentiment. But suppose we agree. If I eventually come to agree with you about the qualities of the *Requiem*, I thereby agree either (outright) that it is religious music, or at least that it is on the way to being such. You may then justifiably accuse me of having previously been imperceptive, unbelieving, and almost blasphemous (in the sense of failing to be properly aware of what is great, dramatic, grim, and so on). If you eventually come to agree with me, you thereby agree that what you had previously taken as religious music was not: you accuse yourself of something like idolatry.

This brief account of the conceptual connections between awe, worship and religion should not be confused with an enquiry about the *origins* of religion, about the reasons or causes which have in fact generated religious awe and worship. There is much to be said here about economic, social and psychological causes which may, indeed, give us a picture of religions having arisen, and being sustained, by many disreputable-looking factors – perhaps economic and physical insecurity, fear of death, guilt, the desire for simple 'answers to life' and various other symptoms of a heteronomous outlook, and more profound and subtle causative factors. Marx, Freud, Durkheim and others are notorious for such remarks. This enquiry, however, is not relevant here: I mention it only to re-emphasize the difference between what is conceptually necessary to religion on the one hand, and what may contingently have, sometimes or always, been part of all religions in practice, or causes of their origin. For, as educators, we are concerned with the concept, the *sui generis* activity: and we are not obliged to incorporate into this activity other elements which may, historically, have accompanied it.

4. The categories of religious belief

We may now return to the problem of identifying religious beliefs, which we left unsolved earlier. A religious belief, we shall feel inclined to say initially, is a belief which is relevant, or taken by the believer to be relevant, to the appropriateness of a feeling of awe towards a particular object, or (more briefly) to the worshipfulness of that object. Just as beliefs in morality, or at least certain aspects of morality, may be formally defined as beliefs about what one ought to do overridingly, so religious beliefs may be defined as beliefs about what one ought to worship. The quick answer to the problems raised by Bambrough's example of Poseidon is this: What makes Homer's belief in Poseidon religious is that, whatever he thought the word 'Poseidon' stood for, he thought it to be an appropriate object of worship and awe: *not*, as Bambrough and many others suppose, that he had empirical expectations of some kind. For, as we saw in our earlier consideration of this example, this is *pro tanto* no more than a (false) *scientific* belief.

It is very important to get a firm grasp of this point, and we may use another of Bambrough's examples, where the goddess Athene appears to Telemachus in the guise of Mentor. This again seems at first sight to present us with only two alternatives. Either (a) we could believe that there was a superbeing, Athene, who took over Mentor's mind (and perhaps an extra Mentor-body); but the difficulty here is that this is an empirical belief, like the belief in Poseidon, and to that extent not religious. Or (b) we could believe that Mentor's words were 'inspired by Athene, that is to say by Athene as goddess of wisdom, that is to say, at the theoretical limit, by wisdom itself, as an animistic abstraction': and of this interpretation Bambrough says that it cannot be 'allowed to count as or to constitute really believing in Athene'. That is, such a belief amounts to no more than saying 'Mentor spoke wisely', or 'Wisdom inspired him': and nobody takes this seriously as a religious belief – it is, perhaps, more like a poetic fiction, analogous to the way in which we may whimsically talk of Cupid when we could just as well talk of being in love.

We should now be able to see what is wrong here. What is non-religious about talking whimsically of Cupid is just that such talk *is* usually whimsical, not that the talker does not believe in an empirical Cupid with real wings and a bow and arrow. If 'Cupid' stood for some object of worship, then a belief in Cupid would be a religious belief: and here it does not matter whether the believer has empirical expectations of seeing a winged boy. One may believe in and worship a winged boy, a mosaic picture of a winged boy, or a psychological force for which a winged boy may be the symbol. Similarly one may believe in and worship a superbeing who is very wise, one's own mental picture of such a superbeing, or whatever it is that we mean by the word 'wisdom' – to which we may not even wish to give a capital 'W'.

To say that the believer must have some 'empirical expectations' is thus either false or misleading. It is false, if we mean that he must expect the object of worship to perform in the world of material objects in the way that, say, Elijah expected God to send down fire from heaven, or Homer expected Athene to turn spears aside. It is misleading, if we mean only that the belief that a certain object, X, is worshipful entails the belief that X exists, and hence that there must be some kind of empirical or factual criteria for determining this, some method of verification or falsification. Of course this is true: if I believe in, and perhaps worship, something I call 'love' or 'wisdom', I have to be able to show that there are such things as love or wisdom – that 'love' and 'wisdom' are not just *words*. But this is just a rather cumbersome way of saying that, if it is a genuine belief or a meaningful assertion, then there must be some sort of evidence that will count for or against it. The truth of this is, in my opinion, undeniable, because it is analytic: briefly, the concepts of asserting, giving information, or claiming existence for something entail the concepts of evidence, verification and falsification. Some may perhaps wish to question this, but I shall not do so here.

This, however, seems to me quite harmless for the believer, *so long as he is prepared to accept that the object of his belief exists in the same sense that any other object exists.* Unfortunately Christian and other believers, especially nowadays and in the recent past, have talked as if there were more than one kind of existence; and nothing but sheer confusion, in my view, has been caused by trying to defend the notion of some absolute God as a concept to which the ordinary rules of logic somehow do not apply – an object of worship which is nevertheless somehow not an object at all. Non-believers have hardly helped by arguing as if this mysterious object-cum-non-object were the only sort of thing round which a respectable religion could form; and by taking it as a model case of religious belief, have often concluded that what passes and passed for religious belief is either bad science, or totally unintelligible.

Exactly what is implied by claiming existence for an object is a complex question. Here I wish only to re-emphasize the point that such terms as 'fact', 'true', 'real', 'exist', and so forth are not tied to that form of discourse which deals with physical objects: in questions of the form 'Is there such a thing as . . . ?' the word 'thing' does not always imply 'object', at least in the sense of something that can be *pointed* at. Such a view would be very much at variance with the way in which we usually talk. 'Is there such a thing as the number seven?' naturally receives an affirmative answer, where there is no question of pointing at an object: and any other intelligible noun-phrase substituted in the question 'Is there such a thing as . . . ?' will, at least, make sense, and cannot be dismissed on grounds of anything like a category mistake, unless the phrase is internally contradictory (as in 'married bachelor'). Existence and non-existence are no more categories than properties. We can ask such questions about love, the highest prime number, unicorns, Platonic relationships between the sexes, and so forth. What answer we give often depends largely on the context, and may take the form of placing the noun or noun-phrase in an appropriate category of discourse. Thus even 'Is there such a thing as a Jabberwock?' (said by a man trying to complete a crossword) may be answered by 'Yes, it's an animal in Lewis Carroll': or (said by a visitor to the zoo) by 'No, it's an imaginary creature'.

To mislead people about the existence of an object is, essentially, to talk in a way that cheats their expectations: to use phrases that imply that so-and-so and such-and-such are true, when they are not true. Thus if I am the author of a bestiary, and talk of unicorns on page 7, when I also talk of lions on page 6 and tigers on page 8, the reader would rightly object by saying that unicorns do not exist. It would be no defence for me to say 'Ah, well, I was talking about imaginary creatures, and these do exist: you'll find one in *Alice Through the Looking-Glass*.' For I did not use 'unicorn' in that way. Similarly if I talk of Poseidon in such a way that I imply, or indeed overtly state, that what I am talking about is an immense person in the bottom of the sea with a trident, then I am talking about what does not exist. I can, of course, use the word 'Poseidon' to mean rather 'the power of the sea', and then of course 'Poseidon' does exist.

This is why the first step in any full discussion of a man's religion must be to pin him down about what object exactly it is that he claims to worship. For on this turns the later question of whether that object is worshipful. Suppose two people with Christian-type views. One of them is quite unworried if it is proved historically that the resurrection never occurred, that Jesus was not born of a virgin, that he did not heal the sick, and so forth. His object of worship is not a material object: what he worships is a picture, an imaginary person, perhaps a story embodying a character whose historicity is irrelevant. The other person, however, worships an actual person, Jesus, in past history. His reasons for worship come in two stages: (i) anyone who rises from the dead, is born of a virgin, heals the sick, etc. is worthy of worship: (ii) there was a man called Jesus who as a matter of historical fact did these things. Empirical facts are not relevant to (i); but they are relevant to (ii). If the facts show that Jesus did not do these things, then (i) – his general tendency to worship anyone that does do them – remains untouched: but the *object* of his worship – a historical Jesus – is now shown not to exist.

It is important to realize that these stages are distinct. To take another example, a primitive believer might hold (i) that anyone who can kill people at a distance is worshipful, (ii) that the witch-doctor can do this. We prove to him empirically that (ii) is false. But we might also take exception to (i): that is, we might think that he was wrong about what was worshipful. And it might be particularly important to persuade him that he was wrong; for otherwise he might simply transfer his worship from the witch-doctor to other killers-at-a-distance – white men with long-range rifles, for instance.

There are thus two different ways (amongst many others) in which a man may be described as 'losing his faith'. First, he may undergo some emotional change, so that the *sort* of thing that seemed worshipful to him now no longer does; and secondly, he may be made aware by the empirical facts that the object of his worship is not (empirically) the sort of thing he thought it was.

Thus a Christian might, first, come to think that the humble, meek and unaggressive qualities of Jesus were not worshipful qualities: or, secondly, that Jesus did not in fact have those qualities.

We may now try to list more fully various types of belief that may have some claim to be called religious beliefs. A man may believe:

(1) That there are some kinds of things – he may not know *what* kinds – in the universe for which awe, worship, and so forth are appropriate.

(2) That any object that has the characteristics p, q, r, would be an appropriate recipient of awe, worship, etc.

(3) That there exists an object X: i.e. that there is something such that m, n, o, are true.

(4) That p, q, r, are true of X.

(5) That s, t, u, are true of X.

(1) To believe (1) is to believe no more than that *some* religious belief *could* be true: it is to accept the possibility of rightly-directed awe and worship. This in itself is not so much a religious belief, but a belief in the possibility of religion. We may leave this on one side, and clarify the remaining types of belief by means of examples.

(2) We have already given examples of (2) – the belief that any-one who rises from the dead, is born of a virgin, heals the sick, etc. is worshipful, and the belief that anyone who can kill at a distance is worshipful. So the characteristics p, q, r, might be 'able to send down fire from heaven', 'able to fill me with confidence and hope', 'having a name which banishes ghosts and vampires', or almost anything.

(3) To believe (3), as we have seen, is to believe that m, n, o, which delimit the believer's use of X, are true. Thus the belief that Jesus existed might be the belief that a man was born and named 'Jesus' in approximately 4 A.D. (m), achieved fame as a preacher and teacher (n), and was crucified in his thirties (o). This might be somebody's minimal meaning for the use of the term 'Jesus': and 'Jesus' in this sense would be shown not to exist only if, for instance, we discovered that the whole story was a late invention. Another man, however, might use 'Jesus' differently: he might not care when he was born, or whether he preached and taught, or whether he was crucified. By 'Jesus existed' he might mean only

that somebody existed among the Jews at some time (never mind his name or date of birth) (m), that he raised someone from the dead (n), and that he himself rose from the dead (o). His m, n, o, are different.

(4) Now we come to the real difficulty which makes religious beliefs hard to disentangle. Belief (4) is that X is characterized by the worshipful features p, q, r. The difficulty is this: that at least some of p, q, r, may be identical with m, n, o. This does not have to be so: a man may use 'Jesus' to *mean* (for instance) someone who was born in 4 A.D., son of Mary, a carpenter, crucified by Pilate, etc. (m, n, o), and keep Jesus' worshipful characteristics quite separate from this list (rising from the dead, healing the sick, etc. – p, q, r). But it is likely to be so: for believers, at least, there is almost certain to be an overlap between m, n, o and p, q, r. In other words, the object that they worship may be at least partly *defined* in terms of worshipful characteristics.

Suppose for the moment that the believer is right about belief (2) – that he is right in saying that any object with characteristics p, q, r, is a worshipful object. Suppose, for instance, that p, q, r, include such characteristics as 'wholly loving', 'able to work miracles' and 'suffering for others', and that we agree that these are worshipful characteristics. Now suppose that when the believer uses the word 'Jesus', he actually *means* 'a wholly loving, miracle-working, suffering person': i.e. his defining characteristics (m, n, o) are the same as his worshipful characteristics (p, q, r). Then the statement that Jesus is worthy of worship is analytically true: and the unbeliever must now argue, not about whether Jesus is worshipful, but about whether 'Jesus' in *this* sense existed.

This of course would be an extreme case, and an unusual use of 'Jesus' (which is normally tied, at least partly, to non-worshipful characteristics). The point is more evident in the case of 'God'. Either 'God' is defined empirically, so that the question can arise of whether God (so defined) is worshipful: or else 'God' is used simply to *mean* 'whatever it is that has worshipful characteristics', in which case 'God is worshipful' is analytically true. But the question can now arise of whether there is anything in the universe that instantiates these characteristics: that is, whether there is any X separately identifiable by the characteristics m, n, o, which also has the characteristics p, q, r.

Unfortunately the cases are usually not so clear-cut. Often believers partly use worship-characteristics as existence-characteristics, and partly use separate existence-characteristics (there is some overlap between m, n, o and p, q, r): and it is a very long job to sort this out. For instance, the 'Jesus' of Christian creeds appears to be partly defined by straightforward empirical characteristics ('suffered under Pontius Pilate'), and partly by characteristics that are at least thought to be connected with worshipful characteristics, if they are not themselves such ('Son of God', 'sitting at the right hand of the Father', etc.). There is of course the added difficulty that, in a fully-formed and sophisticated religion, we simply do not know *how* to take a great deal of the language: the metaphysic has a life of its own, which we can only understand by trying to go back to its beginnings. These are, however, difficulties of interpretation of particular religious beliefs, and do not affect our present classification.

(5) needs to be added, only because one may of course believe things about an object of worship which are neither connected with the identity of the object (m, n, o) nor with its worshipfulness (p, q, r), but just happen to be true about the object (s, t, u). Thus for most Christians the fact (if it is a fact) that Jesus had a beard, or five fingers on each hand, or was a carpenter, is not important, either to whether Jesus existed or to whether he was worshipful. Beliefs of this type, obviously, have little real claim to be called religious beliefs.

Three types, then, survive: (2) (the worshipfulness of certain characteristics) (3) (the existence of a particular object), and (4) (the attribution of those characteristics to that object). A complex belief involving all these elements would be of the form 'X, which exists because m, n, o, are the case, is worshipful, because X has characteristics p, q, r, which are worshipful characteristics'; and the objections that might be made are that X doesn't exist because m, n, o, aren't the case: that X doesn't have characteristics p, q, r: or that characteristics p, q, r aren't worshipful. For instance: either 'Poseidon' does not exist (there is no vast trident-bearing person in the sea); or Poseidon does not cause earthquakes and wreck ships; or causing earthquakes and wrecking ships are not qualities we should worship.

The purpose of this exercise is not the drawing of distinctions for their own sake; rather, we may now hope to see more clearly the kind of logical constituents of which a person's religious belief is made up, and hence how one might set about *educating* him in respect of these different constituents. From the point of view of the educator, we might list them simply as follows:

A. First, people sometimes believe that religious objects exist when they do not. Here we need to get them to say what they mean when they refer to such objects by such words as 'God', 'Poseidon', 'the transcendent', and so on: and then to direct their attention to the evidence for or against their existence. The crucial step here is the first: getting them to say what they mean is, in effect, the same process as getting them to accept certain kinds of evidence as relevant for the verification or falsification of the object's existence. Remembering our cross-questioning of Homer earlier, we must be prepared for them to be uncertain and to dither – not to have made up their minds exactly what object it is they *do* believe to exist.

B. Then we have to get them to say what characteristics they take to be worthy of awe, worship, and so on, and to examine their reasons for thinking so.

C. Then we have to get them to examine the objects of their worship (if they exist) and see whether they measure up to these criteria.

What needs to be noticed here is the particular importance of B and C, as against A, for religious education. For the beliefs in A – beliefs merely about the existence of an object – are relevant to religion, or count as religious beliefs, only if it is a *religious* object: only if the believer then goes on to join them to other beliefs in B and C. Thus the belief in the mere existence of Poseidon is only religiously relevant if a person goes on to say that certain characteristics are worshipful (B), and that Poseidon has those characteristics (C).

To put this another way, the educator needs, of course, to get his students clear about A: in particular, to rescue them from vagueness, woolliness, or sheer nonsense in their use of such words as 'God', 'ultimate reality', 'the transcendent', and so forth. It is also true that their religious and other emotions may be largely responsible for such lack of clarity, so that even in this category (A) the education of his students' emotions is far from irrelevant. But nevertheless, questions about what exists or what does not are not *per se religious* questions: and education in this field would be as much a matter of clear thinking, philosophical understanding, or knowledge of scientific fact as anything else. When, however, the educator is considering his students' tendency to worship (or not to worship) certain kinds of things (B), or certain objects because they have these characteristics (C), then he is right at the heart of religious education – and by the same token, at the heart of one area in the education of the emotions.

Finally, we must be clear that what we have given is a logical skeleton, and not a developmental or any other kind of empirical account. It may seem that we have spoken above as if a man *first* believed in the existence of a certain object (A), *then* took certain characteristics as worshipful (B), *then* came to believe that the object had these characteristics (C), and *then* engaged in a form of worship designed to express all this. But in practice any such person might be a rarity. Thus one obvious objection to taking our logical skeleton as a developmental picture is that most people never consciously make these moves at all; or that they do not necessarily make them in that order. If they are born into a thriving religious tradition, for instance, they may first start by actually worshipping, and then come to believe or take for granted that the object which they and their culture worship exists; and they may never consider whether the characteristics of the object are or are not truly worshipful. A lot of religious belief, one might guess, is in this sense unconscious and uncritical. But I shall say no more here, for fear of trespassing on ground which the psychologist, the social scientist and the historian should more fittingly till.

5. Religious and other 'outlooks'

In earlier chapters I have tried to elucidate a concept of religion as a *sui generis* activity (Chapter 2), which necessarily involves awe and worship (Chapter 3), and which is typified by certain kinds of belief (Chapter 4). I now want to go on to show how this activity, although *sui generis* (because of its particular connection with awe and worship), is nevertheless importantly *like* other activities which it would not be correct to call 'religious'. Most importantly of all, I shall want to show that it is like them in that the same criteria of rationality – the same applications of terms like 'being reasonable' or 'being educated' – apply to both. I shall want to show that all these activities, including those that we have taken to be specifically religious, are based on the emotions: and hence that to be educated in respect of them is, at least centrally, to be educated in the sphere of the emotions. The reader who follows me so far will then be able to join me in Part II of the book, where we shall investigate the education of the emotions in its own right.

Before we proceed, however, I want (at the risk of being repetitious) to make quite sure that the general nature of our task is clear.

1. First, the reader will remember that our interest in elucidating this *sui generis* activity stemmed from our interest in education. If we are going to talk seriously about *education* in religion, as we already talk about education in science, history and so forth, we need first to have elucidated some kind of activity, with its own type of beliefs and attitudes, which is liable in its own way to various kinds of error and unreason. Without this, we would not know what it was we were trying to educate people *in*, or how to help them hold rational beliefs and make rational choices in this form of thought. In particular, we need to have distinguished the activity from others with which it may be confused: to have shown that, even after we have extracted the categories of historical, moral, scientific and other belief from specific religions, there is still something of the highest importance left over. Without achieving

this, we should still be in the position criticized in Chapter 1 (pp. 1-14), where 'religious education' was either no more than a rag-bag title for education in other forms of thought (the history of the church, the moral outlook of Christians, etc.), and there-fore not *religious* education: or – worse – the indoctrination of a particular attitude, and therefore not religious *education*.

Consequently there are two topics with which we have *not* been primarily concerned.

(a) I have not been talking about specific *religions*. The words 'Christianity', 'Islam', 'Buddhism' and so on stand for groups of phenomena (beliefs, activities, institutions, and so on) which may appear to have very little direct connection with awe and worship, and which may seem to be very much more concerned with 'ways of life', 'allegiance to authority', 'commitment', 'pictures of the world', and so on. This is not in question: nor is it denied that some of these phenomena, though having little or nothing to do with awe and worship, may be conceptually necessary for these specific religions (for instance, anything that did *not* offer a particular moral outlook might not count as 'Christianity').

(b) Nor has my chief concern been with the *word* 'religion'. Here I would remind the reader of what was said in Chapter 2 about distinguishing logical types of human activity. I have not been trying to find the 'essence of religion' by just glaring at the way the word is used, but have examined the use of the word only in order to elucidate a type of activity and belief which is *sui generis*, and cannot be assimilated to other activities, for example explaining, making moral judgements, stating historical facts and so forth.

Our account of religion is, then, perfectly consistent with the facts (if they are facts) (1) that specific religions may not be primarily connected with awe and worship but rather with other emotions and activities, (2) that there may be *some* uses of 'religion' which are not conceptually tied to awe and worship at all. Thus Buddhism, certain kinds of Hinduism, and more novel movements such as Subud have perhaps very little to do with awe or worship: yet they are called 'religions'.[1] However, we then want to ask what they *are*

---

[1] Several people have told me that awe is not significant in the New Testa-ment. I find this odd. It seems to me that the whole of the New Testament is

concerned with. We may then say that they are concerned with (i) the practice of techniques designed to produce 'spiritual well-being' or 'mental health', for example ensuring benefits that will accrue if certain alleged facts (such as the transmigration of souls) are the case: and/or (ii) putting forward some ideal for humanity, or a 'way of life'. But then, even though they are *called* religions, it is not clear that these concerns are any different from those of other outlooks which are not called 'religions'. Thus (i) believers in Yoga, 'health cures', and certain rather *outré* forms of mass psychotherapy are concerned to develop 'spiritual well-being', and may adduce alleged facts to back up their practices and techniques; (ii) believers in chivalry, honour, the Superman, or whatever, also put forward ideals and 'ways of life'; yet none of these are commonly called 'religions'. The application of the word, though doubtless not accidental, does not always correspond to the sorts of differences we are concerned with.

There may be those who do not share our particular concerns, and who still feel inclined to say that, for them, religion 'means something else'. I have no quarrel with such people, whose interests may lie not in making sense of religious education but in preserving their own outlooks, faiths, ways of life and so forth. I can only ask them to realize that our own concerns do not threaten theirs, and to remember the distinction between (i) what religion 'means' to a person, to which there may be as many answers as there are people, and (ii) what is the most sensible use for the word 'religion', having regard to all the phenomena. Thus (i) to one man religion may 'mean' simply following the Christian ethic, or going to church on Sundays, or feeling worried about the universe: but (ii) this will obviously not do for any useful *definition* of religion, or for an adequate discussion of religious education. The remark 'When I say religion I mean the Christian religion, and when I say the Christian religion of course I mean the Church of England' is usually quoted as a joke. (He can mean that by it, but that's not what *it means*.)

2. Secondly, the rest of this book does not in any case stand or fall by what we have said about religion as a *sui generis* activity.

---

set in a background of a God-worshipping culture: that the people of Jesus' time were in awe of their God (or at least thought that they ought to be), and some of them in awe of Jesus himself: and that many events described are unintelligible except by reference to this emotion.

For it seems to me, though I cannot prove it here, that *any* plausible view of religion will inevitably relate religion closely to the emotions. If, for instance, it is thought that 'religion' has to do with ways of life, general commitments, morality, attitudes to the world, 'ultimate concern', and so forth, then the connection with the emotions is plain enough. Certainly, if for some people 'religion' still 'means' something which has no, or no very important, connection with emotions of any kind, then what I shall go on to say about the emotions will not for such people be relevant to religion (though it may still be useful in its own right). This would be the case, for instance, if anyone seriously regarded 'religion' chiefly as a matter of explaining certain facts (the design of the universe, creation, and so on). But I should hope that few people would take any such view: and such people may find it useful, before making up their minds irrevocably, to read Appendix I.

3. Finally, I have left it an open question whether we should be in awe, worship, or entertain the prospect of religion at all, and if so of what objects we should be in awe, what objects we should worship, and what our religion should be. This topic is obviously very important, and is briefly discussed in Appendix II. But it is not central to my main argument. My purpose is not to defend or attack religion as an activity and set of beliefs: but first, to elucidate it, and secondly, to show how the educator can deal with it. The educator as such (unlike the private individual) is not, in my view, called upon to take a stand for or against the activity we have out-lined: but he is called upon to be clear about what sort of activity it is, what types of errors and unreason may be manifested in this and cognate activities, and what sort of qualities his students need to develop in order to avoid these errors. This is a very different matter.

I have tried to show, then, that religious beliefs and the religious attitude are crucially connected with the emotions (and with awe in particular). But they are not the only beliefs and attitude to be so connected; and we shall not be able to pursue our task of evolving a rationale for religious education without first being able to see religion as only one phenomenon in a particular class of phenomena, whose nature may give us some guide to the criteria we need. I begin with some important if roughly-stated truisms. For human beings, the world does not consist only of sensory empirical facts.

Things in the world are not only red, square, and heavy, but also frightening, admirable, sad, and glorious. Growing up, we have to structure both our sense-experience and our emotional experience into some kind of reliable and stable pattern. We invest (one might say) our emotions, more or less permanently, in certain objects. Everybody does this. For various reasons, the world of sense-objects is remarkably similar for nearly all of us: but the world of emotion-objects is often very different. Nevertheless, every sane person inhabits an emotional world that is sufficiently constant for him to feel tolerably at home in it. The furniture of this world may consist of people, physical objects, words, ideas, equations, images, or anything to which he may attach emotions: and there are no logical limits to this. Any sane person, then, may be said to have an emotional 'outlook': and the comparative stability and adequacy of this outlook may be said to 'make sense of life' for him. In other words, his emotional life is (a) sufficiently ordered for him not to feel lost, over-anxious, uncertain or disintegrated, and (b) sufficiently adequate or worthwhile for him not to feel it to be boring, pointless, or devoid of pleasure.

'Outlook' is a sufficiently general word to include the whole range of very different cases in which we are interested. This range may be imagined as extending from an inarticulate, theory-free case where a man simply and regularly feels certain emotions in relation to certain objects, to the highly articulated, theory-laden, 'system-building' case where a man casts his emotions into some well-structured form that has every right to be called a metaphysic or a religion. One can move along the range, for example from (i) the man who just doesn't like women very much, via (ii) the man who thinks that women are 'irrational', 'inferior' or 'untrustworthy', and (iii) the man who thinks that 'the place of women is in the home' or that 'women are meant to take orders from men', to (iv) the man who holds a full-blown metaphysical or religious theory, according to which God has made woman to take the lower place (combined with mutually supporting arguments and instances from within his metaphysical system).

The differences in these cases are clearest (because most studied) in mental patients: though even here they are far from being really clear. But we can at least see a plain difference between the extremes: the neurotic, who feels frightened – unreasonably, as he knows – when dealing with other people, and the advanced psychotic, whose

F

fear is cast in the form of a very complex and quite possibly coherent system – he seems to believe that everyone is plotting against him, that they hide their hostility with diabolical cunning, and so forth. The difference is that in the former case the neurotic's emotions do not affect his (conscious) judgement, whereas the psychotic's emotions generate what look like (but may not be properly described as) a set of actual beliefs about other people, which make it impossible for his normal judgement of other people to operate.

The term 'institutionalization', borrowed from sociology, is useful here because it brings out the idea of *giving a form* or structure to feelings and beliefs (just as a political party may give shape to a set of interests, or a political institution give a concrete form to the clash of the interests of different parties, and thus 'institutionalize' the conflicts). Thus the man who gets unreasonably angry and fails to recognize it will have a false picture of the world: he will think, perhaps, that other people are always out to frustrate him, or that he alone is doing the will of God in a world of wicked sinners who bring down the just wrath of God on their heads. As we shall see (p. 134), unreasonable emotions are not only *based on* but also likely to *lead to* false beliefs; and these will be apt to take the form of *rationalizations* – that is, beliefs designed to make his emotions and behaviour look plausible or reasonable, both to other people and to himself.

It is clear enough how well a religious or other metaphysical outlook is suited to this role, and why such highly-articulated outlooks have always been popular as forms of institutionalization. We may mention three general reasons amongst many. First, they are respectable because of this very popularity: the claim to be possessed by devils, inspired by visions, or directed by God is in many societies regarded with more awe than suspicion. Secondly, such outlooks are both capacious and flexible: a supernatural world may be furnished fully enough to suit all our psychological requirements, and the furniture can be changed without any obvious disadvantages ensuing in our relationships with the real world. Thirdly, just because they are not (or at least not directly) related to the world of empirical fact, the outlooks are very well defended against criticism: thus a man who believes that he is being attacked with radio waves has to face the fact that radio waves are not harmful, whereas a man who believes that God is punishing him does not have to face any facts at all.

There is no need here, I think, for a full analysis of the notion of a metaphysic. To discuss the 'normal use' of the word – whatever the 'normal use' may be – would not get us far: though certainly some degree of hypostatization and articulation of belief-structure would be necessary for calling something a 'metaphysic' (rather than, say, a taboo, or an ideal)[1]. However, we may note that it seems unreasonable to reserve the term only for those articulated belief-systems that are either commonly shared or held to be respectable. The outlooks of Nazi theorists, of Swedenborg, Mohammed, Plato, Jesus or the unknown man in the asylum (who might very well be accepted as a prophet in another society) are logically similar in that they are metaphysical, whatever we may think of their merits. It is, of course, highly significant that (in extreme cases at least) we commonly criticize certain metaphysical outlooks as being 'mad', 'lunatic', 'the product of a disordered mind', and so forth. But this does no more than draw attention to the kind of criteria appropriate for assessing metaphysical outlooks in general.

It is perhaps a pity that philosophers have been almost exclusively concerned with highly-articulated and traditional metaphysical outlooks: outlooks which, even if irrational or partially insane, will have been generally accepted by society. But of course there is no necessary correlation between the social popularity of a metaphysic and the intelligence (in the ordinary sense) of its protagonists, on the one hand, and its rationality on the other. Thus there are important respects in which some religious metaphysics are more like being (romantically) in love than they are like, for instance, the metaphysics of Spinoza or Hegel: and a full and detailed analysis might do better to start with such cases. We have *some* idea about how we would discuss the rationality of, say, Titania's being in love with Bottom, or Tristan with Isolde, or even our next-door neighbour with his girl-friend, though full-scale metaphysics may baffle us more.

I do not, of course, intend to deny that metaphysical outlooks

[1] Articulation: for a simple-minded belief in a sun-god, for instance, would not count as a metaphysic; it would become so only if combined with some more or less complex and coherent set of other beliefs. Hypostatization: for such ideals as medieval chivalry or the Japanese *bushido* are complex and highly articulated, yet need not suggest any realm of supernatural entities – they are ideals or codes, not metaphysics. But of course the borderline is blurred.

may be characterized in many other ways. Thus, to mention only a few, we may be interested in the intellectual consistency of some full-blown metaphysical system; or we may regard some metaphysical notions as attempts to approach problems which we now deal with by other disciplines (modern philosophy, cosmology, and so on); or we may take note of the cultural and historical genesis of such systems, or of the political use to which they may be put; or we may observe the way in which some such systems may help to encourage or sponsor work in the scientific or other fields; or in how they may be used as models or pictures of the universe, or of some features of the universe, perhaps useful for some purposes but distorting elsewhere. All these imply different approaches to the very heterogeneous phenomena that we array under the title 'metaphysics'; and it must not be thought that our own approach is uniquely meritorious.

On the other hand, if we are concerned with the *truth* or *rationality* of metaphysical outlooks – rather than with their usefulness, or with empirical facts about their origin and function – there is a strong case to be made out for our particular line of attack. What is *peculiar* to metaphysical outlooks is surely that there is some kind of emotional involvement: an involvement which does, indeed, show itself symptomatically in the well-known philosophical difficulties about the verification and use of metaphysical assertions, but which in fact lies deeper. One may talk helpfully of Freudianism as providing a model for psychological understanding, or of Marxism as sponsoring a certain type of political or economical development, or of some of the metaphysical pronouncements of professional philosophers as dramatic ways of drawing attention to important points. But (one wants to say) what makes these *metaphysics*, rather than just models or sponsors or dramatic philosophy, is that people cling to them emotionally. It does not perhaps matter very much whether we want to make this a necessary condition for the application of the term 'metaphysics': nor is it essential to define more closely the point at which we want to stop talking merely of an outlook and start talking of a metaphysical outlook. These are interesting questions, but not crucial for our own task.

We have already said enough earlier to show that religion is not properly characterized by empirical beliefs, though it may make use of them. The same is true of metaphysical and other outlooks. A set of empirical beliefs is established, defended or attacked by the usual methods of verification and falsification: we talk here of tests, experiments, balancing the evidence, considering the probabilities – and this kind of talk is not at home in metaphysical or religious contexts. Even if metaphysicians or religious believers were to accept it, they would no longer be engaged in metaphysical or religious thinking, but in a kind of science. What characterizes metaphysics is what characterizes other 'outlooks' (in our sense): namely, emotional investment in certain objects.

From our example of the man with persecution mania, it may seem that a metaphysical outlook involves the person in false empirical beliefs. I say 'seem', because he has not arrived at them, and is not prepared to defend them, by normal empirical methods. He is not like the person who mistakenly supposes that there are unicorns, just because he has heard people talk of them or seen them depicted in a medieval bestiary. He has such a strong emotional need, or compulsion, to 'believe' that other people are always plotting against him that he is unwilling or unable to face any facts that might be presented to him in order to convince him that his belief is untrue.

How should we describe this case? Certainly the man acts as if he believed people to be plotting against him, and he says the words 'People are always plotting against me'. But such a proposition, in normal English, is conceptually tied to other propositions that would verify or falsify it, such as 'If given a chance, they attack', or 'They discuss their plots in private', or 'They behave differently towards me than towards other people'. Now if the man accepts no evidence as counting for or against his belief, his belief seems to have no propositional meaning: and then there is, as it were, nothing for him to believe. We may talk here of an unconscious belief, a 'blik', or of a paranoiac attitude, or of a certain kind of emotional outlook on other people. And though this outlook may cause him to utter words which, ordinarily interpreted, would suggest that he holds a false empirical belief, it is more correct to say that he does not consciously hold any empirical belief at all. He is simply *not interested* in the facts. The only way in which one can get at him (and perhaps cure him) is by persuading him to face his emotions themselves.

I do not of course imply that all metaphysical outlooks are cases of mental ill-health, which have to be cured: and the case of the paranoiac is an extreme one. Nevertheless, it illustrates the general point that metaphysical outlooks, like religious ones, generate what look like empirical beliefs, when in fact the crucial beliefs are concerned with the emotions and lie behind the pseudo-empirical assertions. In this example perhaps the crucial belief is something like 'All other people are terrifying'. We could set out the components of this general belief in some such way as we set out the components of religious belief earlier. These component beliefs, and the general belief which is founded on them, can be true or false – in this case, plainly false. More important, however, is the fact that the paranoiac does not realize that this is what he believes: his belief emerges only in the symptomatic form of pseudo-empirical assertions.

I take this to be generally true of metaphysical and religious beliefs. They get off the ground so quickly, as it were, that the foundations of the structure become virtually invisible. This may happen in various ways, amongst which it is important to make at least one rough distinction. First, there may be or have been consciously held beliefs (for example in the worshipfulness of a certain type of object, or in the fearfulness of other people) which afterwards are taken for granted and sink into the background, though they may be recalled by the believer without much difficulty. But, secondly, it may be that part at least of the crucial beliefs are unconscious: that it is, under normal conditions, impossible for the believer to recall them at all. Thus the paranoiac, let us suppose, unconsciously identifies all other people with his parents, who may indeed have been terrifying, whilst at no time does he consciously say to himself 'Other people are like my parents, and also terrifying', which is a crucial component of his belief. In an even more complex case, he may only have seen his parents as terrifying when in fact they were not. We have here a great many different cases, where one or more of the component beliefs, or even the general belief itself, may be at first invisible to us. Whether or not we can talk properly of 'unconscious beliefs' – and this we shall discuss later – it is plain that we can expect no easy assessment of the rationality of any particular metaphysical belief.

As we move away from anything that could reasonably be called 'metaphysics', into the area of outlooks that might better (but still of course far too vaguely) be described as 'ideals', 'ultimate values', 'pictures of how life ought to be', and so on, it becomes much more obvious that the crucial elements are not empirical beliefs but emotional attitudes. A man who believes in the medieval concept of honour or chivalry feels *admiration* for Hotspur and *contempt* for Falstaff: a puritan feels *disgust* or *guilt* about sex: a believer in 'Arab destiny' or 'the spirit of the German nation' feels *hatred* for and *fear* of the Jews, and so forth. As we have seen, these feelings may stand simply by themselves or emerge in the form of a complex system: thus a man may merely feel revulsion at certain sexual acts or parts of the body, or he may subscribe to some very complex sexual code, or even to something which we could properly call a sexual metaphysic. Further, it may be very difficult to know exactly what emotions, and objects of emotion, start the whole thing off: does the Arab or the Nazi begin by hating the Jews, or does he first fear them? Or envy them? These are just a few of the problems that face us in this area.

What we have to deal with, then, is a number of outlooks which differ in many dimensions. We have noticed differences in the degree of complexity and hypostatization, and also in the kind of emotional investment which sustains them: but there are of course many other differences. We might enquire about the degree or extent to which the outlook in fact dictates, or is supposed to dictate, the wants and behaviour of the individual – does it control all his life-choices, or only some? – or about how far the original emotional investment is conscious or unconscious; and of course there could be and have been many enquiries about the social and psychological origins and causes of these outlooks. My impression is that a good deal of conceptual work is needed in the field by way of taxonomy and classification before any very useful empirical work can be done – or, if done already, before the significance of such work can be properly assessed.

In particular, perhaps, what is needed to help the educator is a satisfactory account of the various outlooks or forms of institutionalization that connects them with their original emotional investment. Many writers have nibbled at this task, but the majority seem to have been either doctrinaire or confused and I know of no work that does sufficient justice to the wide variety of such outlooks. (Thus Freud's remarks on religion, although often illuminating, for the most part apply only to a particular brand of Christianity popular in his time, and are plainly inspired by partisan feeling.) Some attempt must be made at a taxonomy in psychological terms, perhaps along the lines suggested by some of this Unit's current researches.[1] But this, of course, is only one of the many tasks which need to be undertaken if religious education and the education of the emotions are to be coherently developed in schools and other institutions.

So far we have been chiefly concerned with the way in which emotions generate metaphysical and other outlooks: but we need also to notice the way in which they generate, via these outlooks, particular *wants* and *behaviour*. This is a large topic in itself: here we shall have to be content with a very brief account. What seems to happen is roughly this. First a man reacts *emotionally* to some object or state of affairs. He feels, for instance, horror or disgust at certain kinds of sexual behaviour: or he feels admiration or respect for a certain kind of person (someone who is sexually chaste, 100 per cent physically fit, and so on). Because of this, he *wants* something:[2] the abolition of unchaste behaviour, or to be 100 per cent fit. To achieve this want may be assumed either to give him positive pleasure (when he is 100 per cent fit) or at least to diminish his dissatisfaction (if society becomes more chaste, so that he no longer feels quite so disgusted). Consequently he directs his choices and *behaviour* towards attaining this end.

Very often it is only the believer's wants and behaviour which are readily available to our inspection: the original emotional investment, and consequently the reasons why he has these wants and behaves as he does, may well remain obscure. It is hence both easy and dangerous for philosophers and others to impose some kind of conceptual straitjacket on various outlooks and metaphysics: to assume, in other words, that outlooks must somehow all fit into one pattern: usually, the pattern which the man with the straitjacket takes to be most 'reasonable'. For instance, a simple-minded utilitarian might be inclined to account for the Jews' attitude to pork as arising from some kind of belief in hygiene, or for the universal horror of incest as following on biological knowledge. Or, in asking why 'reverence towards the elders' is so large

---

[1] See N. Williams, 'Children's Moral Thought' in *Moral Education*, Vol. I nos. 1 and 2, 1969 (Pergamon Press).

[2] We do not need to enquire here whether his emotion is a reason for his want, or conceptually entails it: the answer to this may depend on what emotion-word we use in each case. Thus one might argue that anger entails wanting to attack, but with some words it is not so clear: if 'admiration' or 'pride' entail any specifically identifiable wants, or even wishes, I am not sure what they are.

a part of the lives at least of primitive peoples, he might argue: 'Older people have more experience and knowledge: therefore there are good utilitarian reasons why they should be listened to, respected, and so on. If the outlook persists where the elders cease to be wiser and more experienced, then this is just the inertia of tradition at work.'

This straitjacketing is still more tempting if a single name such as 'religious' or 'Christian' is given to what may be, if we categorize them intelligently, a very wide variety of different outlooks. Thus one writer, whose concern is chiefly with reasons for moral views, says

> ... I suspect that religious views differ from 'humanist' views, not by denying the essential moral relevance of human benefit or harm, but rather by incorporating very different beliefs as to what really is good or bad for human beings. The religious believer finds in a supernatural order a whole extra dimension of preeminently important gains and losses ...[1]

But such research as we have already undertaken suggests that this is over-simple. Some people who would on other criteria count as religious believers take this line; others use or purport to use as their ultimate criteria (a) obeying the authority of God (awe), (b) avoiding the wrath of God and his punishments (fear), (c) living up to the ideal enshrined in the life of Christ (admiration), and so forth. The categories here may be described as those of authority, expediency and a kind of ego-ideal; other categories (in terms of guilt, shame, non-rationalized taboo or inhibition, conformity to laws and rules, and so on) also figure in interview-answers that might be described as 'religious'. Moreover, subjects will give different answers at different stages of an interview.

It is commonplace that when two people with radically different metaphysical or other outlooks argue with each other neither is likely to be convinced: briefly, that what is a reason for one man seems not to be a reason for the other. If I am right in insisting upon the connection between emotions on the one hand and out-looks, wants and behaviour on the other, this is not surprising. To one man the starry heavens above are objects of awe and wonder, to another they are objects only of interest and aesthetic pleasure; to one Hitler (Jesus, Mohammed, Lenin) is admirable and heroic,

[1] G. J. Warnock, *Contemporary Moral Philosophy*, p. 79, note 27.

to another he is contemptible and disgusting: and from these and other emotions flow different outlooks and different choices.

These enormous differences should make us hesitate before too quickly asserting which outlooks and choices are 'reasonable' and which are not. If we make such assertions, we shall have achieved nothing except to set people whose outlooks are radically different from ours against what we call 'reason'. This point, and the general problem we have to face, is well exemplified by Troilus' attitude (based on 'honour') to the utilitarian-type arguments of Helenus and Hector:

> TROILUS: You are for dreams and slumbers, brother priest;
> You fur your gloves with reason. Here are your reasons:
> You know an enemy intends you harm;
> You know a sword employ'd is perilous,
> And reason flies the object of all harm:
> Who marvels then, when Helenus beholds
> A Grecian and his sword, if he do set
> The very wings of reason to his heels,
> And fly like chidden Mercury from Jove,
> Or like a star disorb'd? Nay, if we talk of reason,
> Let's shut our gates and sleep: manhood and honour
> Should have hare-hearts, would they but fat their thoughts
> With this cramm'd reason: reason and respect
> Make livers pale, and lustihood deject.
>
> HECTOR: Brother, she is not worth what she doth cost
> The holding.
>
> TROILUS: What is aught but as 'tis valued?[1]

How are we to judge and assess such cases as these? There are, of course, senses in which an outlook offers a man *some* kind of reason, when he is defending particular beliefs, wants or actions. If a man believes in some metaphysical ideal which might be expressed by him as 'the spirit of the German nation' or 'Arab destiny', then he may defend his action (a) as realizing that ideal in a particular instance, or (b) as promoting some state of affairs which would realize that ideal. Thus (a) if part of what he means by 'Arab destiny' is conquering Israel, then if he joins an Israel-

---

[1] *Troilus and Cressida*, II, 2, 37–52: cf. Martha in Mrs. Gaskell's *Cranford* (Chapter XIV) 'Reason always means what someone else has got to say'.

See also, for this and other points in this chapter, my *Equality* (Hutchinson 1966), pp. 137–52.

conquering army he is *eo ipso* fulfilling Arab destiny; (b) if he stays in Egypt and knits socks for the soldiers, he may prefer to say that, though he is not himself fulfilling Arab destiny, he is making it possible for Arab destiny to be fulfilled. Again, a man who believes in the ideal of a sexually chaste society may object to pornographic literature because (a) a society which sells such literature would not count for him as a sexually chaste society – the existence of such literature would count directly against his ideal; or (b) because, though he does not mind such literature in itself, he thinks that it will incite people to sexual licence: which latter would of course count directly against his ideal.

But what this shows is, again, the importance of obtaining criteria for the original ideal or emotional investment. For the kind of reasons in the example above are (we would want to say) only reasons for *that* man: why should *we* feel like this about Arab destiny or a chaste society? Or, again, even if we grant that one ideal or metaphysic may be right or reasonable for one man, and another for another, must we not also say that (at least in some cases) an ideal or metaphysic may be wrong or unreasonable for any man, or that it may be wrong or unreasonable for the particular man who adopts it? Surely we must say this. To take a parallel, the fact that different drugs suit different medical cases is perfectly consistent, as we very well know, with the fact (a) that some drugs may be harmful for everyone, (b) that a particular drug may be harmful for a particular person. In other words, there will be criteria to be applied for ideals and metaphysics, as for drugs, in each case, even though it may be true that we ought not all to have the same drugs or the same ideals and metaphysics. To the question of how to establish such criteria we shall now turn.

PART TWO

The Emotions

6. Methodology

In the rest of this book my intention is to provide some guidance for the educator in the sphere which may be labelled 'education of the emotions', and which includes education in religious and other emotion-based outlooks. Plainly this cannot be done without at least taking note of such questions as 'What emotions ought one to feel, and on what occasions? What is to count as a good reason for having this or that outlook (and the wants and behaviour which follow from it)?' and so on. I have to commit myself to some kind of approach, some methodology, in the face of such questions: and there is a good deal of philosophical literature which bears on them. On the other hand, this is not the place for a lengthy and detailed philosophical analysis of the various positions that different writers have adopted. The best I can do, therefore, is to give some (inevitably too brief) indication of one possible approach which, though both popular and important, seems to me (for my purposes at least) methodologically unsatisfactory: and then to sketch out the approach which I shall in fact adopt.[1]

I. SPECIFIC CONTENT

This first approach involves trying to establish what we might call an appropriate content, or appropriate objects, for wants and emotions: and hence an appropriate and delimited set of reasons for having wants and emotions. The programme has two aspects, which are often confused. The first (a) is to formulate some kind of logical connection between wanting, fearing, etc. and their objects: to try to show that there are only certain things which a man can ('logically' or 'intelligibly') want, fear, etc. The second (b) is to show that in practice there are only certain things which men in fact can or do want. I shall deal with these in turn, but begin by quoting passages which are relevant to the approach in general.

[1] On this see R. M. Hare, *Descriptivism* (British Academy Lecture, O.U.P. 1963), pp. 122–34.

Now there are, perhaps, no logical limits to what a person may be said to want; and doubtless there is nothing of which it can be said that necessarily everyone wants it; but are there not limits, nevertheless, to what a person may be said *understandably* to want? What does he want it for? What appeals to him about it? In what way, should he get what he wants, does he expect to be satisfied? If we have no notion at all of answers to these questions, then someone's assertion that he wants whatever it may be is, in a clear sense, not intelligible to us; we do not understand what he says, because we do not understand *him*. How would beings from Mars, if set down, say, in London, evaluate what they found there? What would they be favourably struck by, what would they take against? Clearly one has no way of answering these questions, precisely because one knows nothing about such beings; one does not know what their needs would be, what they would want of their environment, what they would like or dislike. Thus, though in a sense one might say that absolutely any feature of their environment might be regarded by them as a criterion of merit or desirability, this is not to say that we could always *understand* its being so regarded: it is rather to concede that we have no understanding of the evaluations of hypothetical Martians. Conversely, a feature, to function as an intelligible criterion of desirability or merit, must surely be such that we could at least understand, say, someone's wanting something to have it; and it is not true that just any feature at all meets this condition. It follows further that it is not true to say, that evaluation rests ultimately on *choice*. For we do not choose to want this or that, to prefer one thing to another; when we have choices to make, we do not in turn choose what are to be reasons for choosing. To take that line, as we suggested earlier that prescriptivism does, is to imply that in the end there *are* no reasons at all.[1]

Again:

But is not anything wantable, or at least any perhaps attainable thing? It will be instructive to anyone who thinks this to approach someone and say: 'I want a saucer of mud', or 'I want a twig of mountain ash'. He is likely to be asked what for; to which let him reply that he does not want it *for* anything, he just wants it . . . would he [the questioner] not try to find out in what aspect the object desired is desirable? Does it serve as a symbol? Is there something delightful about it? Does the man want to have something to call his own, and no more? . . . Imagine saying 'I want a pin' and when asked why, saying 'For fun'; or 'Because

[1] G. J. Warnock, *Contemporary Moral Philosophy*, pp. 66–67: see also p. 55 ff. (his italics).

of the pleasure of it'. One would be asked to give an account making it at least dimly plausible that there was a pleasure here.[1]

(a) *Intelligibility*

My difficulty with this kind of thesis is over the sense to be given to words like 'understandable', 'intelligible', 'plausible', and so on. To illustrate this, let us consider the particular cases of two men. One of them wants 'a chaste society', the other wants 'things grouped in threes': and we are to assume that we have a sufficiently clear description of these phrases to enable us to know what would count as these wants being realized. First, in what sense are these wants 'understandable'?

(1) It is true that 'wanting' is often conceptually connected with 'thinking something to be desirable', itself connected with 'trying to get'. If a person said he wanted something, but denied that getting it would serve some ulterior purpose, or bring him satisfaction, or at least diminish his present dissatisfaction, we would have no grounds, or anyway weaker grounds, for saying that he wanted it (rather than, for example, that he simply *found* himself pursuing it or acted under compulsion). But so long as a man (a) believes something like this, (b) can describe what he wants, and (c) tries to get it, we know that he wants it: the words in which he expresses his want are not unintelligible, however 'odd' the object of his want may be. So the wants of both these men are understandable in that we know (i) what they want and (ii) that they want it.

(2) The former want (a chaste society) is 'understandable' in the sense that we can fairly easily imagine ourselves wanting it, that we know people who want it, that we to some extent sympathize with the man wanting it. (In this sense we talk of 'an understandable feeling of disgust', or 'an understandable desire to make one's own way in the world': roughly equivalent to 'natural', 'acceptable', 'the sort of thing we can easily imagine'.) The latter want is perhaps *less* understandable in this sense: strictly, we *can* (with difficulty) imagine ourselves wanting it – that is, we can suppose ourselves saddled with this passion for grouping things in threes, going around grouping them, and so on – even though we feel no particular sympathy with this

[1] G. E. M. Anscombe, *Intention*, pp. 70 and 72 (her italics).

G

desire and would consider it psychologically odd or curious.
But this seems to be a matter of degree, and it is difficult to see
that anything of philosophical importance follows from it, at
least in the context of our present interests.

(3) Another interpretation of 'understandable' would relate to
understanding *why* these people found satisfaction (or thought
they would find it) in realizing their wants. But this seems
merely a matter of factual knowledge. To take another example,
suppose Martians constantly listen to classical music, and say
they enjoy it and want to listen to it: but they say it gives them
no aesthetic pleasure, and anyway they are tone-deaf. We cannot
understand why they can want or enjoy it. But then we learn
that classical music has certain kinds of purely acoustic properties which affect Martians physically, and perhaps we say
'Ah, yes, the soundwaves affect them rather as alcohol affects
us: now we understand how it is that they enjoy it, it's a sensual
pleasure'.[1]

(4) It is no doubt at the oddity of the *reasons* for these wants that
the thesis directs our attention. We naturally assume that the
man who wants a chaste society thinks unchastity leads to unhappiness and social disorder, or at the very least that an unchaste society would make him personally unhappy or angry
or upset; and conversely, we are at a loss to think of any reason
in virtue of which the other man wants things grouped in threes.
However, these positions might be reversed: if the second man
tells us that he gets paid for grouping things in threes, or that
such groups give him intense aesthetic pleasure, his want becomes
'understandable' in the sense that we can now see what his
reason for wanting it is. And if the chastity-seeker had absolutely
no reason – if he did not believe that there was something about
a chaste society which made it worth having, or which gave him
pleasure, then we should have no grounds for saying that he
wanted it. But we can know, and hence in a very obvious sense
understand, (1) *that* a person wants something, *that* he thinks

---

[1] Following on from this, it might be claimed that there are standard categories of pleasure or satisfaction (perhaps 'physical', 'aesthetic', etc.) or at any
rate stock types of reasons, for all rational entities, to one or another of which
particular pleasures and wants must ultimately be able to be referred. On this
and other points see C. C. W. Taylor's 'Understanding a Want' in *The Business
of Reason*, ed. J. J. Macintosh and S. C. Coval (Routledge 1969).

it desirable or satisfying in some way, and hence *that* he has a reason for wanting it, without necessarily understanding (2) in the sense of sympathizing with him or imagining ourselves in his shoes, or understanding (3) why *this* particular activity gives him pleasure or satisfaction. For, assuming that we could observe and communicate with him at all, we should be able to look at his trying-to-get behaviour, and accept his sincere avowals about what he wanted and thought desirable.

All this seems suspiciously straightforward, and those who favour this thesis may well have a more recherché kind of 'intelligibility' in mind, to which I have failed to do justice. No doubt much more discussion is needed. But in default of further (and more clearly stated) arguments, I should maintain that (i) there are of course logical limits to the concept of wanting and having a reason for wanting – in particular that it is part of the concept that the thing is thought to be desirable or satisfying: but (ii) there is nothing contradictory in the notion of a man wanting any particular independently-specified things. What things are believed by men or Martians to be desirable or pleasure-giving is an empirical matter: and to tie the concept of wanting down to 'recognizable human goods'[1] is to take too short a way.

In much the same way, it is possible to spell out the concepts represented by some emotion-words: to show, for instance, that fear is conceptually connected with the dangerous, pride with a belief in the possession or achievement of something admirable, remorse with a belief in having done wrong, and so forth.[2] But what will have been achieved by this? We shall be able to tell a man who says, for instance, 'I feel proud of possessing this totally undistinguished object' (without additional explanation) that he does not seem to know what 'proud' means in English: just as we can tell a man who says 'I want this, but think it in no way desirable' that it is only in a very peculiar sense of 'want', at best, that he wants it. But this goes no way towards giving us criteria for what people *ought to* feel proud, or fearful, or remorseful about, and so on.

Actually, the conceptual connections of emotions with objects and beliefs are very complex. Thus one writer says:

[1] See A. Kenny, *Action, Emotion and Will*, p. 123.
[2] These connections are not all of the same logical kind: see Chapter 7, pp. 101–105.

In fact, each of the emotions is appropriate – logically, and not just morally appropriate – only to certain restricted objects. If a man says that he is afraid of winning £10,000 in the pools, we want to ask him more. . . . If we can elicit from him only descriptions of the good aspects of the situation, then we cannot understand why he reports his emotion as fear and not hope. Again, if a man says that he feels remorse for the actions of someone quite unconnected with him, or is envious of his own vice, we are at a loss to understand him.[1]

(i) But as this writer himself points out,[2] a fearful or dangerous situation, or (better) the belief that something is fearful, is *not* logically necessary for applying the word 'fear' in all cases. We understand that the man is afraid because he turns pale, refuses the £10,000, etc. – his symptoms and actions are those of fear. The same goes for emotions such as anger and hatred; though it does not go for what we may call the less 'primitive', more 'belief-laden' emotions such as envy, remorse or pride.

(ii) It may or may not be, in particular cases, reasonable to be afraid of what is dangerous, and unreasonable to be afraid of what is not dangerous: but the logical connection between fear and danger (which in the case of fear is not necessary but only characteristic) does not in itself give us moral or prudential reasons. At the very least, it gives us no overriding reasons: it is 'natural', 'understandable', or 'appropriate', that a man should be afraid of what is dangerous, but very often he ought not to be.

(iii) Where there is a necessary conceptual tie, as between 'X feeling remorse' and 'X thinking he has done wrong', then we can certainly say that it is *unintelligible* that X should feel remorse if X does not think he has done something wrong: but for that very reason we cannot say that X *ought not* to feel remorse if he thinks he has done nothing wrong. By this account, he (logically) *cannot*.

(b) *Wants and emotions as 'given'*

Nor must we be put off by the notion that 'we do not choose to want this or that', the force of which would seem to rely on the view that human wants are empirically immutable. But they are not. Of course it is true (and I take this to be the force of the remark)

---

[1] A. Kenny, op. cit., p. 192. See also P. R. Foot, *Moral Beliefs* (P.A.S. 1958-9).

[2] op. cit., pp. 67-8.

that people do very often find themselves in the position of wanting, fearing etc. things of a certain kind, of having to make their choices at that time in virtue of what they then want or fear. But they also have choices to make about what they ought to want or fear. If I am in love with a certain girl, or want to smoke, then (other things being equal) my choices may concern only how to marry her or how to get enough cigarettes: but I may also (in a quite prudential way) think about whether I ought to be in love with her, or ought to want to smoke; and if I decide that I ought not then I can try various means to change my wants or feelings (I can reflect on her bad qualities, or the dangers of lung cancer, go to the hypnotist or the psychoanalyst, and so forth). Sometimes my attempts may be successful, so that I come to want something different: but even if they are not, I can still say 'I ought not to want so-and-so' and imply thereby that it is conceivable – not logically absurd – that I should come not to want it. I can *try* not to want it, and I can choose to try, even if my trying does not succeed.[1]

This last point has the widest possible implications. Examples of being able to change our own wants and emotions seems to me to be very common: but even if there were none, this would merely throw the question back a stage. For we have some control, which is always increasing, over what sort of people we or our children shall *be*, which involves control over what they will want and feel. Thus *I* may have no choice about being in love with a certain kind of girl or wanting to smoke: but I do have a choice about whether to bring up my children so that they follow in my emotional footsteps. Even this, however, fails to bring out all the implications. To face the point fully, we have to imagine a science-fiction type situation in which *any particular* wants or feelings may be changed. This forces us to distinguish between (a) criteria which it is incumbent on any conscious ('rational' in the minimal sense) creature to adopt, and which therefore will form part of *any* reasonable concept of 'welfare' or 'flourishing' in the case of any such creature:

---

[1] This is not to deny that, strictly speaking, we choose only to *do* things, not to desire them. Such fictitious imperatives as 'Want to do X!' or 'Desire Y!', may lack sense. But imperatives such as 'Act so that you come to want to do X (desire Y)' are perfectly good sense: and the same holds of the emotions. With the emotions indeed, the linguistic position is more complex: we can and do, in English, issue such imperatives as 'Love thy neighbour', 'Abandon hope', 'Fear no man', 'Don't be jealous', and so forth, though others seem more senseless ('Be angry', 'Feel ashamed', 'Let it disgust you').

and (b) a list of particular empirically-identifiable activities or states of affairs which are contingently connected with the welfare of human beings *as they now are*.

Some philosophers have taken a hard-headed, down-to-earth line with this problem:[1] but to talk of 'the standard interest', 'generally recognized human wants', and so on seems (for reasons already given) not only unhelpful with regard to the philosophical problem, but also – if the intention is to dismiss the problem as merely academic – empirically naïve. For (1) (a) there are some whole areas of life, for example sexual relationships, where it seems very hard to characterize anything we could call a 'standard interest'; (b) even in those areas often quoted as obviously containing interests, for instance the avoidance of physical pain and suffering, generalizations tend to be facile (what about duels, football, sailing across the Atlantic?); (c) although certain standard interests may be identified in certain areas, people differ very widely about the importance of the areas themselves, and hence about the relative importance of the interests (honour before pleasure, personal relationships before political ambition, adventure before property?). Moreover (2) it is not absurd to suppose that geneticists or other scientists may be able to change any of these 'standard interests' radically, and within the foreseeable future – perhaps before philosophers have settled this particular problem.[2]

We should resist, therefore, any suggestion that the justification of wants and emotions should proceed by identifying a number or class of objects that are 'truly' desirable, pitiable, fearful, lovable, and so on, or the more obviously naïve view naturally following from this that if a man has correct beliefs about an object he will thereby at once know what he ought to feel about it, and feel what he ought to feel. To such general questions as 'What sort of things ought to be desired or feared (pitied, loved, etc.)?' we can return no answer that is of any permanent value to the educator. For either we shall give a purely conceptual answer (e.g. 'desirable

[1] See for instance C. C. W. Taylor's review in *Mind*, April 1965, pp. 296–98.

[2] It ought perhaps to be added that the problem would not be solved by agreeing on what is to count as a 'man' or a 'human being': that, indeed, *is* (in this context) an academic question. For when we discuss wants and rationality, we are not talking about bipeds on a particular planet, but about (any) language-using and rule-following entities.

things', 'dangerous things', 'pitiable things', etc.), which is of no practical use: or else we shall indulge in empirical generalizations, the truth of which is contingent upon (a) particular, and (b) mutable, empirical facts.

2. GENERAL CRITERIA

A much more philosophically attractive programme (to me at least) would be to pursue a suggestion already made, and try to begin by elucidating the concept of a conscious language-using creature living in a space-time continuum, and see if there are any general criteria or desiderata which any such creature ought keep in mind *whatever* his desires and emotions, and whatever their particular objects, may be. For instance, a general desideratum which may be described as 'being able to express oneself as an agent' would apply to any creature:[1] whereas a state of affairs such as 'being able to use one's limbs' would only apply to creatures who had limbs.[2] Similarly, we may not be able to say that such empirically-identifiable states of affairs as 'police protection' or 'having money in the bank' must always be desirable (since individuals and societies could be conceived where this was not true), yet such notions as 'invulnerability' or 'security' seem to apply to any individual or society: that is, the continued and secure enjoyment of whatever are counted as good things seems to be something that any rational individual must (other things being equal) desire.

The elucidation of these criteria or general principles of rationality for practical living is a task that requires a more serious attempt on the part of philosophers than has yet (so far as I am aware) been made. If one tries to list them[3] many of them tend to bear a striking resemblance to the criteria of mental health evolved by those (perhaps rather few) psychologists and psychotherapists who have tried to steer clear both of culture-bound criteria, and of criteria that are too closely tied to particular empirical functions of the mind: and some philosophers have attempted to connect these with the concept of rationality in the way required.[4] This

[1] cf. John Lucas' remarks in *Principles of Politics*, pp. 59–60: also pp. 1–5; and cf. H. L. A. Hart, *The Concept of Law*, pp. 181–95.
[2] cf. P. Foot's remarks in 'Moral Beliefs', *P.A.S.*, 1958–59.
[3] See for instance my *Equality*, (Hutchinson 1966), pp. 139–46.
[4] See R. S. Peters' 'Mental Health as an Educational Aim', in T. H. B. Hollins' collection *Aims of Education*.

parallel is perhaps hardly surprising: but it can hardly be said that the psychologists have produced a list which is either complete or generally acceptable.

Such a list would not include, however, features or states of affairs which psychologists have shown (or have tried to show) to be *empirical prerequisites* for satisfying *any* wants or system of wants,[1] unless these can also be shown to be conceptual prerequisites. The distinction is important, even though in practice it may often be a fine one. Thus, just as any observer can notice that some such feature as 'the use of one's limbs', or 'having a reasonable amount of money', may be empirically necessary for satisfying most wants in human society as we know it, so psychologists may demonstrate that features like 'sensory stimulation in infancy' or 'ability to sublimate sexual impulses' are equally important prerequisites in the case-history of any human being. Such features may be of the highest practical importance: but they are not what we are after here (one could perhaps conceive rational creatures to which the concepts 'infancy' and 'sex' did not apply). We have to be careful, for often the description of such features may suggest that a feature would figure *better* in a conceptual list than in an empirical one: for instance, if for 'ability to sublimate sexual impulses' we substitute another phrase common in the psychological and social sciences, 'ability to defer gratification', we now have something that looks like a conceptual feature. For it is surely a conceptual truth that a rational creature exists in time, and thus should be able to have and tolerate having more or less long-range plans and purposes, as against merely acting on impulse. Anything that could seriously be called a want may take time to fulfil, and this implies some ability to forgo present gratification for the sake of future ends.

This procedure would be to some extent in accordance with a very interesting line of argument developed by R. S. Peters.[2] Peters draws attention to what is implied by the 'serious asking of the question "Why do this rather than that?"' and points out that anyone who seeks an answer to this question must in principle show some concern for what is true or false, appropriate or inappropriate, correct or incorrect.[3] This kind of concern is indeed already

---

[1] See. R. S. Peters, op. cit.

[2] See 'The Autonomy of Prudence', by A. Phillips Griffiths and R. S. Peters, *Mind*, April 1962: also R. S. Peters' *Ethics and Education*, pp. 151–66.

[3] ibid., p. 165.

inherent in the concept of wanting, as opposed to mere wishing: for wanting, at the very least, implies a degree of rationality in as much as it implies a higher degree of conceptualization and a concern for appropriate means to ends. But the man who is prepared to consider whether he *ought* to want this rather than that (rather than just how best to get what he wants) goes further: he seeks criteria for determining what he should want.

Peters uses this argument, not so much in order to make a list of such criteria, but to justify certain types of worthwhile *activities* which are (a) instrumental to answering the question 'Why do this rather than that?' and (b) in some sense embryonically presupposed by the question:[1] and ultimately to justify certain curricular subjects as in this sense 'worthwhile'. We need not here follow him so far. The implications of this line of argument, however, suggest that we could formulate a set of principles or criteria to which a 'serious' man would attend: principles which might ultimately justify certain activities as 'worthwhile', because they are instantiated in and developed by such activities. One might think here of such principles as we have mentioned elsewhere:[2] attention to the facts, clarity and consistency in the use of language, the sense of time and the awareness of causal connections so evidently lacking in psychopaths, and so on.

Unlike 1. above, such a programme seems to me potentially very fruitful. But I shall pursue it only in part: for there is a danger that it will only yield answers of more interest to the philosopher than to the educator. It is one thing to ask and answer (perhaps in philosophical discussion) the question 'How, in general, can we justify particular wants, emotions and outlooks? What are the criteria we can rightly use to assess particular instances of these?' (or in Peters' terms, 'What principles would a 'serious' person use?') and then perhaps move on to the empirical question 'Given these criteria, what particular empirical objects should be wanted, feared, and so on, and what particular outlooks are rational?' But it is another thing to ask and answer (perhaps in the context of practical teaching or educational research) the question 'What qualities and characteristics are logically necessary for a *person* to *formulate* or develop reasonable wants, emotions and outlooks? Where, and in what ways, can he fail to do this?' (or 'What *makes* a "serious"

[1] ibid., pp. 164-5.
[2] *I.M.E.*, pp. 92 ff.

person?'), and then go on to the empirical question 'Given these qualities, what sort of educational content, contexts, methods and arrangements will encourage this development?'

The crucial differences here are two; and both can be observed clearly enough if we remember, what is obvious, that what we educate is not 'emotions' or 'outlooks' but *people*. Then (i) answers to the former question do not, in one way, go far enough. They may give us criteria for reasonable[1] outlooks and emotions, but omit important criteria for the 'emotionally educated' person: just as to achieve clarity about what counts as a reasonable opinion in mathematics or science is not *eo ipso* to achieve clarity about the nature of a good mathematician or scientist. There may be – indeed there obviously are – qualities essential for a scientist which are not *directly* connected with the criteria for a reasonable scientific opinion (accuracy, patience, and so on). Further (ii), answers to the former question, in another way, go too far. For they naturally lead on to an identification of specific opinions, beliefs, desires, emotional states, moral values; but the *education* of people in these areas is not to be conceived simply as a way of getting them

---

[1] Of course the notions of 'rationality' and 'being reasonable' cry out for much more examination than I have given them elsewhere (*I.M.E.*, pp. 102–16) or can give them here. We should need (1) to enquire what was *meant* by 'reasonable' in such phrases as 'a reasonable man', 'a reasonable point of view', etc.; (2) to distinguish between characteristics which counted as 'being reasonable' (e.g. *facing* the facts) and states of affairs which, although not themselves defining 'being reasonable', would nevertheless be those which any reasonable person would seek (e.g. *knowledge* of the facts); (3) to clarify the differences in status between these characteristics ('not contradicting oneself' is different from 'facing facts', different again from 'pursuing appropriate means to ends', and so forth); (4) to defend each of these characteristics or states of affairs by as detailed and watertight arguments as possible; and thereby (5) to consider how far these various types of rationality can, in the last resort, be justifiably pressed upon any or every human being. In the course of this we should also naturally want to look at interlocking concepts, as represented by such words as 'justifiable', 'sensible', 'unprejudiced', 'wise', and many others. I mention this partly to show how much work needs to be done, and partly to acknowledge that from a strictly philosophical viewpoint it ought to be done before we can use these notions with complete confidence in the field of education and research. From a more practical viewpoint, however, I should want to argue that there is – I believe, rightly – little or no dispute amongst ordinary people about the desirability of the characteristics and qualities we shall outline: and that in outlining them I am merely offering reminders and clarifications of what nearly all of us already think, or would on reflection think.

to hold specific opinions or entertain specific desires, emotions or values.

Thus one might construct a practical syllogism on Aristotle's model, for instance:

> Major premise: People who have no food or money are pitiable
> Minor premise: This man has no food or money
> Conclusion (in the form of an emotion): Feel pity for the man.

It is not denied that this model might be useful to *explain why* a particular feeling was or was not appropriate. But to suppose that a syllogistic model of this kind represents how most people actually do (always or even usually) think is obviously absurd: and to suppose that setting out such a syllogism represents the standard case of how a sensible educator of the emotions would proceed is hardly less so, for it would assimilate all cases of education to the case of taking a pupil through a proof in Euclidean geometry or some other sphere of deductive reasoning. There are no grounds for supposing that those who are good at such reasoning are, even *pro tanto*, better educated in their emotions than other people. That the emotionally well-educated man's emotions could be justified by such a model is not in question: what is in question is whether the model is of much use in helping the educator to identify the various types of failure that may occur, and the various types of teaching that might be needed to remedy these failures.

With the general approach,[1] however (particularly as developed by Peters), I am in complete sympathy: the difficulty is how to cash it in a form useful to the educator or research worker in education. We would most naturally think of trying to formulate a list of *qualities* or *attributes* which would be possessed by a man who was thus well educated. This is, of course what educators and observers tend to do in practice. An educator will first notice particular cases of malfunction or irrationality, and then generalize from them. Thus he will see that a boy dislikes taking positions of

---

[1] This approach is not, of course, original. In effect it is to take seriously Aristotle's notion of the serious man (*spoudaios anér*) (see Kenny, op. cit., pp. 149–50). Or as Hector answers Troilus, 'value dwells not in *particular* will'. Briefly: what can reasonably be valued is neither (a) what *must* be valued because of conceptual necessity, or because human nature, wants, emotions, etc. are given: nor (b) a matter of arbitrary choice or 'particular will': but (c) what the reasonable or fully-equipped person values when he is being reasonable and using his equipment.

responsibility in the school, hates the rough-and-tumble of the play-ground, is too frightened to learn to swim, etc.: and he may then write on his report 'Lacks self-confidence'. It is these generalized terms – 'self-confidence', 'determination', 'sincerity', and so forth – that appear in lists formulated by educators and psychologists.

The difficulty of formulating such a list, however, is magnified by three considerations. We have noted some of these already in passing but they need to be listed here:

(a) First, it will not be helpful if the qualities and attributes are too general or cover too much ground. Thus to say that the person who is emotionally well-educated will be 'sane', 'reason-able', 'mature', 'reality-orientated', and so on is sailing too close to the wind of tautology to be of much practical value.

(b) We have to steer clear of the opposite danger of identifying such attributes too closely with contingent facts, and thereby failing to give a list of attributes that are conceptually (rather than empirically) necessary. Thus the ability to earn one's living or enjoy a sexual relationship may, in practice, be excellent empirical *indicators* that a person is emotionally well-educated; or – conceivably – empirical *prerequisites* for a person's becoming emotionally well-educated: but they can hardly be part of what is meant by saying that he is so.

(c) We have also to steer clear of qualities and attributes that would be irrelevant to the notion of *education*. Thus no doubt there are certain physiological and biological attributes (for ex-ample the efficient working of the thyroid glands) that are needful if a person is to be emotionally well-educated. But these would be, at best, preconditions of such education: they would not be attributes of a well-*educated* person, since they would not (nor-mally) be things which a person could acquire by any kind of *learning* – not, at least, by learning in the sphere of *emotion*.

The kind of items that characteristically appear on lists of this sort are:

    (i) Flexibility
   (ii) Moderation
  (iii) Self-awareness
  (iv) Integration, freedom from conflict
   (v) Sincerity

(vi) Forethought
(vii) Resolution
(viii) Ability to relate to others
(ix) Correct perception of external reality
(x) Autonomy
(xi) Freedom from compulsion
(xii) Ability to defer gratification
(xiii) Self-confidence.

But such a list, in my view, would be not so much wrong as unhelpful. It would indeed be possible to show in a general way that these attributes could be subsumed under the general title of 'rationality', and defended as such; but two difficulties should strike us, both due to the same basic cause. First, the attributes *overlap*. For example, if a person acts and feels inflexibly or immoderately (attributes (i) and (ii)) – say, by always getting very angry with his daughter's boy-friends for trivial reasons – then we might also describe this as a case where he lacks the attribute of having the correct beliefs about the nature of the boy-friends (ix), or again as a case where he lacks the attribute of self-awareness (iii). Secondly, the attributes are heterogeneous, in that we seem sometimes to be talking about cognitive abilities or attainments (e.g. correct beliefs), sometimes about what might be called affective abilities, or abilities of the will (e.g. to defer gratification), sometimes about 'social skills' (e.g. the ability to relate to others), and sometimes about factors that could not be described as abilities at all (e.g. integration and the absence of conflict).

The trouble here is analogous to that in the approach to moral education briefly criticized elsewhere[1], in terms of moral virtues. We may, indeed, make out a list of 'virtues of the emotions' – 'flexibility', 'moderation', and so on – but this does not tell us just what (logical) types of constituents are missing: for a number of constituents of different types are required for each 'virtue', as for the moral virtues. What we have listed are qualities which a man may fail to have for a great many different logical types of reason (as well as for many different empirical causes, with which we are not here concerned). It is therefore not surprising either that our list contains logically heterogeneous attributes, or that the attributes overlap each other. What we require is a list of different logical

[1] *I.M.E.*, pp. 215–17.

types of attributes which will, so to speak, cut across the attributes listed above.

It was because of the deficiencies in the approaches briefly criticized above that, in dealing specifically with moral education, we preferred to sketch out a list of 'components' or 'constituents', to which we attached home-made labels (PHIL, EMP, GIG, etc.).[1] The status of these components was not empirical: they were rather to cover sets of qualities or attributes that were logically necessary for the morally educated person. We hoped in this way to avoid the confusion that would be caused (both conceptually and in research) by using terms in ordinary language ('flexibility', 'sensitivity', etc.); and also the possibility that the use of these terms would still leave important logical gaps. In other words, we said in effect, 'If a man has the attributes which fall under the definitions of PHIL, EMP, etc., then it is logically necessary that he will think and act in a morally educated way.' Our task was then both to make quite sure that our components covered all the logical ground, and to begin on the work of producing practicable tests or other assessment-methods for them: our hope being that this would eventually enable us to determine what empirical teaching-methods or other phenomena in schools and elsewhere actually contributed to the operation of these components.

In what follows I shall adopt a similar procedure. But, as will become clear, there are peculiar difficulties about determining these components in the case of the *emotions*; difficulties which did not apply so strongly (though they were hinted at)[2] when we were considering moral thought and moral *behaviour*. Most of these difficulties centre on the notions of sincerity and the unconscious mind, to which we shall have to pay special attention. I should say in advance that I do not feel at all certain that the taxonomy at which we shall finally arrive by this methodology is either complete, or correct at all points: though I feel reasonably confident that, at least for our purposes and for those of other research workers in similar fields, this kind of methodology is appropriate. But all this the reader must judge for himself.

[1] See *I.M.E.*, Chapter 4.
[2] See *I.M.E.*, pp. 94–7.

7. Emotions and Rationality

A. Some points about Emotions

So far as possible, I want here to avoid the very difficult task of giving a full account of what exactly an emotion *is*. Those that wish to take up this question may profit from the work of other writers, on some of whom I have drawn heavily.[1] This evasion may perhaps be partly justified by the possibility that the criteria which we are seeking may apply to more than one of the categories for which the terms 'emotion', 'mood', 'attitude', 'feeling', 'state of mind', and so forth are vague titles: and since for the educator it is the criteria that are important, I do not want to prejudice their use by a mistaken or too narrow view of 'the emotions'. Nevertheless, some attempt must be made to clarify the kind of phenomena I want to discuss.

Although the words 'emotion' and 'emotional' may have uses which are not classificatory, in the sense that they may (to put it roughly) distinguish an aspect rather than a category of mental phenomena,[2] philosophers have rightly tried to distinguish emotions from other phenomena. Two distinctions in particular have been successfully drawn:[3]

(a) Emotions must be distinguished from sensations, though the single term 'feeling' is often used for both, and though the two are often linked conceptually as well as causally. There are characteristic symptoms of (say) fear which are sensations – feeling weak at the knees, or frozen to the spot, or a chill in one's stomach: one feels these sensations *because* one is afraid, and they also contribute to part of what it *means* to say that someone is afraid. But it is clear that things like throbs of pain, tickles, and shivers down the spine are in one category (sensations), whereas

[1] Especially A. Kenny, *Action, Emotion and Will* (see particularly Chapters 2 and 3) and R. S. Peters' 'Emotions and the Category of Passivity' (*P.A.S.*, 1961–2).

[2] cf. R. S. Peters, op. cit., p. 120 *re* 'emotion' and 'motive'.

[3] Kenny, op. cit., Chapter 3.

things like fear, anger, regret, and hatred are in another (emotions). Sensations have a locale: it makes sense to ask *where* a man feels pain, a tickle, and so on; and sensations do not have objects or targets in the way that emotions do.[1]

(b) Emotions can be distinguished from *perceptions*. They give us no information about the external world: and there are no organs of emotions as there are of perception.

We may try to draw further distinctions, for example:

(c) Emotions may be distinguished from moods. Emotions characteristically have *targets* or *objects*: one is frightened *at* an advancing lion, sorry *that* one has made a mistake, angry *with* one's wife, and so forth. Moods or 'states of mind', like emotions, have causes: there is something which may make one happy, sad, depressed, surly, and so on. But they do not have identifiable targets. One is not, so to speak, happy *at* something, though one may be made happy *by* something.

(d) Emotions must be distinguished from attitudes. The very complex concept of an attitude may at least be said to be more closely connected with what other people see of one, or may expect of one, than emotion is: perhaps particularly with the notion of a posture or stance (either in the literal or the meta-phorical sense) adopted in face of the world outside. Hence we call attitudes 'stately', 'hostile', 'friendly', 'uncompromising', etc. Particular attitudes are characteristic of particular emotions and moods, so that we speak of an attitude 'of terror', or 'of dejection'; some are characteristic also of particular activities – an attitude of prayer, or of submission, or of resignation. Emotions are in a sense more primitive and less public: one may be angry without adopting a hostile attitude, or feel afraid and yet strike an attitude of bravery or indifference. Attitudes are shown: emotions need not be.

We can thus distinguish the separate categories in such cases as the following. A man sees a snake (perception): he feels frightened of it (emotion). He feels hot and cold all over and weak at the knees (sensations, symptoms of fear). He cowers, or is rooted to the spot in terror (attitude). While all this is going on he feels miserable

[1] See below, pp. 101–105.

(mood). Or again: a man hears the clapping after his performance (perception). He feels proud of his achievement (emotion). He feels a glow of pride and perhaps feels relaxed (sensations). He stands up very straight and looks down on his fellows in a superior way (attitude). He feels happy (mood).

From the viewpoint of our present interest, the education of the emotions, we need to consider briefly the following points:

1. The first point we have already noticed under distinction (c): it is that some emotion-words imply a target or object (as opposed to a cause). But we need to distinguish here between:

(i) Cases where it is not *sense* to use the word unless there is a target: thus 'I feel proud, but I don't know what of' or 'I feel remorseful, but I don't think I've done wrong' are not intelligible;

(ii) Cases where the word only characteristically implies a target: thus one can *say* 'I feel angry, but not about anything or with anyone in particular', or 'I feel frightened, but not at anything I can think of';

(iii) Cases where there is no necessary or characteristic connection with a target at all: depression, happiness, serenity and so forth, which for this reason we may want to call moods (distinction (c) above).

Just what words are to go under these three headings, however, is not at all clear. Consider, for instance, 'sulky'. Sometimes, one could argue, this means in effect 'resentful', and would come under (i), in that it isn't sense to say 'I feel resentful, but there's nothing I resent'. Sometimes it might come under (ii), in that 'I feel sulky' characteristically (but not necessarily) implies that one resents or sulks about something. Sometimes it may come under (iii), and refer to a mood, without there being any implication of a target ('I feel sulky today'). Sometimes, again, it may refer to a disposition, as when we talk of a sulky child and don't mean that he happens to be sulking at the time.

2. The second point is the implication of a *belief* or a *particular kind of belief*. This goes very closely with the distinction above, but we must distinguish:

(a) Some words imply a particular kind of belief, a belief about the object. It is sense to say 'I'm frightened of X but don't think

H

it dangerous': it is not sense to say 'I regret X but don't think it was mistaken of me to do it', or 'I feel proud of possessing X but don't think X is a particularly good thing to possess'.

(b) The notion of a target or object, as distinct from a cause, of emotion is only intelligible in the context of rational and conscious creatures who are not merely moved by things, but can also pay attention to things and are capable of being influenced by beliefs about them. To have a target for one's emotions – to be frightened *at*, angry *with*, regret *that* – one must be aware of the object: we might say, one must know that, and in principle be able to say that, it is *this* that one is frightened at, angry with, or regrets. This awareness does perhaps imply a kind of belief, but not necessarily – only characteristically – a belief *about the object* – for instance that the object is dangerous, has harmed one, or is something that one has done wrong.

(c) Other cases do not imply any kind of belief. Feeling happy, for instance, does not imply any particular belief about the world or one's future prospects.

3. Thirdly, a point about the *role* of the belief. We have just noticed that certain kinds of beliefs are conceptually connected with emotion-words – sometimes necessarily connected, sometimes only characteristically. This would not be so, were it not typically the case that beliefs not only *accompany* but *generate* emotions (that is, generate the symptoms and actions that we associate with words like 'fear', 'remorse', etc.). It is of course possible that a person should believe X to be dangerous, and at the same time show symptoms and perform actions characteristic of fear, and yet not feel fear *because* he has this belief: the fear-symptoms and actions might be the result of some purely physical cause, such as stimulation of his glands or brain-cells. But such a case would be atypical: if we lived in a world where it was never or only rarely true that beliefs generated emotions in people, we should have no reason for conceptually linking beliefs with symptoms and actions. Whether or not such a world is conceivable (my guess is that it is not), it is not our world, and this would not be our language.

It is not necessary for our purposes here to pursue further the distinctions between emotions, moods, attitudes, and what may be called 'states of feeling'. We are excused from this, partly because moods and 'states of feeling' seem often to be no more than compounds of different or conflicting emotions, but chiefly because there will be nothing specific to be said about the education of moods and states of feeling that is not contained in what may be said about the education of the emotions. Other distinctions that we have mentioned, for instance between emotions, moods and attitudes on the one hand, and dispositions, traits of character, virtues and other categories on the other, likewise do not concern us. It is important for the educator to realize the difficulties involved, which is why we have raised these points: but the reader need only be sufficiently clear that in this part of the book we shall be concerned both with emotions and, by extrapolation, with any states of feeling into which emotions enter.

Before closing this section, however, it must be pointed out that we have taken a very short way with 'the emotions'. The distinctions we have made are adequate for our immediate purposes; but it is possible that they are for other purposes insufficient and in important ways misleading. Insufficient, because there will be other distinctions that need drawing in order to clarify the differences between emotions and other categories of phenomena with which they may be confused. Misleading, first, because they may be based on a too limited sample of emotion-words:[1] secondly, and more importantly, because of the tacit assumption that we already *know* which words are emotion-words, and need only to discover why they are. This latter assumption might be reasonable if, for instance, we were trying to elucidate the concept of a game: we know pretty well what are games and what are not, and need not make a very lengthy list of words that might or might not stand for games. Here we could be sure of our examples. This is not so with emotion: we may feel confident about some cases, but there are very many about which do not. If you ask people 'Is X an emotion?' the answer varies very widely from person to person.[2]

[1] The possible distorting effects of concentrating on a narrow sample are well known in philosophy. See R. S. Peters' criticisms of Bedford's interesting paper ('Emotions and the Category of Passivity', p. 118 ff.).

[2] Here for instance are fifty-odd words and phrases, which certainly do not denote sensations or perceptions, and yet which are reasonable *prima facie* candidates for emotion-words, since they may, in English, intelligibly follow either the phrase 'I feel' or the phrase 'a feeling of'. (That it is reasonable to use either phrase, thereby including both nouns and adjectives, is due to the possibility of linguistic accidents that may be peculiar to English. Thus it is

The relation between emotions on the one hand and perceptions and sensations on the other may be fairly clear (distinctions (a) and (b) above), but the notions of 'moods' and 'attitudes' ((c) and (d) above) are far from clear, and there are many other possible category-headings which need to be thought about – 'states of mind', 'motives', 'dispositions', 'traits of character', 'virtues', and so forth.[1]

It would, therefore, be extremely useful not only to the philosopher and psychologist, but also to the educator, to attempt something like a taxonomy of the emotions. One ought to begin by listing a fair number of words which *might* be taken as emotion-words, and simply noticing some of the conceptual criteria which seem to apply to them (there are many interesting and important conceptual criteria besides those used, e.g., in Roget's *Thesaurus*). To this conceptual framework one could add whatever empirical data about the origin and nature of particular emotions seems of

---

not clear that there are proper adjectives for 'pity', 'hate', or 'grief' ('sympathetic', 'hostile' and 'sad' are not quite right), and many adjectives are just compounded nouns ('panic-stricken'); conversely one can feel brave, but a 'feeling of bravery' is not sense.) Now which of these are emotion-words? The reader might like to try his hand at correlating them with criteria already mentioned, for example, whether they necessarily or characterisically imply a target, or a belief: but I think he will often be in doubt.

Jealousy, grief, anger, fear, terror, panic, anxiety, guilt, remorse, regret, nostalgia, hatred, love, brave, confident, pity, despair, hope, pride, awe, respect, admiration, wonder, surprised, amazement, lust, affectionate, disgust, distaste, grateful, sulky, resentful, irritable, irritated, insulted, lonely abandoned, out of sorts, revengeful, hostile, tender, inspired, vicious, envious, honoured, flattered, responsible, depressed, enthusiastic, optimistic, jubilant, good-humoured, happy, serene, flustered, uncertain, apathetic.

I asked twenty people this question of the first twenty of these. No one word got twenty definite affirmatives or twenty definite negatives: about 35 per cent of the words got about 50 per cent of each: and about 40 per cent of the replies were of the form 'Well, I'm not sure, in a way it is . . .' It should be added that the respondents were not trained in philosophy (in the sense that one might explain this by claiming that philosophers never give you a straight answer anyway).

[1] Consider for example Kenny's reportage (op. cit., p. 12) of what he takes as a Cartesian thesis: 'There is no difference of category between feelings such as joy, emotions such as love, attitudes such as admiration, virtues such as courage and traits of character such as bashfulness'. It's not clear that bashfulness or joy aren't emotions; love might be a virtue, admiration a 'feeling' (whatever that is), and so forth.

particular educational importance. We might then have a clearer picture both of the logic and the psychology of individual emotions: a picture in some ways analogous to a taxonomy of virtues and vices, and one which the educator could use to frame coherent and practical teaching-courses.

We have in fact made some progress in this direction, enough to show that the kinds of things that can be said about the emotions, and perhaps about other categories, by way of criticizing or applauding them, of claiming that they are reasonable or unreasonable, justifiable or unjustifiable, satisfactory or unsatisfactory, are far more heterogeneous than philosophers who talk in a general way about 'the emotions' might imagine. In what follows I shall make some use of the work we have done, though it is too fragmentary to be worth printing here.[1] For our present purposes we may need rather to bear in mind the points made earlier in this section, and go on to see how they are relevant to the educator.

B. EDUCATIONAL OBJECTIVES AND RATIONALITY

Our concern is specifically with the *education* of the emotions: and before going further, we need briefly to discuss one point which is particularly relevant to this whole topic. Educators should by now be familiar with the important differences between educating a person on the one hand, and indoctrinating, conditioning, forcing, or in any non-rational way persuading him on the other.[2] However, someone might say: If we knew what emotions people ought to feel at various times, then why should we confine ourselves to *educational* methods as a way of getting them to feel these emotions? Indeed, would we necessarily need to use educational methods at all? Could we not, in principle, use such means as drugs and brain surgery, and the kind of means implied by some such general title as 'conditioning'? To this it would be pedantic to reply that our topic is defined as 'the *education* of the emotions': for the question casts some doubt upon the importance of the topic itself. There would, for instance, be little point in spending large sums of money and time on investigating the education of

---

[1] See however Appendix II on the inevitability (conceptual and empirical) of certain emotions: and Chapter 10, pp. 149–50 on the justifiability of emotions.
[2] *I.M.E.*, pp. 168–76.

the emotions, if we can more cheaply and quickly achieve all that we wish with regard to the emotions by non-educational methods.

Certain arguments relevant to this question were advanced or hinted at in *I.M.E.*[1] But it is not clear that these arguments, even if valid, would apply to the concept of emotion, as they do apply (in my view) to the concept of moral belief and moral action. It was there suggested that there was not only a practical but a conceptual or logical impossibility in the notion of using brain-surgery, drugs or 'conditioning' methods to get people to act and think morally. This conceptual or logical issue is important: not merely for the sake of philosophical clarity, but for the very practical purpose of deciding what kinds of methods we can sensibly attempt, or what kinds of research are required to investigate the kind of changes in emotion that we want to bring about.

I shall rely on the stipulation (see pp. 101-102) that the characteristic or paradigm use of emotion-words as applied to human beings implies that the person who feels an emotion also has a belief and makes a judgement, and that these are the causes of his emotion. Thus, a man who feels remorse must (logically) believe that he has done wrong, or judge that what he has done is wrong, and *because of this* feel remorse. If this is right, our original question becomes the question of whether it is conceptually possible that the causal functions of judgement and belief are logically consistent with those terms which characterize non-educational methods of bringing about emotional change – methods for which we use such terms as 'condition', 'drug', 'stimulate', 'programme' (in the sense in which we programme computers), and so forth. That is, we want to know whether it is sense to say 'We Xed him to Y', where X is a term like 'condition' rather than like 'teach', and where Y is a term which involves the operation of judgement and belief in the way described. I shall maintain that this is not sense.

What characterizes Y-type terms is that they describe states of mind that a man can (logically) only reach for himself, which he can only reach freely, and which require for their explanation some statement about a man's own perceptions and ratiocination. If a man judges something to be wrong, it is not sense to say that someone else can judge it to be wrong *for* him, or that he is compelled to judge it to be wrong, or that he judges it to be wrong but has not

[1] pp. 45-46.

considered it or thought about it, and has no reasons for his judgement. What characterizes X-type terms is that they describe things that we can do to people whether they choose to co-operate or not, as opposed to processes whereby we initiate people, which demand their active co-operation if the processes are to be successful.

The feeling of logical misfit I am pointing to comes out fairly clearly in such examples as 'I forced the boy to appreciate Shakespeare', or 'I conditioned the man to sympathize with his wife'. The terms 'appreciating Shakespeare' and 'sympathizing with one's wife' are Y-type terms, because they involve making judgements and having reasons of a certain kind. Moreover, the feelings or emotions a person has when appreciating or sympathizing must occur *because of* these reasons: the reasons must cause the feelings. Thus I might, by some process of conditioning, get a boy to feel ecstatic or utter cries of joy while he turns the pages of *Hamlet*: and I might get him to give reasons for his feelings – 'because the plot is so wonderful; because the poetry fits the action', and so on – and these might even be good reasons for enjoying *Hamlet*. But unless it is these reasons which alone account for his feelings, he is not appreciating Shakespeare. Similarly, a man might be conditioned to weep whenever his wife weeps: but unless he has gone through, or at least could go through, some such train of thought as 'I judge my wife to be sad; I love her and want to feel something of what she feels', and unless that train of thought is at least a part-cause of his weeping when she weeps, we would not describe him as sympathizing with his wife. For sympathy is not just a matter of rejoicing with them that rejoice and weeping with them that weep in the sense only of rejoicing and weeping *when* they rejoice and weep: it is a matter of rejoicing *because one perceives* others to rejoice, and so on.[1]

But does this argument apply to the emotions? Let us go back to the point that emotions usually have targets or objects, and involve beliefs. We must distinguish three cases:

(1) The man whose emotion has a cause, but is not directed towards any particular target, and results from no particular belief: thus a man may get frightened whenever a snake is in the room,

---

[1] On this see also *I.M.E.*, pp. 51–52; A. C. MacIntyre, in *P.A.S.*, 1967, and in *British Analytical Philosophy*, ed. Bernard Williams and Alan Montefiore (Routledge 1966): also Kenny, op. cit., pp. 237–39.

but (conceivably) not know that it is the snake that frightens him, and not believe that the snake is dangerous. Here the snake is not the object or target of his emotion. 'Free-floating' feelings of 'fear', 'guilt', etc. are like this.[1]

(2) The man whose emotion has a cause and a target, but is not the result of a belief. Thus a man may be frightened *by* a snake, and (since he recognizes the source of his fear) be frightened *of* the snake: but yet he may know that the snake is not dangerous, and hence have no particular belief about the snake which generates his fear.

(3) The man whose emotion has a cause and a target and is generated by a belief. This is the full-blown case of the man who sees a snake, believes that it is dangerous, and *therefore* feels frightened of it.

Our argument suggests that cases (1) and perhaps (2) may be produced by what X-type terms describe ('condition', etc.), but that case (3) cannot be. That is to say, we may condition a man to feel fear whenever there is a snake in the room, and we may perhaps condition him so that he comes to direct his fear at the snake: but we cannot condition him to judge the snake to be dangerous. We may indeed condition him to *say* that it is dangerous, or even to *say* that he is frightened because it is dangerous; but if he is actually to *be* frightened because it is dangerous, he will have himself to have gone through some process of reasoning which leads to this conclusion ('I see the V-mark on the head, noticed what happened to a dog when a similar snake bit it, *therefore* . . .'), and which is causally effective.

Whether our X-type terms apply to emotions, then, will depend on what we are after. Suppose (to take an example from our particular concern in Part I) that we want a child to feel awe at a religious object (O) (the life of Jesus, a cathedral, love, or whatever). Then if we mean by this (1) simply that we want the child to feel awe whenever he is in the presence of O – that we want O to *cause* him to feel awe – or even (2) that we want O to cause him awe, and we want him to know that O is causing him awe, then we may

---

[1] These words may have to have inverted commas, because it is arguable that in their proper uses they do involve targets and/or beliefs, as remorse and pride seem evidently to involve targets and beliefs.

use those methods that are covered by X-type terms. But if we want (3) the child to believe that O is awesome (for which he will have to have reasons) and *therefore* to feel awed by O, we can only proceed by those methods which would be described by such words and phrases as 'educate', 'bring him to see that', 'show the reasons for', 'explain to him why', and so forth.

As our example from 'appreciating Shakespeare' may help to show, it seems fairly clear that our objectives in educational practice often are of type (3) above, and not just of types (1) and (2) We want his emotions not just to be felt on appropriate occasions, but to be directed by his own belief that the occasions *are* appropriate. Thus, we would not be satisfied with (1) free-floating guilt occurring whenever he breaks a window, nor even with (2) guilt directed by the child at the event of his having broken a window, but only with (3) guilt directed by the child at the event of his having broken a window *because he believes that he has done something wrong*. Indeed, as we have noticed, many emotion-words (pride, regret, remorse, hope, jealousy and many others) are only used in their full sense when the element of belief, as in (3), is present.

We are not, then, simply making a point about the way in which words like 'educate' prescribe certain methods that are not prescribed by words like 'condition': we are, rather, suggesting that many phrases which we use to state our educational aims in this area are Y-type phrases, and logically necessitate those methods which are implied by 'education' rather than X-type terms. 'Appreciating a poem' is only one such phrase: others are 'taking pride in one's work', 'sympathizing with one's friends', 'being in awe of God', 'respecting one's superiors', and so forth. Nor, again, are we saying that X-type methods may not have an important part to play in, or be necessarily prior to, this process. If we want a child to appreciate Shakespeare, it may be very useful to make him learn some lines by heart, or to develop a warm feeling whenever he sees the word 'Shakespeare' written on a book: and this we may be able to do by hypnosis, or hypnopaedia, or some form of conditioning. But methods that do more than this will always be required.

By 'methods' we refer not to the physical nature of the techniques used, but to the logical nature of their effect. Thus, if we described some direct action on the brain-cells as one 'method', and the use of words in conversation as another, we should be open to the obvious objection that each of these methods may be used either to educate or to condition. Words may be used to explain, or to act merely as stimuli and signals in a process of conditioning; direct action on the brain can be used to condition, but might in principle be a quick way of communicating, explaining, clarifying and doing all those things which at present we do by words.[1] This is not what we mean by 'method', however. Our concern is with what (logical) sort of way we may act on other people, not with what tools we use. We may act on them in a way which in itself enlarges their perceptions and develops their reasoning, or in a way which does not, but merely changes them in some other manner (though such a change may be a useful preliminary or a later reinforcement, for the former process). The point about words like 'indoctrinate', 'condition', and so on is simply that these words normally imply giving a person either no proper reasons at all or reasons which are not causally operative. They exclude the possibility of giving them causally operative reasons: for such processes we should talk in terms of 'teaching', 'clarifying', and so on.

This is not to say that other objectives may not also be very important, either in themselves or as preconditions for effective education. For example, suppose a man whose irrational anger or fear is so great that he never listens to what anyone says and goes round hitting people: or a man whose fear is so great that he never listens to what anyone says and is too frightened to go to a doctor when he is ill. Suppose further that they could in principle be educated in respect of these emotions, but that such education would involve their listening to other people (perhaps particularly

---

[1] Whether or not there are brain-states, or physiological states, which 'correlate' or are in some sense 'identical' with what we describe in ordinary language as 'having reasons', 'understanding', 'being aware' and other educational objectives and processes, is a vexed question: partly a philosophical question, and partly an empirical one. But in any case, if there were a brain-state (B) which correlated or was identical with (say) 'understanding Pythagoras' theorem' (U), then *ex hypothesi* we have some other, non-physiological, way of identifying U – some independent way of knowing that a person understood Pythagoras' theorem: for, if we did not, we could not know that B correlated with U. In other words, whatever the advance in physiological knowledge, we should still have to marry up that knowledge with the educational objectives we wish to attain: and this involves identifying such objectives, which we cannot do in physiological terms.

the psychotherapist). Then there are two obvious justifications for diminishing his anger or fear by drugs or conditioning: (a) that by so doing we may enable him to listen to other people, and hence stand at least some chance of being educated, and (b) that anyway we do not want the first man to go around hitting people, or the second man to suffer because he is too frightened to consult a doctor. This general point has already been touched on elsewhere[1] and need not be developed here.[2] We shall need to look more closely at these matters in relation to the unconscious mind, in Chapter 9, where they present peculiar difficulties: but we have said enough to enable us to begin a general investigation of the education of the emotions.

---

[1] *I.M.E.*, pp. 155–68.

[2] It has, however, a special relevance to the treatment of mental patients, delinquents, maladjusted children and others, which will be briefly considered in Appendix V.

8. First sketch of a taxonomy

The considerations in Section B of the last chapter may seem to create a peculiar difficulty for the educator of the emotions. For it may be wondered how the educator can actually affect, or induce a *change* in a person's emotions, if he is not permitted to bring about such a change by what we have called 'non-rational' methods. Thus I can stop Peter being frightened by giving him tranquillizing drugs, or abolish Johnny's envy of Molly by giving Johnny the same sort of toy that Molly has: but how (it may be asked) can I *educate* or teach Peter not to be frightened, or Johnny not to be envious, in the sort of way I can teach them to read or to do long division? To put it another way, 'reading' and 'dividing' are things that a person *does:* and I can teach them to do them by a series of orders or invitations ('put down 3, carry 4', and so on). But fear and anger are things that a person *feels* or that *happen* to him. He does not *choose* or *decide* or *obey an order* to feel them or not to feel them: they are not under the direct control of his will. So how can an educator issue any instructions or commands or invitations that will make a person feel differently?

Yet it would be curious if this were the whole story. For moralists and others do appear to issue orders or invitations, such as 'Love your enemies', 'Be not angry', 'Fear not', and we do not regard these as absurd. Moreover, we can think of a great many different kinds of instructions about how to achieve particular emotional states. They are indeed instructions about what to *do*, or what to *reflect upon*, but we carry them out with the aim of affecting or changing what we *feel*. Thus we say 'Don't feel sad about it – look on the bright side', 'Don't be angry with him – think what an awful time he's had', 'Don't worry about it – think about something else', 'Get to know him better, and then you won't be so jealous of him', 'Do some mountaineering and you'll learn not to be so frightened of heights', 'If you're angry, count up to ten before doing anything', and so forth. In other words, although we cannot *directly* obey a command to alter our feelings, we can and do obey commands and instructions to do things by which our feelings will in fact be altered or affected. The educator of the emotions is concerned to discover and use those methods of teaching and instruction by which people can be effectively helped to do this.

The first thing to notice is that these instructions are of very different kinds, and have different objectives; and this should make us hesitate before putting our money on any *one* way in which the emotions may be educated. Thus for many people, the phrase 'education of the emotions' may call to mind various devices for 'controlling one's feelings' – learning to keep one's temper, learning how to stand up to enemy fire, and so on. Others, including philosophers who have a special interest in the reasonableness or appropriateness of particular emotions in reference to particular objects, may be inclined to stress the role of correct belief *about the object* of emotion. Both of these are obviously important, and give us two rough categories from which we may start. The instructions we characteristically give people relate either to (a) what a person should believe, judge or consider about a situation, which is likely to affect the kind or amount of emotion he feels; or to (b) what a person should do by way of handling, controlling, inhibiting or expressing the emotion he feels. We say, for instance, (a) 'Don't be angry with him, he's a nice chap', or (b) 'You may be angry, but at least try to act like a gentleman', or 'Count up to ten very slowly'.

We may talk, then, about two different *areas* in which we may succeed or fail: (a) an area of cognitive belief or appraisal, and (b) an area of the expression or the control of actions and symptoms. But it would be a mistake to suppose that the education of the emotions consisted entirely (or even chiefly) of improving a person's *abilities* or *attainments* in these two areas. This supposition is not absurd in simple cases: thus (a) my fear of spiders may simply exist because I have not attained to the relevant knowledge – that they are not dangerous, and (b) I may be able to avoid or diminish my fear of heights if I learn the simple trick of looking up rather than down. But in other cases mere *information*, or mastery of a *technique* – 'knowing that' such-and-such is the case, or 'knowing how' to do certain things – is not enough.[1]

Indeed the instructions we give people are plainly intended to do more than this. Not only (A) do they give information ('he's a

---

[1] See Bernard Williams, *Morality and the Emotions*, p. 20.

nice chap') or set out a technique of control ('count to ten very slowly, take a deep breath', etc.), which the hearer may or may not already know; but also (B) the utterance of them in their context *reminds* the hearer of the *relevance* of the fact or the technique: the injunctions suggest that it is this fact or technique that should guide his feelings and conduct. We might say that they attempt to get the hearer to bring the knowledge in (A) above to bear on the situation. Obviously enough, it is of little help to *have* the relevant abilities and attainments if one does not actually *use* them, and use them effectively, when the situation arises.

But there is a further complication still. For a man may (A) have the relevant abilities and attainments ('knowing that' and 'knowing how'), and (B) bring these to bear on the situation, and yet (C) still fail to feel the right, or the right amount of, emotion, and fail actually to control his emotional symptoms and the behaviour that flows from them. We thus have three logical types of failure, which we can clarify by an example. Suppose a father is angry with his daughter's boy-friend, apparently for a trivial reason (perhaps because he has long hair). First, he may be *incompetent at judging* the person or the situation: he may hold mistaken views about people, for example that long hair is always a sign of a degenerate character. Secondly, he may be quite competent at judging people and situations, but nevertheless *fail to make* a judgement at all: thus he may just explode with anger, perhaps triggered off by the memory of the long-haired boy yesterday who stole the fish-knives. Thirdly, he may possess competence in judgement, and actually make a competent judgement, but nevertheless fail to *feel and act* in accordance with his judgement: here he might say 'Yes, I know he's a nice chap, but somehow I just get very angry when he's there.'

This already gives us the beginnings of a taxonomy. We can represent these three categories of failure in the form of three questions. Of anyone who fails to feel the 'right' emotions or fails to handle his emotions properly, we may ask:

A. Does he have (a) the relevant cognitive abilities or attainments ('knowing that'), and/or (b) the relevant skills and aptitudes ('knowing how')?

B. Does he actually use and bring to bear (a) and/or (b) on the situation?

C. Are his emotions and their expression actually affected or altered by his use of (a) and (b)?[1]

These categories are, so to speak, cumulative. To possess whatever attributes are required for A is a necessary, but not a sufficient condition for B and C: and to possess whatever attributes are needed for B is a necessary but not a sufficient condition for C. Thus if a person lacks an A-type attribute, we still do not know whether he has or lacks B- and C-type attributes: if he has A-type ones, and lacks B-type ones, we still do not know whether he has or lacks C-type ones. This is obvious enough: it is perhaps worth mentioning only because we may be tempted to think that there need be only *one* category in which the person is inadequate. But as we all know, the fact that a person lacks an ability does not mean that he would use it even if he had it, nor that his emotions would be significantly affected even if he had it and used it.

They are also cumulative in another important sense. For it is not just that we want the person to have and bring to bear the relevant abilities and attainments (A and B) *and* feel the right emotion (C): it is that we want him to have and bring them to bear *and therefore* feel the right emotion. It would in principle be possible (and perhaps useful), once the angry father has gone through stages A and B and knows he ought not to be angry, to give him a tranquillizing drug and thereby make him calm; and so with other cases. But then he would not become calm because of his knowledge and its application. As we have seen,[2] most actual educational objectives necessitate that stage C occurs *because of* stages A and B; so that the cumulativeness of these categories is of great importance.

In principle, therefore, we could ask of any case 'Why did the man fail?' and give an answer in terms of one or more of the categories A, B and C. What particular answers we gave would of course be an *empirical* matter: we should have to look at the facts

[1] In the case of emotions for which a particular kind of belief is conceptually necessary (e.g. remorse, pride, envy, but not fear, anger, hatred), A and B alone would be sufficient to make a person change the *name* of his emotion. If I (A) know that I have not done wrong, and (B) bring this knowledge to bear, then it cannot (logically) be the case that (C) I nevertheless still feel *remorse*. I should have to say something like 'I have the symptoms of remorse', or 'I feel urged to apologize' or 'I feel as if I had done wrong'. This has to be noted: but I am not clear that it is of great importance for the educator.

[2] See Chapter 7.

of the case. It appears that any item which might reasonably feature on a list of 'emotional virtues' can be cashed out in terms of these types. Thus the notion of 'autonomy' or freedom from psychic or social compulsion boils down to the notion that a man's feelings and acts are dictated by his cognition (perception of reality), and not by factors which are not rationally relevant (involving A, B and C above): 'integration' might be covered by C: 'self-awareness' and 'perception of reality' by A and B; and so forth. This task need not be pursued here: but it may be worth noting that the 'emotional virtues' or 'criteria of mental health' usually listed tend to be a mixed bag: that is, some fall wholly under one logical type (A or B or C), some under two, and some under all three. Insofar as educators, psychologists and others find it helpful to work from such lists, it seems to me important that care should be exercised in determining into just which logical types items on the list are supposed to fall.

We now have to ask to what extent *education* (rather than conditioning, indoctrination, brain surgery, biochemical treatment, and so on) is relevant to these categories. The answer to this depends partly on how purist a view we take of the word 'education': but I do not want to enter at any length into this problem here, particularly since it seems to me a terminological rather than a substantive issue. All we need note is that some reasonable degree of cognitive awareness and development on the part of the person is required if we are to speak of methods of *education* (as opposed to conditioning, indoctrination, brain surgery, or biochemical treatment on the one hand, and mere training, drill, habit-forming, and so forth on the other). This knocks out, at least, all those cases of failure in *any* of the categories A, B and C which are due to purely physical causes – to what we might call lack of basic equipment rather than lack of teaching. For instance, in A a person may lack some relevant ability, not because he has not been taught to develop it, but simply because part of his brain is missing. Similarly in B: it may be that he has not been taught to bring his abilities to bear, but it may also be simply that he is drunk or drugged. And finally with C, it looks prima facie plausible to say, not only that there may be some cases where his failure to feel the right emotion is due to lack of equipment rather than lack of education, but that all cases in this category must be such. For (we might think) if the educator has taught him to develop all the relevant abilities, and taught him to bring them to bear, what else can he do? Must not any failure be due to some physical cause? Does the person now need not the teacher but the doctor or the brain-surgeon?

We shall deal with this last problem in the next chapter: for the moment I shall assume that there can be cases of both kinds. We can, then, repeat our taxonomy as follows:

	I Not educationally remediable	II Educationally remediable
A. (i) Relevant cognitive abilities and attainments ('knowing that') (ii) Relevant aptitudes and techniques ('knowing how')		
B. Bringing (i) & (ii) to bear		
C. Feeling rightly as a result of bringing (i) & (ii) to bear		

The educator of the emotions needs first to be able to identify particular cases of failure. This is of course an empirical matter, but any cases should be able to be (and for the sake of clarity ought to be) located within this simple framework.

We need now to notice that we seem to have set up (at least so far as A and B are concerned) a scheme for the successful performance of a person educated in *any* sphere. For such a person will always need (A) some cognitive ability, attainment or skill, and (B) attributes in virtue of which he deploys these when the situation arises. It is only in C that we seem to be specifically concerned with the emotions or emotional states: for it is not normally considered a part of (say) scientific education that deploying scientific abilities should generate any particular feelings on the part of the pupil, only that the pupil should be adequately *motivated* by some feelings.

This is inevitable, however, because of the connection of emotion with belief. We have to face the fact that any belief, cognitive ability, attainment, aptitude or skill *may* be relevant to a man's emotions. We may incline to suppose that, in practice, it will be his beliefs about himself and other people that are particularly relevant: but he might, for instance, feel depressed or angry because he thinks he has a low I.Q. or is illegitimately born – and hence the kind of cognitive abilities which are relevant to knowing

I

one's own I.Q. or the facts about one's birth are also in principle relevant to the rationality of one's emotions.

At the same time, there are practical (or what might be called 'administrative') reasons why we should not allow our scheme to cover an absurdly wide area. Some distinction, however pragmatic, must be observed between 'the education of the emotions' and other educational spheres in which practical educators or research workers may be interested: and we may well make such a distinction without losing sight of the fact that these spheres of education overlap – that, for instance, a person's emotional education may largely depend on his ability to use language or his general intelligence (attributes which are equally relevant to other educational spheres). It might well be argued that we shall not be in a position to say just what attributes we ought to single out for inclusion until a good deal more effective research has been done: but we can make sensible guesses about which are likely to be the most important items in the category of cognitive abilities and other aptitudes (A). Perhaps we might list the following:

cognitive grasp of emotion-words and concepts;
ability to identify one's own emotions;[1]
knowledge of 'hard' facts related to what is normally dangerous, advantageous, and so on for human beings as they are;
skills and aptitudes related to communication with other people, linguistic expression, techniques of self-control, and so forth.

This is a purely *ad hoc* list of suggestions for improvement, and I shall not pursue it here. In the same way we are not concerned here with plausible guesses for B and C. Much could be said about the importance of forming habits and sentiments, and of giving the child sufficient security and confidence, which will help him to bring his abilities and aptitudes to bear (B) and produce right feeling (C). But this is primarily a matter for the psychologist rather than the teacher.

Let us now go back to our problem about category C. That we recognize cases in this category does not seem to me doubtful. We often say, and mean, such things as 'Yes, I know it's not dangerous, but I still feel frightened'; 'I'm fully aware that he is kind, but he

---

[1] This ability seems, for reasons given in the following chapter, to be of particular interest and importance: and I have considered it more fully in Appendix IV ('Insight'). See also Appendix VI.

still makes me angry'; 'I keep telling myself I've done nothing wrong, but I still feel as guilty as if I had'. We often have the knowledge, and bring it to bear, but still fail to feel rightly. Moreover, it seems to me that such cases are both common and important. There are indeed other common and important cases, where a person actually has some false belief about a situation, or fails to bring his correct belief to bear: for instance, an adolescent may genuinely think that his parents persecute him, or fail to remember on relevant occasions that they do not. But there are plenty of other cases where this is not so: where (we feel tempted to say) the adolescent 'acts as if he believed' his parents were persecutors, or that even if he denies that he believes it, nevertheless he 'really' or 'unconsciously' believes it.

The relationship between belief and emotion is not always straightforward. To take just one example, when we consider the notion of *prejudice* we distinguish the person who genuinely believes that negroes are inferior, or that Jews are plotting to overthrow the State, from the person who is prejudiced against negroes or Jews: but it is not at all clear, at least prima facie, how we should describe the latter. Are we to say that he has no false belief about them, but acts and/or feels as if he has? Or that he does have a false belief, but fails to recognize it?[1] Is the belief specifically about negroes and Jews, or about 'outsiders' generally (negroes and Jews being only particular instances)? And do we say that the belief (if it exists) generates the feeling of antipathy, or that the antipathy generates the belief? If the latter, what sort of answer should we give to the question 'Why is he antipathetic?' – is it the kind of antipathy that exists between cats and dogs, or does it rest in turn upon another belief? Here are conceptual as well as empirical problems.

It is of great importance how we are to describe cases of this kind. For if we deny that the adolescent previously instanced or the prejudiced person really has anything we could call a *belief* –

---

[1] We have also to recognize that unreasonable emotions are not only *based on* but *lead to* false beliefs. Thus it is at least an open question whether (to use the example above) racial prejudice is based on (caused by) the false belief that (say) the Jews are plotting to overthrow the State, or whether we ought not rather to say that this belief is a rationalization arising from an already existing prejudice against Jews, itself perhaps based on a quite different false belief (e.g., perhaps, 'they are different from us and therefore dangerous').

anything which he is or has ever been conscious of and conceptualized – then we shall want to say simply that, though there
are failures in category C, they can only be failures due to lack of
equipment, and cannot be *educationally* remediable. The adolescent
or prejudiced person has been wrongly conditioned, or perhaps his
glands or brain cells need attention: for if all his beliefs and cognitive
faculties are in order, then the failure cannot be anything to do
with lack of *education*. And more follows from this. The failure
cannot be (if we say this) in any sense his *fault*: nor is he being
unreasonable, for he cannot help it. He is simply unfortunate. On
the other hand, if we accept the existence of unconscious beliefs and
emotions, then there may be educationally remediable cases in
category C: and we may want to say that in an important sense the
person *does not want to* feel rightly – as opposed to saying that he
cannot: that he is, in a very deep sense, being *unreasonable*.

These cases (if they exist) merit special attention for another
reason also. For in any such case the whole process of identifying
a category of failure and a category of reasons for failure would
have to be *repeated*. For we now have a situation in which one
emotion, or an emotion at one level, is misplaced *because of* another
emotion or an emotion at another level. Thus, to use our example
again, the angry father may be angry because he is frightened that
the boy-friend will take his daughter away from him: to deal with
his anger we would first have to deal with his fear. And this fear
may be something he does not admit even to himself. Hence the
person would have to be taught to bring to bear his abilities and
attainments, not now on his anger, but on the underlying fear
which inspires it.

For these reasons, then, we will temporarily put our taxonomy
on one side, and take a look at such cases. They are important not
for a coherent and intelligible categorization of attributes relevant
to the education of the emotions, but also for the practical task of
education. They are closely connected (1) with the concept of the
unconscious mind, a concept which nearly always appears in the
immense literature relevant to this general topic, and which educators and others can hardly avoid facing: and (2) with the concept
of sincerity and the so-called problem of 'weakness of will' (*akrasia*).
Although we cannot do anything like full justice to all the problems
here, a somewhat more detailed account is necessary.

9. The unconscious mind and sincerity

We saw at the end of the last chapter that there seemed to be cases, like the case of the father angry with the boy-friend, which formed a category of particular relevance to the educator. We also saw that we sometimes described such cases, either by saying something like 'he *unconsciously* . . .' or by saying something like 'he doesn't *sincerely* . . .' Now, as we shall see in this chapter, it does in fact make a great difference to the practical educator whether we describe such cases in this way, or in other ways: and in particular, how seriously (and with what *sort* of seriousness) we take the notion of the unconscious mind. I make no apology, therefore, for going into this in some depth: though of course it would require a whole book to do it full justice.

A. The Unconscious Mind

'The unconscious mind' may be used as a peg on which to hang a great many different phenomena, to which we refer in a great many different words and phrases. It is important to remember that these phenomena and phrases are not the exclusive monopoly of Freud or his followers: and we shall not here be concerned with offering any kind of exposition, defence or disproof of Freud's own theories – the logic of which is, indeed, highly obscure. Almost everybody, however, says such things as 'he doesn't really love her, although he thinks he does'; 'he doesn't genuinely mean to do it, he's just deceiving himself'; 'he says he's fond of me, but in fact he acts as if he hates me'; 'he professes to despise his boss, but unconsciously he's frightened of him', and so forth: and there is much in the work of psychological phenomenologists such as Sartre, and novelists such as Tolstoy, which leads one to suppose that such remarks stand for phenomena which are as baffling to analyse as they are interesting to observe.

We can hardly suppose that all these phenomena are essentially of the same logical nature, and we shall not undertake the task of classifying them all and matching each with an appropriate and unambiguous description. Rather I shall attempt to describe *one* general type of phenomenon. It could, I believe, be argued that this type is extremely common: that it has a very good claim to give serious significance to the notion of the 'unconscious mind': and that it makes more sense of Freudian theories and psychoanalytic practice than other phenomena. But I shall not argue this: I shall argue only that it exists, and that it is of peculiar importance to educators.

It is natural to interpret such phrases as 'he unconsciously fears' as equivalent to 'he fears, but is unconscious (unaware) of fearing', ('. . . loving', '. . . being jealous', etc.). But at this point a difficulty strikes us. Is it not part of what is meant by 'fear', 'love', and 'being jealous' that these are conscious activities? Not, indeed, that a person must necessarily know that what he feels *is* fear, love or jealousy – it is conceivable that he might not know how to describe his feelings correctly, perhaps through lack of the necessary vocabulary: but rather that (as we saw in Chapter 6) human emotions are directed towards *objects* and characteristically involve *beliefs*. Hence, if a person feels fear in the full sense of the word, his feelings must be consciously directed towards an object, and he characteristically believes that the object is dangerous. Indeed, as we also saw, there are some emotion-words where the connection between the emotion and a particular kind of belief is not only characteristic but necessary: thus 'remorse' and 'pride' logically entail certain beliefs. How then, we might ask, is it intelligible to talk of 'unconscious emotions' at all?

To this there are two possible lines of approach, which I can give here only in their most general form:

(1) We may use the emotion-words in a sense whereby they are tied only to actions and symptoms, playing down (so far as we reasonably can) the conceptual role of target and belief, and regarding emotions primarily as passive experiences. On this view, we shall say that a man is frightened if he trembles at the knees, turns pale, runs away, and so on, whether or not he consciously directs his feelings towards an object, and whether or not he believes that the object is dangerous. Similarly we shall say that a man feels remorse if he looks shamefaced, avoids the scene of the crime, and

so on: and though this will not be 'remorse' in the normal sense (which conceptually entails a certain kind of belief), some sense can be attributed to it. (Some might prefer to say, in these cases, that the person *behaved as if* he felt remorse: the implication being, not that he was pretending or insincere, but rather, simply that his behaviour was what one might expect from somebody who felt remorse in the full belief-entailing sense.)

This interpretation uses emotion-words in what I shall call a 'thin' or diminished sense: that is, in a sense which implies no element of propositional belief or conceptualization. In particular, there is no question here of a person feeling fear *because* he believes an object to be dangerous, or remorse *because* he believes that he has done wrong. A model case would perhaps be that used in Huxley's *Brave New World*: very young children are given electric shocks when they are confronted with flowers, and subsequently express fear and discomfort in similar situations when they are adult. The children do not believe that the flowers are dangerous: or if they come to believe this later, the belief would only be a rationalization and not a cause of their fear. They simply evince certain symptoms and behave in certain ways when confronted with flowers, responding to stimuli with a characteristic behaviour-pattern.

On this view, to say that somebody 'unconsciously fears X', is open to two interpretations. (a) It may be simply to say that the fact escapes his own notice, or he is not aware that he is afraid: in much the same sense in which he might not be aware that he is scratching his ear, or that a nerve in his face is twitching, or that he has turned pale. It is to say that he is unaware *that* he is frightened. Here the 'unconsciously' qualifies the verb 'fears'. However, it is also (b) open to a more sophisticated interpretation: that the person is not conscious or aware of what he is frightened of, not aware of the object of his fear. This would apply, for instance, to cases of what is sometimes called 'free-floating anxiety', where a man is aware of being afraid but not aware of being afraid of anything in particular. Here the 'unconsciously' qualifies the 'X': 'he unconsciously fears X' means 'he is afraid (and knows it) but is unconscious (unaware) that X is what he fears'.

This latter interpretation (b) might perhaps be extended to make some sense of many of the cases commonly referred to by psycho-analysts. For example, suppose that a person is afraid of his employer: and suppose that (in a way similar to the Huxley case mentioned above) when he was very young he had certain experiences in relation to his father which set up the response pattern (not the *belief*) 'when you encounter men in positions of power with moustaches, then fear'. Then, if his employer fits this description, he will react as he reacted to his father, without knowing that his reaction is due to his early experience. We might express this by saying 'he is unconsciously frightened of his father', meaning that he is unaware of how he comes to be frightened of his employer – unaware that the fear-generating stimulus-pattern was originally based on fear of his father.

On this interpretation, we are still using 'fear' and other emotion-words in the same 'thin' sense: we do not have to suppose that his original fear was generated by any particular *belief* about his father, any more than that Huxley's children had any belief about flowers. There is no question of the person at that time *saying* to himself 'I judge my father to be very dangerous because he can do so-and-so to me', and consequently coming to be afraid of him. Because of this, it is only in an equally 'thin' sense that we can talk of the person *learning* to be afraid of people in positions of power with moustaches: for there is no question of cognitive awareness, but only of a person's coming to adopt (or having forced on him) a certain behaviour-pattern or set of responses. The sense of 'learning' here is more like what we mean when we say that a bull has 'learned' to charge at cape-waving matadors, or that a dog has 'learned' to salivate at the ringing of a bell. Similarly to say that we can 'teach' such behaviour-patterns to people is only to say that we can, by some process of training, conditioning, giving lumps of sugar, administering blows ('rewards' and 'punishments' again only in a thin sense), and so forth, simply *induce* this behaviour and these symptoms in them.

Again, if we talk of a person first feeling fear of his father and then *repressing* his fear (so that, when he is afraid of his employer, we can talk of his 'unconscious fear' of his father), we are not – on this interpretation – talking of any conscious or conceptualizing process. The person does not *say to himself* 'My father is a dangerous man, and I'm frightened of him: but I mustn't think about this any more, and I'll try to forget about my fear.' What happens is that the fear immediately vanishes from consciousness, or perhaps is never conscious at all: it is not so much that *he* represses it, but rather that it becomes repressed. Repression, on this view, is something that *happens* to him, over which he has no conscious control.

(2) The second line of approach is to retain the fuller sense of emotion-words, and to hold that there may be at least some cases in which a man may first entertain a belief which generates a certain emotion, in which he may then come to forget (or deliberately repress) this belief, yet in which the belief continues to be causally operative in his behaviour. The difference between this view and (1) above is very important, though hard to express precisely: we may adumbrate it at this stage by saying that this view implies that the man's behaviour may be purposive and rule-governed, in the sense that he is not just behaving in accordance with a regular pattern, but (albeit unconsciously) following a formula which he has at one time consciously learnt, and which depends on his having had certain conceptualized beliefs. The following example may help to make the difference somewhat clearer.

Suppose I have been conditioned always to make certain moves in chess, and then been made to forget this conditioning (this might perhaps all take place under hypnosis). Then I will make the moves: but the cause of my making them will not be anything to do with any beliefs I had or have about the game itself (though I may of course invent rationalizations *post eventum* in order to make the moves seem justifiable to myself and to others). But now suppose instead that I have at one time learnt (in the full sense) or come to believe that I ought always to make certain moves: that I said to myself, for instance, 'I must always get the queen out early, so as to develop a strong attack'.[1] Then I forget having learned and believed this, but nevertheless still go on bringing out my queen on the second or third move, without really knowing why I am doing this (though of course I might invent rationalizations in this case also). Note that in this second case the 'why' bears a different sense: I am in fact acting as the result of a belief, purposively and intentionally, and part of any explanation would have to include some such phrase as 'in order to develop a strong attack'; whereas

---

[1] This is in fact a bad rule to follow in chess. But I might equally have given an example of a good rule. The concept of the unconscious is not only relevant to the abnormal cases, or cases of failure to behave appropriately. One may behave *appropriately* for unconscious reasons.

in the first case it would be sufficient to say 'because he was hypno-
tized or conditioned into making such moves – goodness knows
whether there is any point in them'.

Another simple example would be this: a person says to himself
'My unpaid bills are up in the attic: I ought to go up there and
find them.' He dislikes the idea of paying his bills, and starts
thinking of something else. He gets to the attic and begins vaguely
looking for something, but has forgotten (repressed) his belief that
the bills were there and that he ought to find them. He forces
himself to think about what he is doing and why, and eventually
remembers. Or: a person comes to believe that it is appropriate
to hate and be suspicious of Germans (because they were enemies
of his country); in the changed atmosphere of peace and brother-
hood he represses this belief, maintaining stoutly that he thinks
that 'Germans are just like anyone else', but still continues to act
on it. Under certain circumstances he may come to admit that he
still believes Germans are hateful, and remember how he came to
formulate this belief.

If we adopt this view, then the interpretation of such phrases as
'he unconsciously fears', '. . . wants', '. . . is jealous of', will be
significantly different. We are now saying, not just that the person
evinces a behaviour-pattern which we can call 'fearing', 'wanting',
or 'being jealous' in a thin sense, a pattern (a) of which he may be
unaware or (b) that was originally set up in a context of earlier
experiences of which he is now unaware: we are saying that his
emotion (as in standard cases of emotion) is the result of a particular
belief, but that he is not aware of having this belief. Further, if we
advance the proposition that he 'unconsciously fears X' as part of
an *explanation* – if, for instance, we say that he is frightened of his
employer because he is unconsciously frightened of his father – then
we are giving an explanation of a somewhat different kind from that
implied in view (1) above. We are saying that his present behaviour
(his fear) is the result of a particular *kind* of cause: namely, his
original conscious beliefs. And this is different from saying that
his present behaviour is the result of a particular, behaviour-
pattern, syndrome, set of responses to stimuli, or whatever.

This may not seem to lessen the appearance of paradox and
unintelligibility which we noticed earlier. The question may be
raised of whether the notion of 'unconscious belief' now makes any
sense. Is there any difference (it might be asked), even in principle,

between a person who has an 'unconscious belief' and a person who merely behaves in a certain way? Once we abstract the element of consciously entertaining a proposition from the notion of a belief, is anything left except the man's behaviour-pattern (his disposition to do certain things, and certain symptoms which affect him)? And if this is all that is left, will it not fit perfectly well into the first of the two views above? But now the answer to this will be reasonably plain. To say that someone has a belief of which he is unconscious is to lay oneself open to methods of verification which are different from the methods by which we verify whether a person has acquired a *behaviour-pattern* of which he is unconscious. To verify the first, we would want to observe (in so far as this would be possible in practice) whether or not, in the person's earlier history, he thought (however vaguely or quickly) something like 'My father is dangerous': or else (and this is the method used by psychoanalysts) we would have to create a context which would enable him to *remember* having formed this belief. To verify the second, we should need only to observe external (not conceptual or linguistic) behaviour, in order to establish that the original-pattern was set up on such-and-such an occasion and has persisted into adult life. The difference between the two methods is roughly similar to the differences between the kind of explanation used by biographers, novelists and (according to some) historians (in terms of conscious intentions and purposes), and explanation in the natural sciences (in terms only of causal laws).

In order to verify the further claim that it was the original belief that generated and continues to generate his fear, we should have to determine whether the absence of the belief would have resulted in an absence of fear. This, again, may in practice be very hard to determine. But in principle it is possible to do so: and apart from what we may induce from direct observation of children, it may be that by reconstructing (as it were) the conditions under which he came to hold the belief, and then encouraging him to change it, we can see that the fear vanishes. This too is the kind of verification (however uncontrolled and in a sense 'unscientific') that is supposed to take place in the psychoanalytic consulting-room. I do not propose to examine the actual evidence for such cases: my intention here is simply to show that they are logically possible, and to distinguish them from the cases that would better fit the view outlined in (1) above.

Since the fashion in many philosophical and psychological circles is to over-emphasize view (1), it may be worth reminding the reader that there are prima facie grounds for supposing that much human behaviour which may at first sight seem to be mere malfunctions or lapses from rationality, or the result of early conditioning, is in fact meaningful and purposive. Freud himself used such phenomena as slips of the tongue and dreams to make this point: and there are plenty of examples. Thus if I type to my girl friend 'I don't think I need to be mithered any more', this is intelligible as a straightforward mistake for 'mothered', since the letters 'o' and 'i' adjoin each other on my keyboard. But if I type 'I don't need to be smothered any more', one suspects a piece of unconscious communication. Perhaps I believe that girls, like my mother, are apt to smother me. But this is no more than a (plausible) suspicion. To verify it, we would need to have observed me formulating this belief in childhood, or to enable me to admit or remember having formulated it, in the way described above.

The importance, for our purposes, of the overall distinction between (1) and (2) – whatever may be the incidence of either general type of case in practice – is not far to seek. For (2) involves the notions of belief, reasons for belief, and conceptualization in a way in which (1) does not. A person who fits (1) – who, let us say, has been forced by conditioning or archetypal traumatic experiences into an unsatisfactory behaviour-pattern or set of responses – we should be more inclined to describe as 'ill' or 'malfunctioning'; a person who fits (2) – who has made some use of reason and language to form beliefs, albeit false beliefs, which generate certain inappropriate feelings – we should be more inclined to describe as 'unreasonable'. Similarly in (1) the person is less *responsible* for his feelings than in (2), since (to put it somewhat metaphorically) they are in no way the product of his own consciousness and reasoning. This suggests that, whereas cases of type (1) might in principle be dealt with by methods which we should not want to describe as *educational* (as for instance reconditioning, 'behaviour-therapy', hypnosis, or brain surgery), cases of type (2) necessarily involve paying attention to the man's beliefs and reasons for belief, since it is these which generate his feelings and behaviour.

We must be careful, however, not to claim too much for those cases which come under interpretation (2). Two points need to be briefly made:

(a) The abolition of *false* beliefs can, in principle, be achieved not only by the 'educational' methods of increasing a man's awareness, pointing out the evidence, verbal persuasion, and so on, but also by non-educational methods. We might be able to abolish a belief or set of beliefs by cutting a nerve in the brain, treatment by electric shock, drugs, and so forth. We might, as it were, wipe the slate of his mind clean by such methods. But what we cannot, logically, do – as we explained in Chapter 7 – is to give the man *true* beliefs of the required kind in this way. For example: a man may have false beliefs about his wife – that she is plotting against him, hostile, wants to betray him, and so on. We may remove these by non-educational methods: for instance, we might induce total amnesia about his wife. But if our ultimate objective is to get him to build up a relationship of trust and understanding with his wife, then this involves his holding true beliefs and making correct judgements about her, which are to function as the cause of his emotions: and this necessarily involves *learning* or *relearning*. This process of building up rationally learned relationships constitutes a large part of what goes on in some forms of psycho-analysis; and it is logically requisite for the attainment of any objectives describable in such terms as 'trusting other people', 'understanding one's wife', etc.

(b) More obviously, the mere *coexistence* of a false belief with inappropriate emotions and behaviour does not enable us to classify a case under interpretation (2): for that belief may not be the cause of the emotion, but only its effect. For instance, the man in our example may have false conscious beliefs about his wife, and these may in turn be traceable to false unconscious beliefs (perhaps about his mother). This would come under (2), where the false beliefs, whether conscious or unconscious, are the cause of the paranoid symptoms. But equally it may be the case that the man is in a general state of anxiety due to purely physical causes, and simply cashes out that anxiety in the form of false conscious beliefs about his wife: roughly, he feels free-floating fear, and attaches it to the nearest object in order to anchor it somewhere. If his original free-floating fear is not the result of any unconscious belief, then it comes under interpretation (1), and is amenable to non-educational treatment.

Remove the fear by drugs or electric shocks, and the belief (which was only a symptom of the fear) vanishes: just as the beliefs of alcoholics that there are snakes or beetles climbing up the walls may vanish, once they are thoroughly weaned from their physical addiction.

We may use this example to draw attention to one other important point, involving a further distinction which we have slurred over in the general distinction between (1) and (2). There are two possibilities: (i) I originally believe something like 'My mother smothers me'; this belief sets up a behaviour-pattern (resentment, anger, desire to escape) towards my mother; this behaviour-pattern continues when I meet other women in adult life: (ii) I originally believe something much more generalized, for instance (roughly) 'If long hair, skirts, and so forth, then smothering': this sets up a behaviour-pattern *both* towards my mother and (potentially) towards other women. In the first case my adult behaviour is directly caused by an imprinted behaviour-pattern which is simply *triggered off* by other women (because they are like my mother) – I do not believe, and never have believed, anything about women *in general*. It is true that the behaviour-pattern was originally set up by my belief about my mother, but after that it leads a life of its own. But in the second case my adult behaviour is the *direct* result of a more general belief about women (or whatever identification-signs I as a child have for 'women' – long hair, skirts, etc.).

This distinction comes out more clearly if we assume the particular belief to be true (perhaps my mother was peculiarly liable to smother me) and the general belief to be false (it is false to regard all women as peculiarly liable to smother me). For now, if (i) I only hold the particular belief, then I have no *false* beliefs at all: what has happened is that I had (and unconsciously still have) a true belief about my mother, and no beliefs about women in general at all. My (true) belief about my mother has generated a behaviour-pattern which is inappropriate for other women. Here psycho-therapeutic treatment might consist of strengthening my rationality – getting me to recognize my belief about my mother, and to recognize that it does not apply to other women, and hence to evolve new and more appropriate behaviour-patterns towards other women: but the treatment *might* merely employ the non-rational method of inhibiting or 're-training' my adult behaviour towards other women, since I have no beliefs *about women in general which cause* that behaviour. On the other hand, if (ii) I hold the general belief, which is responsible for that behaviour, it will be necessary for effective treatment that this (false) belief should be changed.

There is, then, considerable scope for non-educational methods in a great many cases: I have been concerned only to show that for *some* cases educational methods are logically necessary. But they may, of course, also be useful for other cases where they are not logically necessary. Thus strengthening a person's reason by making him aware of what he feels and why, and showing to him the inappropriateness of such feelings in particular contexts, is certainly *one* way of encouraging or enabling him to change them. The man's own reason is *one* force that may be deployed, and deployed successfully, in an attempt to change his emotional behaviour and symptoms. But this may not work: it is, indeed, a common experience (though not quite as common as we sometimes suppose) to be perfectly aware of what one feels and why, and aware of the inappropriateness of such feelings, and yet still to display the behaviour and symptoms of the feelings. It is here that the non-educational methods of drugs, 'behaviour-therapy', conditioning, training and so forth may be of the utmost value: and our only reason for not saying more about them here is that they are not relevant to the educator as such.

We must now relate all this to those categories that are relevant to the educator. We saw in Chapter 7 that for attaining certain objectives in the upbringing of children ('appreciation', 'sympathy', etc.) we require methods that are rational, or educational, or involve *learning* (in the full sense of the word) rather than the application of drugs, brain surgery, or conditioning – even though the latter may facilitate the former. However, this by itself suggests only a straightforward two-stage process, corresponding to the distinctions made at the end of the last chapter (p. 116) in the types of reasons for emotional failure:

I. Non-rational methods used to put the student in a state in which he can easily learn;
II. Simply filling in his ignorance (so to speak) by teaching of the required kind.

But the notion of the unconscious, in so far as interpretation (2) applies, suggests that it is over-simple to regard the student's mind as a *tabula rasa*. It suggests that he already *has* false beliefs, unconscious if not conscious, which he needs to be educated *out of*. In other words, he has *mislearned* a good deal already in the sphere of the emotions, in a way in which (perhaps) he would be unlikely to have mislearned anything in the spheres of mathematics or Latin. For (it is held) there are obvious reasons why people are likely to have false or irrational beliefs and emotions in the former case, and less likely to have them in the latter. If this is true, it would require us to supplement II above, as follows:

III. Helping the student *unlearn* or correct his false beliefs, and only then II, helping him to replace them by true beliefs.

And it may be that III is as difficult, and requires as much attention from the educator, as II.

B. SINCERITY

The above remarks derive from an attempt to make some sort of sense of what is commonly said by psychologists and others under the heading of 'the unconscious mind'. Much the same conclusions would, I believe, be reached by a full examination of other writers whose orientation is not psychoanalytic at all, but who are concerned with a number of concepts and phenomena for which they use such phrases as 'insincerity', '*mauvaise foi*', 'self-deception', and – more illuminating – 'double-think'. In the brief discussion that follows, we shall try to reinforce and illustrate from a new angle some of the points made above: in particular, that interpretation (2) of 'the unconscious' which involves unconscious beliefs.

A man's emotional rationality is frequently *displayed* in the way he talks. It is misleading to speak of 'care in the use of words' as if this were always a criterion of rationality, distinct from other criteria (such as freedom from false unconscious beliefs). For though this is sometimes the case – that is, although a man can be quite free from other kinds of irrationality, yet still careless or confused or simply ignorant about the proper use of words – yet often the case is quite different: it is *because* the man has conflicting beliefs operative at different levels of his mind that he uses language in the way he does. Indeed, from this point of view, there is a sense in which it would be inappropriate for him not to speak as he does, for he has to voice more than one belief: in the extreme case, if the beliefs conflict, he has to contradict himself. Self-contradiction is of course a model case of one type of irrationality: but the root of such self-contradiction is the existence of two conflicting beliefs which the man's ego has failed to reconcile, or even to recognize. Thus it is frequently observed that arguments with a certain type of person are often not worth pursuing, since any attempt to lead them into an admission of obvious contradictions, or to get them to clarify statements of belief (perhaps resisted precisely because such clarification might lead to contradiction), always ends in failure. (Often it is the adherents of a highly articulated metaphysic, such as Roman Catholics or theoretical Marxists, who are said to fall into this category: I mention them here for the sake of example, and not because there is any evidence at all that this phenomenon is in fact found in their case more often than elsewhere.)

It is here that the notion of sincerity is in place. To compress the relevant points as much as possible: 'sincere' is applied to people and their speech-acts, and is often used to mean (a) telling the truth about yourself, not lying, not deceiving another person by your utterance or use of signs. But this is only one common case of the more general meaning, (b) doing as much justice as you can to your beliefs, feelings, wishes, and so on by your utterance or use of signs, or saying in public what you have said to yourself. Both of these are included in the notion of 'meaning an utterance'[1]: but they are distinct. 'Sincere(ly)' and 'insincere(ly)' are used not only (a) when a man is deliberately *misleading* other people about his beliefs, etc., but also (b) when a man is only (deliberately) *misreporting* them, for example understanding his feelings by means of a joking or light-hearted or casual reportage of them. These latter reports are insincere (not *meant*), and the man who makes them is *pro tanto* insincere, even though he sets out to deceive no one and in fact deceives no one. In both cases, however, the notion of insincerity implies that a person *deliberately* or intentionally misleads or misreports. If he fails to mean what he says through linguistic incompetence, stupidity, ignorance of the English lang-

---

[1] See Kenny, op. cit., pp. 218 ff.: note however that what is in question here is not just words, but any signs usually understood as having meaning. Thus Kenny says (p. 220) that 'there are no such things as insincere coughs or insincere snores'; but plainly there are such things as insincere smiles, where the smile is taken to *mean* something, and the same is sometimes true of coughs, snores and any other act that *may* be intentional.

uage, or carelessness, the notion does not apply.[1] The insincere person is responsible for his insincerity.

Notions like self-deception or 'double-think' are extensions of the concept of insincerity. We are concerned here, not with any kind of incompetence or psychological misfortune, but with either deliberate misleading or deliberate misreporting. A man must, at some time and in some sense, know or believe p: he must then, deliberately and consciously, put this knowledge or belief on one side, and tell himself that not-p. For example, a boy may be very frightened of learning to swim, because he believes that other boys may drown him. But he may feel guilty about being frightened – most obviously perhaps in the form of feeling guilty about confessing his fear to other boys, but also in the form of not wanting to confess it to himself. So, under the influence of this guilt, but still deliberately, he puts on one side the proposition 'I am frightened of learning to swim' and substitutes (say) the proposition 'I think swimming is boring, I'd much rather not bother to learn'. Examples of this kind are common.

It may be questioned whether we are right in describing such cases as (a) deceiving oneself and/or (b) misreporting to oneself. Here we need to observe a stock ambiguity in the phrase 'deliberately doing X', as between (i) 'deliberately doing X, whether or not you know that X is what you are doing', and (ii) 'deliberately doing something which you yourself know to be X'. It seems that the only impossible combination here is (a) (ii). For (a) (i) the boy can deceive himself without knowing that deceit is what he is engaged in: (b) (i) he can misreport his own feelings to himself without knowing that he is misreporting them: and even (b) (ii) he can know that he is misreporting his feelings, but still deliberately do so. What he cannot (logically) do, however, is (a) (ii) be aware that he is being deceived; for this implies that he is both deceived and not deceived at the same time.

In these extended cases of insincerity, then, we are dealing with a situation in which a person himself (under the pressure of a par-

---

[1] Insincerity or self-deception is only *one* reason for a man giving a false *account* of his own feelings. Sincerity applies to *utterances*: *statements*, even about one's own feelings, may be false because one is careless, lazy, etc. about observing what one feels. *Expressions* of feeling, of course, are neither true nor false, but only genuine or misleading. See my 'Happiness' in *Analysis*, October 1968.

ticular feeling) generates a new belief in himself. But we have to remember that new feelings may go along with these new beliefs. Thus the boy in our example not only feels guilty about being frightened, and not only persuades himself to believe that he is bored rather than frightened, but may (at least consciously) come to *feel* bored rather than frightened. We are thus dealing with different levels on which both beliefs and feelings operate: and it is primarily because the beliefs are both induced by, and themselves generate, these feelings that it is natural to speak as we did earlier (ch. 5) of an 'emotional investment', rather than merely of submerged beliefs which could be easily recognized and reconciled. Hence also the extreme difficulty of dealing at a practical level with the kind of irrationality which is our present topic.

If we lean heavily on extended uses of 'sincere' and 'insincere', we may perhaps follow those philosophers who maintain (to put it very briefly) that if a man sincerely assents to some course of action, then either he will do that action or else it will not be in his power to do it – that is, he will be under some kind of compulsion. For if the concept of assenting is screwed up tightly enough (to include, *inter alia*, assenting at the time and not on some previous occasion which may be forgotten), and if the concept of sincerity is screwed up tightly enough (to entail sincerity at all levels of belief and commitment), then it can be made to follow logically that the man will act. If a man appears to assent but does not act, then either (a) at some level of his personality he has denied rather than assented (i.e. he has not 'genuinely' or 'sincerely' assented), or else (b) he has assented, but there is something which prevents him from acting or causes him to act otherwise. This latter may be described as a 'psychological compulsion' if and only if it cannot be categorized as an 'unconscious desire' (fear, wish, etc.) in the sense outlined in interpretation (2) of the previous section (pp. 125-8). If it is an unconscious desire in this sense, i.e. if it is something that he has at some time verbalized but subsequently repressed, then it is less misleading to say that *he* did not (sincerely) assent, rather than that something *caused him* not to act. The extreme difficulty, in practice, of determining whether a particular case is to fall under (a) or (b) should not blind us to the importance of the distinction [1]

[1] See P. L. Gardiner's 'On Assenting to a Moral Principle' in *P.A.S.*, 1954–55. Because of the pull of unconscious desires, fears, etc., correct descriptions of what actually takes place, in those cases commonly dealt with by

Thus suppose a person who, by his actions, produces a certain result which we identify as 'murdering an innocent man' (for example, a Pharisee who helped bring about the judicial murder of Christ). Now take the phrase 'thinking that one ought not to do something but doing it'; give the first part of that phrase ('thinking that one ought not to do something') the fullest possible sense, and if necessary add to it, as follows:

(i) The person identifies his choice, at the time of his choosing, in the same way that we do: namely as a choice between 'murdering an innocent man' and not doing so.

(ii) The person says to himself, at the time, that he ought not to do it: he uses 'ought' as a genuine prescription, telling himself (as it were) not to do it: he is wholly sincere; and so on.

Now it will necessarily be true that, if he does do it, he cannot help doing so. For in screwing up the phrase 'thinking that he ought not to do something' so tightly, we have excluded any possibility of the man himself failing as a rational being. He identifies the situation correctly, has the liveliest possible sense of the prescriptiveness of 'ought', is wholly sincere, and so on. A man who is so well-armoured

---

philosophers under the title of 'akrasia', are likely to be more complicated than philosophy has generally allowed. In particular the dichotomy often forced on such cases, e.g. in some such form as 'Is it that he *can't* do X or that he hasn't really *chosen* to do X?', seems to be a straitjacket, because it uses 'he' in far too monolithic a sense, and without regard for the notion of different levels – conceptualizing and purposive levels – of the human mind: one might say it implies a forgetfulness that human beings persist through time. (cf. R. M. Hare, *Freedom and Reason*, pp. 72 ff., particularly the remark on p. 81, that a man may be 'in his *whole personality* or real self, ceasing to prescribe to himself (though there may be *a part of him* that goes on prescribing . . .)' [my italics].) The difficulty of analysing such cases is largely due to the difficulty of obtaining an honest and clear account of what actually goes on in a person's head when he is about to perform this or that action. For people have a vested interest in misdescribing the situation, usually in such a way as to deny their autonomy – it is the fault of the gods or of Ate, of the 'flesh warring against the spirit', it is 'no longer I who do the action, but sin that lodges in me', 'Love conquers Reason', and so on. These are more in the nature of dramatic summaries, bird's-eye (and often retrospective) views, or semi-metaphysical explanations of what happens, rather than straightforward, honest, detailed accounts. For these we should turn rather to autobiographies, certain types of novels (Tolstoy, Dostoevsky, Proust, Sartre, etc.), or to what actually transpires in confessionals and psychoanalytic sessions.

can only have met with some superior force or compulsion: he must, as it were, have come up against a brick wall.

By the same token, such a man is not *unreasonable* or *weak-willed*. For we can only describe what he does as 'his action' in a very weak sense. If the words 'Crucify him!', or 'Not this man, but Barabbas!' issue from his mouth, it is only in this sense that we must say that *he* has spoken them: and if he finds his hand going up in the Sanhedrin, it is only in this sense that he has 'voted'. For if we give these a fuller sense, we shall have to say that he was at some other point insincere, which is *ex hypothesi* inadmissible. If he finds himself walking and shouting and throwing stones with the rest of the Pharisees, then it must be against his will: for otherwise he would not be sincerely trying to do the opposite. This, then, is a case where the man *cannot* do X: and, significantly, a very implausible one – for the actions of the Pharisees plainly *were* intentional, and connected with their own wants and psychological posture. It will be readily seen that the qualifications we have so liberally added to the phrase 'thinking that one ought not to do X', themselves contain all the cases that interest us that is, the cases where the man simply *does* X, or *wants* to do X (rather than can't help doing X), even though in *some* sense he thinks that he ought not to.[1]

Thus of course it is true that if the Pharisee goes through an

---

[1] And in some very strong sense. Consider Hector's speech in *Troilus and Cressida* (II, 2, 163–93):

> The reasons you allege do more conduce
> To the hot passion of distemper'd blood
> Than to make up a free determination
> 'Twixt right and wrong . . .
> If Helen then be wife to Sparta's king,
> As it is known she is, these moral laws
> Of nature and of nations speak aloud
> To have her back returned: thus to persist
> In doing wrong extenuates not wrong
> But makes it much more heavy. Hector's opinion
> Is this, in way of truth; yet, ne'ertheless,
> My spritely brethren, I propend to you
> My resolution to keep Helen still;
> For 'tis a cause that hath no mean dependance
> Upon our joint and several dignities.

It is hard to say here that Hector does not think that he *ought, morally*, to give Helen back. Yet this is not what he decides to do: and he has conscious reasons for his decision: i.e. he follows a different and overriding syllogism, concerned with 'honour' or 'dignities'.

Aristotelian practical syllogism, sincerely and at the time of action, as follows:

> Major premiss: 'Condemning an innocent man to death is always wrong',
> Minor premiss: 'Christ is an innocent man',

then his conclusion can only be the action of voting against condemning Christ to death. But there may be various ways in which the syllogism fails to operate for him, or in which he fails to operate it. Two common phenomena, which may be loosely described, are relevant here:

(a) The Pharisee may simply not bring these *or any other* premisses to bear at the time of action: he may, as it were, 'forget' one or both of the premisses, and (to a greater or lesser extent) fail to think rationally at all – he drifts, or 'sleepwalks', or *finds himself* acting rather than having planned his actions;

(b) He may fail to bring them to bear because he is operating a quite different syllogism which leads to a different conclusion, e.g.

> Major premiss: 'Trouble-makers ought to be put down, and killed if necessary',
> Minor premiss: 'Christ is a trouble-maker',
> Conclusion (action): Vote for condemnation to death.

The minor premiss here is *another way of describing something*: it may be positively false (Christ was not, let us assume, a trouble-maker in the sense intended by the Pharisee): or else it may be true (assume Christ was a trouble-maker in the sense intended), but morally irrelevant, since his (overriding) moral principle is assumed to be that killing innocent people is *always* wrong (*sc.* even if they are trouble-makers).

The chief point about these and other similar cases – for the variety is much wider than we have shown it to be here – is that each may be interpreted as either a case of moral failure, or as a case of sheer incompetence. For instance, the 'forgetting' in (a) above may be what is sometimes called 'deliberate' or 'psychological' forgetting: that is, the premisses do not occur to him because he is intent on his own (selfish) wants and therefore thrusts aside other considerations; or it may be genuine forgetting, if he happens to have a very bad memory, or is very stupid. Again, in (b) the Pharisee may simply be misinformed or very stupid about Christ, mistakenly but blamelessly supposing him to be something which he is not; or it may be that he has a (usually unconscious) *reason* for his mis-description – it fits in too well with his own selfish desires if Christ can be described as a blasphemer – or a reason for not seeing that the description, though true, is morally irrelevant.

This, then, is the justification for the chief distinction made in the last section; and when general descriptions of failure in practical thought and action are given, such as 'lack of resolution', 'lack of will-power', 'lack of forethought', etc., we must always remember that we may be talking about two quite different things: (I) and (II), categories of failure where the person is simply not mentally *equipped* to succeed – he is drunk or drugged or brain-washed, too stupid, has a bad memory, is misinformed, has not been taught for long enough, etc., and (III) a category where the person *does not want* to succeed, and where his submerged wants and beliefs destroy the effective operation of the practical syllogism at different points or in different ways. Again, what actual instances fall into which category is often a very difficult empirical question: but it is one which has to be answered against this background of categories.

10. Second sketch of a Taxonomy

The points made in the last chapter do not invalidate our taxonomy, but make necessary a more sophisticated version of it. Our original sketch was:

	I Not educationally remediable	II Educationally remediable
A. (i) Relevant cognitive abilities and attainments ('knowing that') (ii) Relevant aptitudes and techniques ('knowing how')		
B. Bringing (i) & (ii) to bear		
C. Feeling rightly as a result of bringing (i) **B** (ii) to bear		

What requires sophistication here is column II. For in the last chapter (p. 132) we distinguished between cases of failure which required only straightforward teaching and learning to be remedied (as if the person concerned was emotionally a *tabula rasa*), and cases where there was unconscious resistance – where something had to be *re*learned. We need therefore to add another column (III) alongside columns I and II.

The relationships between columns II and III are important, however. There is a sense in which these categories, though they differ significantly in the ways described above, nevertheless coalesce for the educator: or to put it another way, category III exists only as a category for *diagnosis*, not as a category requiring a totally different kind of process or treatment (in the way that category I requires medical or scientific techniques). Suppose we ask how to deal with a case diagnosed as one in category III, where a person has an unconscious system of beliefs and emotions that militate against what it is rational for him to feel on certain occasions. Plainly, if what we have said about the unconscious mind is at all on the right lines, what he requires is some kind of *education* (rather than conditioning, behaviour-therapy, brain-washing, etc.). This education may be a long and difficult business, just because the beliefs and emotions are unconscious: it may require special contexts of communication and specially trained educators. But the job of the psycho-analyst (with whom we normally associate this sort of case) is not logically different from the job of the ordinary educator. The fact that the beliefs and emotions are unconscious – and this itself, indeed, is no more than a matter of degree – is extremely important from the diagnostic point of view: but it is, *pro tanto*, no more than one of many practical difficulties which the educator of the emotions has to face.

Secondly, suppose that the educator succeeds with cases of type III sufficiently to expose most or all of the relevant unconscious beliefs and emotions that form the resistance to learning. We will remember, of course, that he may well find yet another unconscious system lurking behind the one he has already exposed: but let us assume that he has gone as far as is necessary for practical purposes in this direction.[1] What has now happened is that category III has disappeared. *Ex hypothesi* the man is now no longer motivated against acquiring the relevant abilities and attainments (A), or against learning to deploy them and actually to feel those emotions that fit the real situation (B and C). And for these purposes, now that the unconscious resistances are gone, the man will need only straightforward *teaching*, which is wholly contained in category II.

We shall correctly put column III, therefore, under the general heading of 'educationally remediable', whilst remembering its importance for diagnosis, and also that special techniques may be required. We shall now write our taxonomy as shown in the sketch on following page.

The reader will remember from Chapter 6 that our taxonomy was to be set out in terms of a number of components; and a somewhat more sophisticated version of the components used in our first publication[2] seems adequate for this purpose. Thus:

1. Category A of the scheme fits in well with our components EMP and GIG. EMP we use to stand for the ability to identify one's own emotions (AUTEMP) and the emotions of other people (ALLEMP):

---

[1] See Appendix IV.
[2] See *I.M.E.*, Chapter 4.

	I Not educationally remediable	Educationally remediable	
		II No un- conscious resistance	III Un- conscious resistance
A. (i) Relative cognitive abilities and attainments ('knowing that'). (ii) Relative aptitudes and techniques ('knowing how').			
B. Bringing (i) & (ii) to bear			
C. Feeling rightly as a result of bringing (i) & (ii) to bear			

GIG to stand for an attainment, the mastery of those 'hard' facts (GIG(1)) and of those social and personal skills (GIG(2)) that are relevant and necessary for the morally educated person (here to include the 'emotionally educated' person as well).

2. Category B concerns the deployment of the abilities in category A. This fits in well with the component KRAT. This component was used in a very general way to bridge the gap between moral abilities and moral action: but we need here to distinguish between what we may call KRAT (1) (those attributes required for the deploying of the abilities in category A) and KRAT (2) (those attributes required for the later stage of feeling and acting rightly *after* he has deployed the abilities). Given the relevant abilities plus KRAT (1), then, the person will have deployed or brought to bear his abilities on the situation, and will then know what he ought to feel and how he ought to act. We represented this stage by the terms DIK and PHRON (DIK being used for those situations where other people's interests are directly and importantly involved, and PHRON for other situations).

3. Category C is concerned with whether a person actually feels rightly, and expresses and controls his feelings rightly. For this he may need other attributes, to which we may attach the general label KRAT (2).

This may be represented as follows:

$$
\left.\begin{array}{l}
\text{AUTEMP} \\
\text{ALLEMP} \\
\text{GIG(1)} \\
\text{GIG(2)}
\end{array}\right\} \begin{array}{l}
+\text{KRAT(1)} (=\text{DIK or PHRON})+\text{KRAT(2)} = \text{right emotion} \\
\text{(and expression and control of emotion).}^{1}
\end{array}
$$

To return to our old example: the father who really thinks long hair to be an infallible sign of decadence lacks the attainment GIG(1) (category A). If he knows better than this, but somehow fails to bring this knowledge to bear, he lacks KRAT(1) (category B). Either of these would emerge in a lack of DIK or PHRON: i.e. he does not know, or has not decided, what he ought to feel. If he does bring the right knowledge to bear, yet still cannot or will not feel anything but angry, then he lacks KRAT(2) (category C).

So we can write our taxonomy in these terms:

	I Not educationally remediable	Educationally remediable	
		II No un-conscious resistance	III Un-conscious resistance

A. AUTEMP
    ALLEMP
    GIG (1)
    GIG (2)			

B. KRAT (1)			
C. KRAT (2)			

---

[1] I have not here mentioned the component PHIL (roughly, 'concern for other people as equals', or 'weighing other people's interests equally with one's own'). PHIL is of crucial importance for interpersonal morality: but I am here concerned with a wider range of cases, in many of which other people's interests may not be significantly relevant. Moreover, PHIL is itself one sort of attitude or 'outlook', whereas we are here interested in criteria for attitudes, outlooks and emotions in general.

Nevertheless, I believe there to be arguments (both conceptual and empirical) which show PHIL to be necessary for any reasonable person, and to some of which I briefly drew attention in *I.M.E.* (pp. 102–8). The relationship of one such argument to the area of ideals and outlooks in general is discussed in Appendix III.

It may still be thought by some that two of the KRAT(2) squares have no logical existence – those under columns II and III. For (one might argue) if a man has *really*, *fully* or *effectively* brought his EMP and GIG to bear on the situation – if, in other words, his KRAT(1) is properly and fully used – then the only logically possible reason for his failing to have the right feeling must be in column I, the lack of basic equipment or physical defect. A full and proper use of KRAT(1) would include bringing to bear his EMP and GIG not merely on the facts and feelings of which he is conscious, but also on those of which he is unconscious. All his desires, emotions and beliefs will be known to him: there is nothing more that the educator (or the psychotherapist) can do.

I do not want so much to deny any force to this argument as to point out the disadvantages of using it. First, it distorts the way we usually speak. We do in fact say that a man has 'brought his abilities to bear', even if (to put it dramatically) he has not spent five years finding out about himself with a psychoanalyst. In other words, there is a more or less arbitrary cut-off point at which we are prepared to say, or stop saying, that a man has 'thought about the situation', 'considered his own feelings', or whatever phrase we use. We would not say this, for instance, of a man who acted entirely on impulse: nor, perhaps, of one who made only a very superficial use of his EMP and GIG. In other cases we might say that he had not thought about it 'seriously' or 'properly'. But we would say it of a man who, under normal circumstances, made what would normally be called a serious attempt. Of course 'normally' and 'normal' do not give us any exact rules: but they would not include, for instance, that the man must meditate for weeks, or talk it over with *all* his friends. As we noticed in Chapter 9, we can if we like screw up the notion of a *serious, sincere* or *proper* use of EMP and GIG so as to make it a logical truth that, if a man then does not feel rightly, it must be because he cannot. But as we have pointed out, this is not how we commonly use such words as 'serious', 'sincere', or 'proper'.

The second objection to using this argument was also noticed in Chapter 9: briefly, that if we insist on screwing up these concepts so tightly we thereby dismiss the very cases that interest us. It is important, for research purposes and for practical education, to be able to distinguish *amongst* those cases where a man is consciously sincere, serious, etc. in bringing his abilities to bear

(KRAT(I)) the particular class of cases where, despite this, he fails to feel rightly because there is some unconscious system of beliefs and emotions – where, in our language, he lacks KRAT(2). Thus we want to distinguish the father who, having brought his abilities to bear, knows quite well that his daughter's boy-friend is a nice chap despite his hair, knows that he ought not to feel angry, but still feels angry for unconscious reasons, from the father who has not bothered to think about whether he is a nice chap at all. To say that in the former case the father does not 'really know' or does not 'really think he ought not to be angry' seems to me both to violate normal English and to assimilate importantly different cases.[1]

As more than one philosopher has pointed out,[2] there is a whole range of different cases in this area; and it would require a whole book to distinguish them properly. So far we have found it sufficient to distinguish KRAT(I) and KRAT(2) as we have done: one distinguishing mark being that, given KRAT(I) and the abilities and attainments (GIG and EMP), the man will know what feelings are appropriate for the situation – he has reached the DIK or PHRON stage: but that KRAT(2) is required for him actually to *feel* rightly. Nevertheless, it would be useful to be able to distinguish as far as possible between various logical types of KRAT(I): not just for conceptual clarity, but for severely practical reasons. For it is, I think, fairly obvious in a very large number of practical cases that failure occurs in *some* area of KRAT(I).

[1] It is also worth pointing out that, for purposes of practical research, this issue is likely to be at least partly academic. Tests or assessment-methods of *any* kind for KRAT (1) and (2) will be hard to come by; and the strategy and results of empirical research will have to be governed by those assessment-methods which prove valid, reliable and practical to administer. Even in laboratory-type situations, it will be difficult to discover whether a person 'brings his abilities to bear' – and this even in a fairly straightforward or superficial sense of the phrase. It will be harder, or perhaps impossible, to discover by any specific test whether he brings them to bear in any profound or sustained manner. In other words, it is likely that we shall be able to test for EMP and GIG, and to some extent for KRAT(I); but it may well be that we can only induce an absence of KRAT(2) by comparing the presence of all the other components with a person's actual behaviour or symptoms. (In other words, if he has all the other components but still does not feel or act rightly, then it must be a lack of KRAT(2)).

[2] See, e.g. R. M. Hare, *Freedom and Reason*, Chapter 5: P. L. Gardiner, 'On Assenting to a Moral Principle', in *P.A.S.*, 1954/5: Aristotle, *Nicomachean Ethics*, Book 7, C. C. W. Taylor's review in *Mind*, April 1965: also Chapter 9 above.

First, there are plenty of occasions on which a man's *abilities* and *attainments* (be he never so simple-minded) are wholly adequate for the situation – it is just that he does not make proper use of them, because he is counter-motivated by various more or less conscious desires, the operation of which we describe in such phrases as 'not stopping to think', 'being carried away', 'being wrapped up in one-self', 'impulsiveness', 'fecklessness', and so on; in brief, cases of straightforward ignorance or unintelligence seem to me less common, and of less practical importance, than has sometimes been supposed.

Secondly, it is certainly possible, as we have said, for a man to succeed in KRAT(1), so that he knows what he ought to feel (the DIK- or PHRON-stage), and yet because of unconscious desires (which we should regard as 'normally inaccessible' to him) fail in KRAT(2), and hence fail to feel rightly: but there are as many, or more, cases where the man never gets to this stage at all – where, in other words, he does not even do what we would *normally* call 'bringing his abilities to bear'. I am not here saying that failures in KRAT(2) are unimportant: and in Appendix IV I shall try to say something about one type of ability ('insight') the development of which may help to reduce such failures. But it must be acknowledged that this ability and the contexts or methods of developing it are (one might say) somewhat recherché: and perhaps what the average case needs is not 'insight' so much as more straightforward qualities such as thoughtfulness, patience, carefulness, alertness, and so on – qualities which are partly (though by no means entirely) coextensive with the component KRAT(1).

Here I can give only the most general account of the logical sub-categories of KRAT(1), and I do so with some hesitation. The variety of cases is very wide, even in philosophical discussions: strategically, it may well be that a purely conceptual, 'armchair' approach is inadequate, and that we need a good deal more empirical data before attempting a serious taxonomy, if we are not to miss out important sub-types. It is true that literary or imaginary examples may carry us some of the way: but there is always the possibility that our examples may be preselected and biased by our own unconscious preconceptions of what these sub-types of failure *must* or *ought to* be.

Nevertheless, there do seem to be three logically distinct sub-types, or three general ways in which a man may fail in the area of KRAT(1):

(a) He may fail to *notice* or *be alert* to the relevant situation at all, so that he does not even make a start on bringing his abilities to bear: thus he may be drunk, day-dreaming, or 'wrapped up in himself' in one way or another.

(b) He may be alert to the situation, but fail to put his abilities adequately to *work* on it: this might result in his misdescribing the situation, or not describing it fully enough.

(c) He may avoid failure in (a) and (b), but nevertheless lack a sense of the seriousness or *importance to him personally* of the whole procedure: that is, he may not end up by thinking, in a fully prescriptive and personal way, that *he ought* to feel pity or remorse (or whatever he ought to feel). Here we may mention two possible sub-divisions of failure, corresponding to failures to use the phrase 'he ought' in a fully prescriptive and universalizing sense:

(c.i.) thinking that he 'ought' (as it were, in principle) to feel (e.g.) pity, but not that it is really *important* that he should feel it;
(c.ii.) thinking that the situation calls for pity, that *one* ought to feel pity, but not that *he* ought to:

And there will no doubt be further complexities within these categories.[1]

These three sub-types might emerge in cases such as the following. Suppose a Pharisee sitting in the Sanhedrin during a discussion of what to do with Jesus. If he is very sleepy or day-dreaming or bored, he may not face the situation at all: he may just sit there and say nothing, or vote as he is told without bothering to consider the case. This would be failure in (a) above. Then again, he may start to think about the case, but not think about it adequately or fully enough: for various reasons (with which we are not here concerned), he may end up by saying 'Oh, he's just a trouble-maker' or 'I expect he's guilty if the high priest says so'. This is failure in (b). Finally, he may come to realize that Jesus is innocent, that he ought to pity and not condemn him, but his realization is (so to speak) merely theoretical – it is as if Jesus were more like a character in a novel than a real person, not someone whom he

---

[1] These and other cases are mentioned by R. M. Hare, *Freedom and Reason*, p. 83. See also P. L. Gardiner, op. cit.

himself seriously ought to feel pity for. This would be failure in (c), perhaps (c.i.).

Or again: an older pupil is present when a nervous new boy comes into the playground. He may (a) be so out of touch with the real world that he fails even to notice the new boy, or fails to notice that he is new or that he is crying: or (b) he notices this, but doesn't bother to think seriously about what it must be like to be a new boy, surrounded by strangers: or (c) he does all this, and thinks vaguely 'Poor kid', or 'It must be rotten for him', or 'Somebody ought to go and talk to him', but these thoughts do not represent any serious belief that *he* ought to feel (and display) sympathy: (c. ii).

Or again: a girl is approached by a man who is trying to involve her in some relationship or other. She may (a) not even start to think about whether she should let herself feel attracted towards him or get involved: or (b) she may say 'Wait a minute, this needs thinking about' but not in fact take the trouble to think about it very much: or (c) she may get to the stage of saying 'This isn't the sort of man one ought to feel attracted by', but say this only in a theoretical way, taking no real responsibility for her feelings (c. i or c. ii).

Note that, in all these cases, failure in (c) is still failure in KRAT(1), not in KRAT(2). The Pharisee could seriously think he should pity Jesus, the older pupil that he should sympathize with and help the new boy, and the girl that she should not be attracted – and yet they might still find their actual feelings largely unchanged. There might be something about Jesus – perhaps his air of cool unconcern – which prevents the Pharisee from actually feeling pity. The older pupil's (perhaps largely unconscious) contempt and belief that new boys 'don't really count' might inhibit his sympathy. And (notoriously) the girl's firm, serious and sincere belief that she should not feel attracted to the man is quite consistent with her continuing to feel attracted.

These types of KRAT(1) raise a further problem which merits a short discussion. It would be absurd to suppose that a man must, consciously and deliberately, face and think about *every* situation: that he must confront and deal with every occasion on which he feels or fails to feel an emotion by (1a) 'noticing' the situation, (1b) 'thinking thoroughly' about it, and (1c) 'thinking responsibly' about it. For, first, life is too short for anyone to 'face every situation': the number of 'situations' in the world is infinite, since a question can always be raised about how we should respond (in feeling and action) to any phenomena. Secondly, we may respond correctly but out of habit, or semi-consciously[1]: such responses may be perfectly rational (in the required senses), and perfectly 'emotionally educated'. We have, therefore, the question of what or what *sort* of situations he should notice and think about: the question of what area we expect KRAT(1) to cover.

The three examples quoted above are (I hope) reasonably convincing, only because we would normally suppose that the areas which they cover are *important*. It is important to pity rather than condemn innocent men: to sympathize with rather than despise new boys: to be indifferent to, rather than compulsively attracted by, the wrong sort of man. We expect, or at least hope that people will notice or be alert to such cases and think about them: whereas we do not much mind if they are not alert to other areas, e.g. whether they like or dislike beer or cricket, are attracted by the town or the country, feel slightly envious of another man's success or slightly frightened of the dark. We expect them to *preselect* the important areas: to have, as it were, a kind of warning bell which sounds in their minds whenever a really significant situation confronts them.

But now, what is to count as 'important' in this sense? In the first two of our examples (perhaps indirectly in the third also) we would feel it important that the person should be alerted and think about it, because other people's interests are at stake – Jesus' or the new boy's: the situations have an overriding *moral* importance (in the narrower sense whereby 'moral' relates to interpersonal morality). In the third case, we would think that the girl would make herself (and perhaps the man also) seriously *unhappy* if she could not change her feelings: this seems to be a case of *prudence* rather than of morality in the narrower sense, or else a case where her feelings are symptomatic of some more or less mild kind of mental ill-health. We have discussed these different types of case elsewhere,[2] and argued that it is reasonable to use these two criteria of importance – other people's interests and one's own happiness.[3]

In particular reference to 'important' areas of the emotions, there is of course a lot more to be said. We are concerned with emotions

---

[1] See *I.M.E.*, pp. 50–2.

[2] *I.M.E.*, pp. 76–92.

[3] *I.M.E.*, pp. 102–16: see also Appendix III in the present work.

L

as (a) pleasant or painful in themselves, (b) inspiring or failing to inspire right action, (c) conducing or not conducing to understanding, (d) predisposing to other emotions which might be (on other grounds) desirable or undesirable. The reasonableness of these *external* criteria for the justifiability of emotions (as against the *internal* criterion of correct belief) could not, in my view, be seriously denied: at any rate I shall not question it here. It is these criteria which we use to determine the 'important' areas; and when some emotion offends against them – by being very unpleasant, or conducing to serious future unhappiness, or leading to behaviour which causes significant damage to others – we expect a person to be alerted to his own emotion and to the situation which confronts him.

To say this is not to renege on our remarks in Chapter 6¹ concerning the autonomy of emotions and their objects. It is not proposed that *we* should decide what specific situations are 'important' and what specific emotions a man should feel in these situations: it is not *we* who have the ultimate right of preselecting those areas which a man needs to 'notice', 'be alert to' or 'think thoroughly and responsibly about'. It may well be true that most people do have 'standard interests' in (say) not contracting unhappy marriages or lung cancer, not finding themselves bankrupt, and so on; and certainly it is true that every individual will have *some* specific ends or values of his own, whether like or unlike those of his fellows: so that we can say which areas, for that person if not for most people, are 'important' and worth his while to notice and think about. Even if a person has ends or values which are not 'standard' and which we may disapprove of, we shall determine the 'important' areas in terms of his own outlook, and not in terms of ours. This will not prevent us from being able to educate him in respect of that outlook itself – to help him to consider, for instance, whether he really ought to pursue 'honour' or 'achievement' at the cost of losing his health or making his wife a widow.

It may still be objected that, in the case of children, we are virtually compelled to equip them with a particular set of wants, outlooks and emotional reactions (however haphazardly and inefficiently we now do this): that we have to *form* their outlooks, so that we cannot use their (as yet non-existent) outlooks as a

¹ pp. 83–91.

criterion for the areas of 'importance' that we want to make them alert to. Since we can hardly suppose that it does not *matter* which outlooks, or what set of emotional reactions, we generate in them from birth onwards, must we not decide beforehand, on their behalf, which outlooks and reactions are right or appropriate? The answer to this is both yes and no. Yes, if we mean that we must generate those outlooks which, while also giving them physical and psychological security, will best enable the children to become 'emotionally educated' – that is, to think for themselves, to acquire the various components we have mentioned, and (if they wish) to change or modify those outlooks when they are older. We have, indeed, that criterion or set of criteria for generating the outlooks: briefly, we choose those which will help children to develop into rational and autonomous adults: and this is the only criterion that would justify us as educators rather than partisan moralists. But the answer is no, if we mean that we must decide on specific outlooks to generate in our children because we happen to think those outlooks are right *by some other criterion*.

In practice, the crucial difference is likely to be, not between particular 'outlooks' in the sense of publicly identifiable creeds or ways of life (Christianity, 'honour', Communism, Stoicism, Epicureanism, etc.), but rather between different *styles* or sets of reactions *within* these public creeds. Thus it seems probable that some Christians, Communists, or Stoics bring up their children in accordance with these creeds in a way which encourages rationality, and that others fail to do this. For instance, two sets of Christian parents might both always take the children to church and express a certain emotional attitude to divorce, gambling and swearing: but one set might encourage their children to discuss these matters, and allow the possibility of different behaviour and emotions, whilst the other might discourage all questioning and regard alternative points of view as wicked or rebellious. Many 'outlooks' (in the sense of public creeds) would, I should guess, come into this category: though of course there are some – the Nazi creed might be an example – where it would be hard to see how a child could be brought up as a Nazi in any serious sense without crippling his chances of rationality and autonomy. These and connected problems have been discussed more fully elsewhere.[1]

---

[1] *I.M.E.*, Chapter 3.

If then we can allow these sub-types of KRAT(I), at least as a first step towards a fuller enquiry involving phenomenology as well as logic, we can write them into our taxonomy as follows:[1]

	I Not educationally remediable	Educationally remediable	
		II No un-conscious resistance	III Un-conscious resistance
A. AUTEMP ALLEMP GIG (1) GIG (2) etc.			
B. KRAT (1) (a) ('noticing') (b) ('thinking fully') (c) ('taking responsibility')			
C. KRAT (2)			

And we must note, once again, that the *reasons* for failure in one or other of the components are not built into the components themselves, though they are specified to some extent under columns I, II and III. Failure in KRAT(I) (a), (b) or (c) are all of cases where the man *does* not do something: whether this is because he cannot or because he does not *want* to (or want to enough) is another question. This is important, because there is a natural temptation to use ordinary English words to describe KRAT – 'patience', 'seriousness', etc. – which because they have moral implications, may also imply that it is within the man's power to exercise KRAT. No such implication, however, is built into the components as here listed.

Some may feel that we have concentrated unduly on the cognitive aspect of emotions: in particular on the importance of conscious and unconscious beliefs. They might say: 'But is it not the case that, in practice, a large part of the education of the emotions must consist of what we might call "training the will" or "forming good (emotional) habits"? And this may have very little to do with

---

[1] A fuller list of the components is given on pp. 261–2.

cognition or belief.' This is not to be denied. But we here enter upon the question of what *methods* are, in practice, likely to generate these components. A person who is, so to speak, emotionally un-disciplined or uncontrolled will lack KRAT(1) (and perhaps other components as well); and it is plausible to maintain that this lack can only be filled by the formation of good habits ('self-control'), such formation being chiefly a matter of training or conditioning, or of generating in him certain desirable and 'self-transcending' emotions which will keep him safe from other emotions of a more disturbing and misleading kind.[1] Equally the 'over-controlled' person may need practice in being spontaneous, or may need to develop habits of a different type. I express no definite opinion on the merits of such methods as against (for instance) the methods of psychotherapy: indeed without further research any definite opinion appears premature.

Nor would I wish to maintain that such methods are not, in some sense of the word, 'educational'. But it seems important to appreciate the distinction between increasing cognitive awareness (which is perhaps the paradigm case of what 'education' is) on the one hand, and processes of training, habit-forming, and conditioning on the other. Further distinctions among these latter processes are of course required; for instance, it is one thing to *teach* a child the *habit* of stopping to think before he works himself into a rage: another thing to *condition* him (in some quasi-Pavlovian sense) so that he checks himself at the first signs of anger: and another thing again to ensure, by drugs or brain surgery, that he is then checked. There are no doubt degrees of cognition, awareness and intention-ality in most of these processes, rather than a fixed gulf between two radically different types of method. Nevertheless, the rough dis-tinction between increasing cognitive awareness and other processes generally holds. It is true that we have been chiefly concerned to elucidate the former rather than the latter. But as we have said, here and earlier, this does not imply that the latter are not of great practical importance. I should myself prefer to describe their importance as that of 'setting the stage' or 'establishing the pre-conditions' for educating the emotions, rather than as itself 'educational': but I do not want to quibble on a linguistic point.

[1] Pointed out by R. S. Peters (following A. Koestler), in a private paper. Such emotions would include love, a sense of justice, a passion for relevance, and so on.

As a matter of strategy, I should be inclined to say that there are so many 'preconditions' of this kind, and in consequence so many practical methods that may be required to 'set the stage', that we ought not to make premature guesses. Hence I have (in the main) confined myself simply to explicating a definition, as it were, of what it is to be 'emotionally educated': to listing the (logical kinds of) ways in which a man may fail. It may well be that relevant considerations for generating the components include not only habit-forming or 'training the will', but also certain kinds of experiences in infancy, features of the body-chemistry or brain-structure, and many others. But to investigate these is not our task. For present purposes, we shall stick to the components.

This, then, will be the final sketch of our taxonomy: and it is worth noting that we have not produced a *phenomenological* or *chronological* model. It is not implied, in other words, that our categories A, B, and C or the components that fit into them either do operate or must operate *in that order*. Consider the following example. A man thinks he is in love with a girl. For one of many possible different reasons – perhaps because he wants to have a happy marriage, perhaps because his mother is worried – he begins to think about whether she is really the right girl for him: in other words, he brings to bear (KRAT(1)) his cognitive abilities. He thinks about his own feelings – does he really love her, does she really make him happy, or is he frightened of her, anxious to conquer her, or what (AUTEMP)? What are her feelings (ALLEMP)? What about the 'hard' facts – is she rich, or infertile, or stupid (GIG(1))? He considers all these, and (let us suppose) attains a stage at which he realizes that he ought not to be in love with this girl (PHRON). If his feelings do not immediately change, he may then use certain more or less effective techniques to try to change them: perhaps he keeps reminding himself that what he really wants is only to conquer her (AUTEMP) or that she doesn't really love him (ALLEMP), or that she is too stupid (GIG(1)): and perhaps there is a certain 'know-how' or skill which helps to stop him being in love with her (he counts to ten before kissing her, or pretends to himself and behaves as if she was just another girl) (GIG(2)). Here he 're-uses' the other components, brings them to bear again (KRAT(1)), not this time to work out what he should feel, but to stop himself feeling what he should not. Finally, perhaps he actually stops loving her (KRAT(2)): though of course he may not – he may have done his best, but either (I) from lack of equipment or some basic physical cause (as it might be, a love philtre), or (II) from lack of practice or instruction, or (III) because there is still some unconscious part of him which wants to go on loving her and which predominates over all his conscious efforts, he may still be in love.

Here the components 'come in' at different stages, and some of them 'come in' more than once. What needs to be stressed is that this is a phenomenological model about what *happens* in a particular case: not a logical model about what must, logically, be true if a man is to be 'emotionally educated'. As such, the model would only fit certain cases or classes of cases: plainly there are many men who think they are in love who do not actually behave or think like this at all.

Equally ours is not a deep *empirical* model of the psychological '*structure*' or '*factors*' which actually operate: rather it is for the psychologist to tell us what empirical states of affairs are necessary for the development of these components, or what empirical causes there actually are for their non-existence. We must not slip into believing that they are psychological forces which a person *used* or *had*. It is fairly harmless to talk (as I have sometimes done) of a man 'having', 'developing' or 'lacking' GIG, EMP and KRAT: but strictly speaking this is only a (perhaps misleading) way of saying that certain things are or are not the case about his thought and behaviour. The temptation to hypostatize these components into empirical existence must be resisted. For similar reasons, the same cause or 'psychological force' may be responsible for different category-failures. Thus suppose psychologists had reason to identify a general factor which they called 'ego-strength' or 'reality-testing': then this factor would be likely to operate in more than one of our categories. Similarly the same sort of empirically-identified counter-motivation would operate in both KRAT(1) and KRAT(2): obviously, for instance, fear of an enemy would prevent one both from thinking properly about what one ought to feel towards him, and from actually feeling what one ought to feel.

It will be apparent that bridging the gulf between logical components and empirical facts is at least as philosophically important, and as difficult, as establishing the components themselves. The business of test-construction and test-validation involves constantly asking the question 'If a person thinks or behaves in such-and-such a way empirically, does that satisfy what we *mean by*

GIG, EMP, etc.?' This is a general question that faces all research which takes its starting-point from what we *mean* by (say) 'an aggressive person', 'a religious person', 'a morally educated person', and so on; and as I have pointed out elsewhere,[1] even if research does not take this starting-point, the gulf between concept and empirical facts has to be bridged at some time if the research is to be safely and correctly applied.

Meanwhile I put this taxonomy forward tentatively, in the hope that it will be useful not only for 'the education of the emotions', but also in the still more vaguely defined area labelled 'mental health'.[2] Only a fool would claim either completeness or certainty for it: but I would like to end this chapter by pointing out the necessity for *some* scheme of this kind. The time is now past when educators and research workers can permit themselves to talk vaguely about encouraging children and adolescents to 'develop their will-power', 'increase their sensitivity', 'become more responsible', and so forth. If we are to get anywhere at all, we must have a clear set of aims and objectives: and this has so far been conspicuous by its absence. Similarly, I do not at all wish to imply that empirical researchers must, in the meantime, call a complete moratorium on all their work: but I would suggest that, without very close attention to some coherent conceptual framework, the relevance of such work is always questionable: and it may well degenerate into a mindless and unstructured collection of logically heterogeneous facts. Philosophers have often, and rightly, been castigated for lack of concern with the empirical world: but the converse accusation – that psychologists and social scientists need to be aware of conceptual problems, and willing to accept the help of philosophers in solving them – could, I suspect, be substantiated at least as easily. We can only hope that improved communications, and a good deal more self-education on both sides, will enable us to make a proper use of the very considerable academic resources that are available in this country and elsewhere.

Meanwhile I make so bold as to say that teachers and other practical educators, as well as research workers, should find this taxonomy of value. To be clear about what you should be trying

[1] See *I.M.E.*, Chapter 4; research methods are discussed in more detail in 'Problems of research in moral education' (1968) (available from the Farmington Trust Research Unit).
[2] See Appendix V.

to achieve is more than half the battle in getting clear about the merits or demerits of the practical methods you are using or could use. I would suggest that those many people – and there are far more than just teachers – who are concerned at all with this area should take a hard look at what they are doing, to see if in their view they are helping to develop the components listed in this taxonomy. We have looked at this area, originally (in Part I) from the standpoint of a person concerned with religious education, and subsequently (Part II) under the general title of 'education of the emotions'. But the title does not matter very much: the taxonomy, and what practical workers may do to realize the aims it incorporates, matters a great deal

PART THREE

From Theory to Practice

11. Teaching 'R.E.'
and educating the emotions

A. THE LOGICAL CONNECTION

The reader who has followed us so far should now be able to see more clearly the points made in Chapter 1, about the connection between religious education and the education of the emotions. Above all, he should now be able to see that we do not have to choose between (a) teaching children some facts *about* religion, which saves us from indoctrination but fails to get to the emotional heart of the matter, and (b) persuading children *into* religion, which is more likely to involve the emotions but is indoctrinatory and not a satisfactory educational aim. We have a third choice, (c) that of educating them *in* religion – that is, of helping them to become more reasonable[1] in respect of those emotions and attitudes that are central to religion, so that they may more reasonably make or not make their own religious commitments, and assess those of other people. In other words, we can make 'religious education' into a *respectable subject*, by recognizing that the criteria of rationality appropriate to it are similar to those appropriate to the education of the emotions, and by devising teaching-methods to fit those criteria.

It should also now be clear that 'religious education' and 'the education of the emotions' are not on all fours. For a large *part of* 'religious education' will precisely *be* 'education of the emotions' – that is, of those many emotions which are characteristic of religion: and conversely, a part of the 'education of the emotions' can take place *under the heading of* 'religious education'. Religion, we might say, provides us with an *arena* or a topic-area in which we may try to educate our pupils' emotions: although there may be other things we want to do also. In the same way, topic-areas like 'sex', 'money', 'war', or 'the family' may include logically distinct types of education, including the education of the emotions, as well as other matters: thus in 'sex education' we should be partly (perhaps

[1] That is, to develop their moral 'components' (EMP, GIG, etc): see below.

primarily) concerned with how our pupils *felt*, though also with whether they knew some elementary biology.

In order to get quite clear about this, I should like to refer the reader to Appendix VII (on the meaning of 'moral').[1] I there explain why I thought it sensible to take 'moral education' in a very wide sense: that is, education about what a person ought over-ridingly to *do*, and about what he ought to *feel*. Now during the course of the book we have seen that not only religious beliefs but all other ideals and 'outlooks' come into this area: for they are all ultimately based on the emotions. Hence we were forced to turn to the topic of the education of the emotions in general, in order to make sense of religious education. When we considered this topic, we found that the best way to proceed was to list and clarify a number of 'components' or qualities which we needed to develop in our pupils – EMP, GIG and KRAT. And these components are among those which we have outlined elsewhere[2] as forming the objectives of moral education. We have, indeed, concentrated on certain components (especially, EMP and KRAT) as *particularly* relevant to the emotions, and hence to religious and other 'outlooks': but we have, nevertheless, remained within the area of moral education all the time.

In our terms, then – and it does not perhaps matter very much if the reader prefers other terms, so long as the logic is clear – we begin with the concept of moral education, which we might divide into (a) education of behaviour (what to do) and (b) education of the emotions (what to feel). We have been chiefly concerned with the latter. 'Moral education', in this sense, is *defined* as education which develops or is intended to develop the moral components (EMP, GIG and so on). To this form of education a large number of curricular subjects and topics, as well as many of the social and psychological features of the school, will contribute. Among these topics, as we have seen, will be 'religious education', 'sex education', and many others – perhaps 'health education', 'social education', and so on. Education in these topics will be chiefly a matter of developing the moral components, each topic being particularly concerned with those components most relevant to it (religious education with EMP and KRAT, 'social education' perhaps with GIG, and so forth): though, of course, in so far as any topic is taught

[1] pp. 251–7.
[2] *I.M.E.*, Chapter 4.

without any particular concern with what the pupils ought over-ridingly to do or to feel, the topic may include other things that would not come under moral education at all.

We may represent this logic in schematic form, thus:

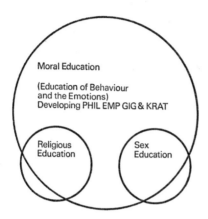

Here the topic-areas 'religious education', 'sex education', etc. are chiefly concerned with developing at least some of the moral components: but there is room also in each, outside the 'moral education' circle, for education that is not concerned with the pupil's behaviour or emotions. Thus one might want to discuss certain heresies, or certain aspects of church history, without this in any way bearing upon the pupil's own feelings, behaviour or religious awareness: and similarly one might want to discuss the sex practices of the Polynesians for the subject's own sake, and not with a view to educating the pupil's own sexual behaviour or emotions. Such discussions could still, in a loose sense, count as 'religious education' or 'sex education'.

But only in a very loose sense. For as soon as we step outside the circle of moral education, as defined by the moral components, we immediately find ourselves confronted by the question of what *other* aims, if not those of moral education, we are trying to satisfy. Any answer we give to this question will have to be in terms of particular disciplines, or what Professor Hirst[1] has taught us to call 'forms of knowledge'. Thus we can, of course, use the topics of

[1] See his essay in R. Archambault's *Philosophical Analysis and Education*.

'religion' or 'sex' to make our children better at history, or science, or the appreciation of literature, or sociology. Somebody who thought (as we do not) that there was no form of thought and feeling peculiar to religion outside these other disciplines (history, etc.) could, I suppose, use the title 'religious education' to name a topic-area in which these disciplines or forms of knowledge were taught. In the case of some topic-areas, of which perhaps 'sex' may be one, this move might be plausible: but we have tried to argue that religion is *centrally* concerned with questions about the appropriateness of various objects of awe and worship, and with other human emotions. Hence the larger and more important part of anything we could sensibly call 'religious education' would fall within the sphere of the education of the emotions, and hence of moral education. Indeed I should argue that other forms of knowledge that are not peculiar to religion – history, sociology, etc. – should only be brought into the area of 'religious education' in so far as they contribute to this larger and more important part and relate to the education of the emotions.

We cannot discuss at length here the merits or demerits of the topic-area 'religion', as against other topic-areas, for the education of the emotions; but there are good prima facie reasons for believing that it forms an excellent arena in which the educator can work. Nearly all the important emotions – love, hate, fear, guilt, anger, etc. – find a place in most religions: indeed one might almost say that a religion can be regarded from one viewpoint as an institutionalization of these emotions. Secondly, there are two areas that religious education seems peculiarly well adapted to cover: (a) the area of the specifically religious emotions and attitudes (awe and worship), and (b) the area concerned with this whole process of institutionalization itself – the whole business of 'finding a meaning to life', or 'making sense of the world', which we have mentioned earlier (pp. 7–8), and discuss in Appendix I.

Now it is of course obvious that the moral components (EMP, GIG, etc.), which define the aims of religious education and the education of the emotions, are not likely to be developed *only* – perhaps not even chiefly – in R.E. lessons, religious assemblies, or anything else that might go on under the official title of 'R.E.'. For the components are not to be represented as constituting a particular 'form of thought' or 'form of discourse' which can be, as it were, insulated from other forms, and taught separately (in the way that, perhaps, mathematics may be). They represent qualities which can be, and no doubt are being, developed in many other contexts – in the teaching of other curricular subjects, in the social organization of the school, the day-to-day contact with teachers, and so forth. What attitude is the R.E. teacher to adopt towards this?

The R.E. teacher will first *recognize* that this is so: that he must rely, at least to some extent, on other teachers and other factors beyond his immediate control for the development of the moral components. But he must also appreciate that the components represent *his* particular aims as an R.E. teacher. Other teachers concerned with moral education and the education of the emotions may specifically adopt these aims: but it is likely that most will be concerned with teaching subjects – mathematics, history, French, etc. – with more specialized aims that have little relation to the moral components. So the responsibility for developing the components is his, *qua* R.E. teacher: and he should be concerned to do what he can to make such changes in the school generally as he believes will contribute to this end. (Most R.E. teachers and chaplains have long recognized this, even though they may not have associated the point specifically with our own aims.)

What the R.E. teacher will actually do in his lessons, or in whatever contexts he has under his immediate control, will thus depend on what he thinks is being done, or not being done, elsewhere in the school. For instance, if he thinks that (say) the children learn enough 'hard' facts (GIG(1)) elsewhere, he will be more inclined to concentrate on whatever methods he believes will assist the development of emotional awareness and insight (EMP). Or if he thinks that EMP is adequately taken care of by English teachers, perhaps in the form of impromptu acting or group discussion, he will make some attempt on the area of KRAT(1) or (2). He will, in fact, have to fill the crucial gaps: and since this whole topic is still very much under-researched and obscure, there will be plenty of gaps to be filled in. He might profitably begin by looking critically at the curriculum and social organization of his school, to see how they stand with reference to the moral components.[1]

Further, it is very much to be hoped – and this should be borne in mind during what follows – that the teacher of R.E. will not confine his attention solely to those emotions, ideals or 'outlooks'

---

[1] For this particular purpose my *Moral Education and the Curriculum* (Pergamon Press) may be found helpful.

M

that may properly be called 'religious'. As we have seen in Chapter 5, religious outlooks are only one sub-class of emotion-based outlooks in general. We must include not only near-religions, like Communism or the Nazi movement, but (for instance) ideals like the ideal of 'honour' (not losing face), or 'Stoic' ideals of nobility and self-sacrifice, or 'Epicurean' ideals concerned with pleasure and a quiet life. So what we shall now go on to say about R.E. will apply to this wider area of 'outlooks' also.

B. CURRICULUM, METHODS AND CONTENT[1]

I shall here simply enumerate a number of general points, each of which would merit discussion in much more depth.

1. First, we have to face the problem of how we can best organize our curricula and school practice so as to do justice to the connections between the education of the emotions (and moral education in general) and religious education in particular. As we have said, 'religion' is a topic-area within which we may try to educate our pupils' emotions. Some may hold that the best plan is to retain this topic area, add others ('sex', 'money', etc.), and divide up 'the education of the emotions' in this way. Others – and a case for this has been advanced elsewhere[2] – may feel that the division should correspond, not to topics, but to some at least of the *logical* components relevant to the education of the emotions, which of course cut across all the topics. Thus one could envisage separate types of teaching – perhaps even separate curricular periods – devoted to (a) the development of insight (AUTEMP), (b) the development of skills and aptitudes in expressing and controlling emotion (GIG(2)), (c) psychotherapeutic or 'counselling' sessions designed to free pupils from unconscious counter-motivation and hence developing KRAT: and so forth.

Decisions of this sort must surely depend on practical considerations. It is too early to say, without a great deal more research and experimentation, whether the distinctions should be made in terms of topics or in terms of logical constituents: though the connection between the two must always be borne in mind. Certainly it would be most unwise, in my view, to abandon 'religious knowl-

---

[1] See also Appendix VI.
[2] See *I.M.E.*, pp. 448–58.

edge' as a subject – or topic-title in the hope that the education of the emotions will be adequately dealt with elsewhere. The very least that can be said about 'R.E.' is that it offers us a chance to educate the emotions, if only because it is an accepted title for an accepted topic. This is not to criticize those who wish to practise such education under quite different titles: it is only to say that we must be careful not to throw out anything that may be of value.

I am optimistic enough to believe that such problems will not be hard to solve, provided educators are clear about what they are trying to achieve, and try hard enough to achieve it by *some* means and under *some* titles. The most suitable means will in the course of time become clear: and the question of what one is actually to *call* curricular periods, though not unimportant (because titles, like other words, generate expectations), will in a sense solve itself, once we know what we ought to be doing and how to do it. Hard work in this field is likely to profit us more than sterile arguments between believers and non-believers, or by reactions to the mere *words* 'moral education' and 'religious education' or 'education of the emotions'.

2. What sort of content do we need for R.E.? Earlier we dismissed some features of religious education as not central to the problem. But we can now see how these features may contribute towards the central aim of the education of the emotions. Briefly, the position is that, although *in themselves* these features seem to be of little educational importance, and certainly would not merit a supposed subject called 'religious education', they may nevertheless be highly relevant to that subject *if they are attached and related to its central concern with the emotions.* For example, the case for teaching children about church history, getting them to learn the Psalms by heart, or increasing their understanding of Christian doctrine as represented in the creeds, is a very weak one if it is based on the view that they ought to know about these things 'because it is part of our common culture'. (The same argument would apply to children learning astrology in Babylonia, or voodoo in Haiti.) Similarly, to teach comparative religion may be useful as a kind of sociology or anthropology, but could hardly be justified as specifically *religious* education. But if these things are relevant to a better understanding of religious and other emotions – to an understanding of what it is, or what it feels like, to have a religion – and if they are taught in that light and with that aim, then it is plain

that we shall hesitate before throwing them out of the window. Thus, to choose an instance at random, we might reasonably think it important for children to be able to entertain the kind of feelings represented in, and evoked by, the Psalms or the first chapter of Genesis (perhaps Haydn's *Creation* would be better?), if they are to have an emotional grasp of what one type of religion, at least, is actually like.

The teacher will thus probably want to *use* much of the traditional material as subject-matter, or as affording examples of particular religions (in much the same way as the teacher of morality may wish to use particular moral codes or *mores* as illustration-material). But the selection of material will depend on whether it fulfils this particular purpose. Probably the most important kinds of material here will not consist of 'hard' historical facts (the journeys of St Paul, the history of the rise of Islam, etc.) but of psychological illustrations (what it felt like to believe in Jehovah or Aphrodite, – do we feel anything of the same kind nowadays? – and so forth). We are concerned here with making real to the child such considerations as what sorts of objects (gods) various people, today and in past history, are or have been in awe of and worshipped; why they have done so; how the children themselves feel about various objects of emotion (their parents, nature, artistic productions that evoke emotion, etc.); what beliefs, conscious or unconscious, underlie these feelings; whether these beliefs are reasonable, and so on. Psychological illustrations from primitive and polytheistic religions may be particularly important here, at least as important as the study of the 'higher' religions.

As many readers will be aware, a good deal of work is already being done along these lines. This is not the place to discuss the various ways in which emotional awareness can be taught: but it is a reasonable guess that those methods that employ the techniques of group discussion, mime and dance, arts such as literature, music and drama, media such as film, tape and TV as well as the printed word are most likely to be effective. In general we need to know the most useful methods for the education of the emotions as a whole, and apply these to the area of religious education in particular. One very plausible suggestion for syllabus-construction would be to organize the contexts and methods of education round a number of concepts – worship, awe, guilt, forgiveness, etc. – so as to give children a genuinely educational grasp (both intellectual and emotional) of the stuff of religion; but no doubt there are others, including many not in current use, which the imaginative teacher will be able to devise for himself.

3. This leads to a widening of the task of the R.E. teacher. For though he will be concerned with objects of emotion *as found in religion*, he will also need some methods of getting the pupil to admit to, and hence to be more able to understand and control, his own emotions (awe, fear, loneliness, admiration, guilt and so forth) *in relation to the objects to which they are already attached*: for these will be the stuff out of which his outlook – whether eventually religious or not – will be made. The relevant type of education is in general more analogous to certain types of psychotherapy than to subject-teaching. Naturally one must be careful in dealing with the child's feelings here, but enthusiasm is just as important: and to give up this task altogether would be, in effect, to give up the notion of any serious religious education.

For example, suppose we are dealing with adolescent boys whose 'outlook' is some form of 'honour ethic'. They are concerned not to lose face with their peers, to prove themselves to be tough and daring, to fulfil the code of honour which the gang or the group subscribes to: rather like the Japanese samurai, or gunfighters in Western films. This concern, we may think, is partly caused by their position as adolescents: they do not really feel big, tough, potent and adult; they have internal doubts about their own powers and their own security, and are anxious to prove to themselves that these doubts can be laid to rest. Now here we have, if not exactly a religion, at any rate an outlook that incorporates many of the emotions which some religions (such as Christianity) would wish to be reorganized or redirected. These adolescents may be in awe of, and even worship, the biggest and toughest person in their environment – perhaps the gang-leader, or some hero in the world of films or TV. They may repent and feel guilt – but not about their daring robberies, only about not being daring enough. They have their rituals, their conventions, their code – but these are not concerned to celebrate a loving God or a forgiving Christ, only to bind them more tightly to the service of honour.

Plainly, the only way in which the teacher can hope to introduce them effectively to other outlooks or religions would be to start by making them more conscious of the outlook that they already have.

If they are really to 'get the feel' of any other outlook (the Christian, for instance), they must be able to let go of their own, if only temporarily. They must be secure enough to detach their emotions from the 'honour ethic', and at least consider what it would be like to attach them to other objects. Otherwise, although we may *tell* them about other outlooks, these outlooks will seem to them mere oddities, and not appear as real and viable alternatives. The teacher has to begin by getting them to understand their existing outlook, and the (often unconscious) reasons behind it, so that their emotions are no longer *compulsively* directed in the way they are.

Of course this is only one example: it is not only adolescent boys whose outlook is compulsive, and who hence find it virtually impossible to make any really free choice of outlook. But it suggests strongly that teachers should think hard about the *conditions* and the *context* in which this sort of education can flourish. Obviously a relationship of trust and closeness, in which the pupils are prepared to take even the first steps in trying to understand themselves, is essential: and it is equally plain that an attitude of *detached concern* (rather than a moralistic or wholly unconcerned attitude) must be adopted by the teacher. As soon as one even starts to think seriously about what is required, one is already thinking in terms with which psychotherapists are familiar: and the intelligent teacher will not be surprised that, in these very fragmentary suggestions, I want to direct his attention to this field.[1]

4. Thus, in this context, it will be as well to issue a warning against one common but over-intellectualized picture of 'R.E.', stemming from an over-intellectualized picture of religion itself. Many seem to believe that 'learning about religion' is essentially a matter of intellectual maturity, a cognitive grasp of fact and doctrine, philosophical ability, historical understanding of the major or 'higher'

---

[1] In particular the psychoanalytic notion of the *transference* is of great importance for the teacher, for both conceptual and practical reasons (see Appendix IV, pp. 233–5). Without creating conditions under which the transference may occur, and understanding how to use it for the benefit of their pupils, schools are not likely to do much more than scratch the surface of this kind of education. It is hence a great pity that psychotherapy and psychoanalysis are still widely regarded primarily as *medical* or *clinical* techniques, when in fact they are mostly *educational* and very much within the teacher's domain. (On this see Appendix V: also my *Education and the Concept of Mental Health*.)

religions, and so on. From this it seems to follow that only in the sixth form, if then, can we seriously hope to deal with the reasonableness or unreasonableness of particular religions, or to give our pupils any adequate conception of what it is like to believe in them. But, as we have seen, there are certain quite ordinary emotions, common to all human beings even when they are very young, which underlie these complicated metaphysical and doctrinal structures: and any picture of 'understanding religion' which makes it similar to understanding the Nicene creed or Spinoza's metaphysics is a false picture. The metaphysical or doctrinal superstructure is, in one very real sense, unimportant in itself: it is the kind of emotions to which it bears witness that we have to detect and educate.

Granted this, there seems no *a priori* reason to believe that age, I.Q., or intellectual maturity and sophistication are of crucial importance. Characteristics such as insight and self-awareness (EMP), or the bringing of these to bear on specific instances (KRAT(I)), are to be found amongst younger children as well as in the sixth form: indeed one might argue, rightly or wrongly, that some of these may actually diminish as pupils become more intellectually sophisticated and psychologically well-defended. In fact we do and should expect young children to understand their own and other people's emotions and outlooks: by getting them to act out their emotions, role-playing, the use of video-tape and other methods of 'showing them to themselves', film, simple literature, games and simulated situations, we believe that it is possible for them to become more 'emotionally educated'. And if emotionally educated, to that (very important) extent educated in religion, if the teacher is concerned with those emotions that are central to most religions, and which have often been institutionalized into a religious form.

5. Again, once we are thoroughly weaned from the notion of R.E. as a means of inculcating the religious attitude or a particular religion, we shall easily see that we shall want to put before the child not only what we take to be 'good' religions or outlooks, but also ones which we take to be thoroughly wrong-headed, or even lunatic. Just as we think it possible for the child to learn from the conduct of villains as well as heroes in literature, so it would be useful to show him (for example) the irrationalities of the Nazi movement, the Inquisition, Baal-worship, and so forth. For we

want the child to internalize, to appropriate for himself, the *reasons why* some religions and outlooks are sane and sensible: and this cannot in principle be done without the child also being able to see why others are insane and stupid. Once we stop thinking that 'religion' or 'Christianity' is something which we hope in a vague way will *rub off* on the child, all this becomes reasonably plain.

6. I do not propose to discuss at length any 'agreed syllabus', since (to speak frankly) nearly every such existing syllabus seems to be based on various confusions and misconceptions, including the one that I have just criticized – namely, that learning about religion is primarily an intellectual matter: or, more precisely, a matter of learning facts – since of course to become more 'emotionally educated' is in an important sense 'intellectual': that is, we aim to give children a better cognitive grasp of their own and other people's feelings, rather than just encouraging 'self-expression' for its own sake.[1] But of course a good deal of excellent work is being done by teachers, which is much more in line with the kind of thing we have been suggesting. There is, I think, a strong case for encouraging imaginative and clear-headed teachers to start or carry on such work, without the trammels of an agreed syllabus. What we want is not so much a syllabus, as a proper assessment of the methods and contexts in which this sort of work is done.

7. Lastly, it is worth noting here that many elements in existing religions themselves seem prima facie likely to contribute to the general aim of the education of the emotions: consider for instance the notions of confession and self-examination in Christian practice; or the study of such Biblical features as the parables, which plainly function as means of teaching awareness of feelings (repentance and forgiveness in the Prodigal Son, love in the Good Samaritan, etc.). It is not possible or relevant here to investigate the extent to which this is true of particular religions. But that it may be true is of great importance to the educator. In particular it should help to dissuade us from adopting *a priori* views about the merits or demerits of particular religions or particular sects within a religion. What the

---

[1] A fault on the other side and one often committed by 'progressive'-type schools. To encourage expression in emotion and behaviour, if it is to be seriously educative, can only be a preliminary to helping the children to *understand* and *control* their emotions and behaviour: one might say, it gives them the data or subject-matter on which to work. See Appendix VI.

educator has to do is *first* to gain a clear understanding of the criteria of rationality, and what general methods of education are likely to develop rationality in children, and *then* to take a close look at particular religions or features of religions. Only then will he have some idea of how far the latter are likely to be beneficial, or could usefully form a basis for providing either useful teaching-material, or valuable contexts of communication.

C. The Social Context

Our last point leads us on to a consideration of the *context* of such teaching. In devising practical methods for education in religion and the emotions, the teacher or research worker will find it helpful to use a tripartite distinction between content, methods, and context. The fragmentary suggestions so far mentioned are primarily suggestions of content and method: that is, (a) what sort of things the pupils are supposed to learn (awareness of emotions, control of emotions, etc.), and (b) what sort of activities, teaching devices, etc. enable them to learn this (mime, drama, films, discussion, and so forth). The social or psychological context of such education, however, may be more important than either of these: and it is worth while for the teacher to get clear about how such contexts do in fact operate, and how they should operate. Social contexts have of course been widely discussed by social scientists of various kinds: here I wish only to make clear the connection with the aims of religious and emotional education.

1. In practice many religious groups, or groups who attach themselves to some other type of ideal or metaphysic, do not *educate* very much at all: that is, they do not deliberately use particular methods or contexts to develop the rationality of their adherents. Either the methods or contexts are not used deliberately at all (but just uncritically accepted); or else they are used to indoctrinate or reinforce some particular set of attitudes, beliefs or emotions. What the teacher has first to do is to free himself from both of these mistakes. The question is *not* 'What contexts (church services, meetings, etc.) are somehow in themselves right and proper, or traditional, or correctly reflect and reinforce the beliefs of a particular sect or religion?' but rather 'What contexts will help our particular pupils to become more reasonable and sane?' This is an

open question, and (partly) an empirical one, the answer to which will depend very much on the kind of pupils we are dealing with.

The history of religious and metaphysical groups has in general shown them either hostile to this approach or ignorant of it. Characteristically most adults, responding to external social pressures and internal psychological ones, have adopted a religion or an ideal which suits (or appears to suit) their own mental make-up, used those contexts of worship or group activity which fit the religion of the ideal, and been content or anxious for their children to use the same contexts. For example, some people appear to need an external authority to whom they submit, and who will decide moral and other questions for them. The orthodox Roman Catholic church supplies (or used to supply) this need not only by Papal pronouncements, but also by a type of ritual and hierocratic structure in which the authority is very evident. People with a more egalitarian bias may be members of a nonconformist sect, where more stress is laid on the individual conscience and less on obedience: and the services of such sects, as well as their doctrines, reflect this preference. We may trace here a dimension on various points of which we may place certain sects, creeds, ideals and so forth: the authority-freedom dimension. It would of course be grossly oversimplified to put (say) the Roman church and the Communists at one end, and at the other the Quakers; but the point is plain enough.

2. Now there is a similar dimension, at one end of which stands the notion of *reinforcement*, and at the other the notion of *education* or *therapy*. In many, perhaps most, social contexts we do not *learn*: we enjoy ourselves, make ourselves feel more secure, get rid of excessive emotions, and feel at one with our neighbours. The purpose (whether conscious or not) of a Nazi rally, a dinner party, a fiesta, and most of the features of religious services is not to improve our emotions by cognitive understanding, but (in various ways) to keep the participants happy – to relieve their guilt, uplift their spirits, give them a sense of social solidarity, inspire them to communal action, and so forth. These objectives are of the greatest importance, and educators must not decry such contexts simply because they are not educational. Human beings cannot spend all their time learning: and it is not clear that they should even if they could. Everybody needs these contexts, not least children and

adolescents; and the wise teacher will arrange for his pupils to have them. Indeed, there is a very strong case for saying that schools fail to give their pupils enough of them – particularly enough of the unsophisticated, physical, warm, communal activities that the young above all need, as a solid base of security from which they can move into the very difficult area of learning, exploring and understanding the world and themselves.

But such contexts, although necessary *for* education, are not themselves educational contexts. Thus a church service with a fixed pattern of ritual and symbolic acts may help an individual's security, by offering an institutionalized form which fits his mental state: but it will not *pro tanto teach* him anything. The sermon and the private confessional may tend to be more educative: and the kind of discussion and meditation that takes place in some sects (for example the Quakers) is still more so. Usually, however, religious contexts are not contexts of learning, but contexts in which (at the least) a certain type of atmosphere is, as it were, expected to sink into and influence the individual of itself. This atmosphere may be encouraged by music, decor, dress, ritual silences, bodily postures and so forth: even in the lowest of the low-church sects the context is not quite that of a seminar or a discussion-group.

Once we get rid of the idea of uncritically accepting particular contexts (which may make neither for security nor for therapy) simply because they are not there, or are part of some tradition for which we still have some hankering, it will be seen that teachers have a far wider choice in practical matters than might have been supposed. Thus the question 'What shall we do about morning assembly?' has to be tackled in an appropriately wide framework. The right questions to ask are: 'Do we want to have the whole school together in one place? Where? When? For what sort of purpose – reinforcement (social solidarity, etc.) or educational? What sort of activities will achieve this purpose?' These questions go far beyond such issues as whether to have hymns or not, or whether to allow other literature besides the Bible to be read.

3. For teaching 'R.E.' is not a matter merely of *instruction*: the child also requires *experience*. In trying to educate children in those areas commonly called 'musical appreciation' or 'drama', we are not content merely to instruct them about music and drama: we also require them to take part in concerts and plays. So too with

religion. Provided we keep our aims clearly in mind, there is an obvious case to be made out for giving children that experience of religion that may be gained by particular forms of worship. 'Communal acts of worship' in the school may in principle be thus justified: and the experiences which a child might gain by taking part in many different types of worship – not only Roman Catholic, Church of England, Methodist, etc., but also Jewish, Mohammedan, Buddhist and so forth – are obviously valuable. Like other aspects of religious education, this falls into place once we realize that we are out to educate children in religion, not to inculcate a particular religion; and again, much imaginative thinking, and much trial and error, is needed before we know just what experiences are educative for what sorts of children.

4. Finally, I have said nothing here about whether the school itself as an institution should be 'Christian' or 'religious', or what difference will be found in the position of schools which are committed in one way or another (either to Christianity or to agnosticism). This is partly because I have nothing to say that I have not said elsewhere.[1] Briefly, all that is important is that, whatever the partisan commitment of the institution, its social arrangements, teaching contexts, 'ethos', 'atmosphere', and so on should be such as to give the children the best chance of security and development into autonomous and rational adults. It is this (educational) criterion that schools must use, not any criterion derived from partisan commitment.

This does not of course imply that the commitments, arrangements, 'atmospheres', of all schools should be *the same*. For we do not know – and shall not know without a good deal more research – which arrangements are in fact the best for developing children in this area: that is, for increasing their EMP, GIG, KRAT and so on. It would be possible to argue that Catholic, or Quaker, or Communist, or atheist schools satisfy this criterion better than others (though the truth is more likely to be that *some* Catholic, Quaker, etc. schools satisfy it and others do not). The important points is that it is *this* criterion that must be borne in mind by those in charge of schools, or those influential in them. There is all the difference in the world between the man who says that a school should have a 'Christian atmosphere' because it produces

[1] See *I.M.E.*, Chapter 3.

good Christians (Catholics, Quakers, Communists, etc.), and the man who says that a school should have this atmosphere because (in his view) this atmosphere is the best for religious *education*. The former has partisan aims, the latter does not.

I am of course very much aware of the practical difficulties for those schools which are founded on the basis of a partisan commitment. But this is only one case of a general problem which may be put thus: 'How can one *educate* when governors, parents and perhaps society in general want one to indoctrinate or inculcate specific partisan beliefs and behaviour?' This is a practical problem and has no short answer: as a teacher, one has to do the best one can. But at least conceptual clarity about the issues involved may make for a re-thinking of the whole area of R.E., and perhaps make life easier for the teacher who wants to get on with the business of educating.

D. Three Objections

The foregoing should be acceptable, if I have succeeded in making clear to the reader what is involved by the concept of 'religious education'. Some, however, may still feel uncertain: and there are three objections in particular which I should like to clear up.

I. '*How can one understand a religion without being committed to it?*' Some have maintained that a person cannot 'understand religion' in the full sense – perhaps not even in the most important sense – without being personally *committed* to a religion. This seems to present us with an impasse: for (a) unless he is in some sense 'committed', he cannot understand it fully; yet (b) unless he is in some sense *not* 'committed', he cannot assess it objectively and rationally. To try and settle this by saying that religion 'is not a rational matter anyway' is, as we have seen,[1] as false as it is fugitive. We need rather to distinguish the senses in which somebody who is to 'understand religion', or to be 'educated in religion', needs to be committed or otherwise.

1. Different people have different beliefs, and attach their emotions to different objects. They have different gods, different moral codes, like different kinds of music and literature, believe different

[1] pp. 4–6.

things about the physical world, fall in love with different people, and so forth. We do indeed sometimes say 'I can't understand how he could believe that', or 'I can't understand what he sees in her', or 'I can't understand why he should worship such-and-such or approve morally of so-and-so'. But in fact we also think that, given patience, insight, imagination and practice, we can come to understand such things. As we have shown earlier,[1] some cases demand much more imaginative effort, and are much more a matter of 'getting the feel', than others: but as long as people speak intelligibly and have human emotions, it is always possible to understand them, even if some cases seem to us extremely odd.

2. It is true that, if I am not a totally committed worshipper of (say) Hitler and am trying to understand someone who is, I shall not have 'personal experience' of what it is like to be totally committed in this way. But this is only to say that I cannot *be* the other person and *have* his commitment, any more than I can have his headache. This is a logical truth, not a regrettable empirical limitation; and it may tempt us to say things like 'I can never *really* know what it's like to worship Hitler' or 'One can never fully understand another person' (since one can't *be* that person). But this temptation must be resisted. If one could not understand people without being them, one could never understand them at all. I can know what it is *like* to have a total commitment to Hitler, if I learn enough about the Nazi movement and use my imagination: I can, in any normal sense of the word, *understand* it; just as (though in a more complicated way than) I can understand a person's beliefs without actually sharing them.

3. Indeed it is sometimes (perhaps often) the case that the totally committed person, so far from being in the privileged position of having unique knowledge about his situation, may in many ways understand himself and his situation *less* well than an outsider. He may be too involved, biased, prejudiced, unable to see himself objectively and compare himself with others, and so forth. This is surely a commonplace with human emotions generally: it is doubtful whether Hitler or Hitler's followers understood themselves better than a competent and uncommitted psychologist understands them.

[1] pp. 42–3.

4. Nevertheless there is one way in which we may say that someone who wants to understand religion (or many other emotion-based activities) must be 'committed'. He must be committed fully to the business of 'getting the feel' of such activities, and this (as we have said) involves far more than just learning some bleak psychological or sociological or other empirical facts about them. In the same way, someone who wanted to understand music or drama would have to do more than learn the dates of Beethoven or Shakespeare: he would have to launch himself into the world of the Eroica or *Fidelio* and *Hamlet*, to 'commit' himself to it imaginatively. This is sometimes said, in the case of drama, to involve 'suspending one's disbelief': but it is better to say that one believes when one is *in* the world, and suspends all questions of belief or disbelief *about* the world as a whole until later, when perhaps one may want to criticize or assess it. Learning what it is like to be a Christian would certainly involve engaging in characteristically Christian activities and forms of thought – going to church, praying, being moved by the words of the Bible, and so on: just as, for a full understanding of Fascism, one would go to the rallies, march with the goose-step, try and think oneself into the mental postures demanded by 'racial purity', 'German destiny', and so forth.

5. But this is perfectly consistent with, indeed necessary for, the ability to *assess* these things objectively at *other* times: just as, to use a humble example, one may 'get the feel' of cricket by actually playing quite a lot of it, yet at other times make judgements about whether it is a good or a bad game. If we must use the word, we can say that one is 'committed' to it *at the time of playing*. Conversely, the ability to make these objective and (in one sense) 'uncommitted' assessments is itself necessary to the concept of *understanding* the phenomenon fully. For understanding involves being able to stand outside, as well as inside, the game: being able to make comparisons, determine where the game is silly or neurotic and where it has point and reason, and in general evaluate it. A person could not be said fully to understand Christianity and Fascism unless he could do *both* of these: just as, for instance, a mother who fully understands her daughter's being in love with a man must both be able to see it from her point of view, *and* be able to look at it objectively.

II. *Shouldn't the form of religious education be Christian in this country?*

This is rather a difficult objection to phrase, because it can easily be muddled up with others. I shall not take the objector to be saying 'Children should be turned into good Christians' or 'Children should be indoctrinated with Christianity': that represents a point of view which we have dealt with elsewhere.[1] I shall rather take him to be saying something like 'Children should be taught Christianity because it is part of our common culture'; or, more fully, 'Look, we teach English children English and not Chinese: we even think it right to concentrate to some extent on English history, rather than the history of the ancient Aztecs or the contemporary pygmies. Since this is a Christian country – in some sense, anyway – shouldn't our R.E. be chiefly concerned with Christianity? So surely you are wrong in suggesting that children should be taught to "get the feel" of lots of other religions?'

1. The point here depends on a clear understanding of the concept of education and educational aims.[2] As we said before,[3] this might justify teaching about Christianity because it is helpful to historical, or sociological, or some other form of understanding: but these reasons have nothing to do with *religious education as such*. To put it briefly, the notion of 'cultural transmission' is only relevant to any *educational* aim in so far as it is the transmission (or simply teaching) of various forms of thought and factual information. And these are not themselves culture-bound; they may or may not flourish in particular cultures, but that is not why we transmit them – they are valuable in their own right.

2. Of course it may be granted that there are *other* sorts of aims. Not everything we actually do and should do in schools is to be justified specifically on educational grounds. Part of the point of teaching the British system of weights and measures, for instance, is simply that it will be useful for a child in Britain to know these. But it is not on those grounds that we would justify if *as education in mathematics*. The aims of education in mathematics, as in all other subjects, derive from the nature of the subject itself. Certainly teaching about British weights and

---

[1] See pp. 1–4, 9–10, and 15–16.
[2] See R. S. Peters, *Ethics and Education*, Part I.
[3] See pp. 8–9.

measures may be a useful *method* of achieving those aims; but that is not the point. Similarly the notions of 'education in history', 'education in literature', and so on are not culture-bound: 'education in history' does not *mean* 'education in British history', but something more like 'education in the principles and skills which history as a subject involves'. Again, it may be the case that one of the best ways of teaching a British child history and literature is to start, at least, by using British history and literature: but this implies no difference in *aim*.

3. Exactly the same goes for 'religious education'. Our aims are to get the child to be better able to understand, assess and develop his rationality in respect of religion: and I have argued that our central concern here is with the education of the religious emotions. It *may* be that this aim can best be achieved, in Christian or quasi-Christian countries, by making a good deal more use of Christianity, as subject-matter, than of other religions: and the same might go for Buddhism in Buddhist countries, Baal-worship in ancient Palestine, and so forth. But equally this may not be so: it may be that presenting children with less familiar examples has an equally valid claim on the teacher's time – on the grounds, perhaps, that the child needs a good many different examples if he is to get a grip on religion in general at all. In the same way, some historians would argue that, to give the child a good grasp of what history is and how to do it, we should proceed better by taking fairly remote examples (ancient Greek history, for instance) than by taking familiar ones. I am not arguing any specific empirical thesis here: I am arguing only that it is a question about methods, which cannot be settled *a priori*.

III. *Surely teachers who are committed for or against a religion can't be non-partisan?*
Although this question also presents no difficulties once we are clear about the concept of religious education, it is very commonly asked: so perhaps something needs to be said even at the risk of being repetitious.[1]

1. When teachers are trying to educate pupils in various subjects they are very likely to have particular views of their own on

[1] See *I.M.E.* on indoctrination, pp. 168–76: also pp. 176–83.

N

particular points. Thus I may favour one scientific theory of the origins of the universe, or one historical interpretation of the fall of the Roman empire. I may like or dislike Shelley or Dickens: I may be thrilled or bored by pop music or Bach. The same is true in the spheres of morality and religion. As an individual I am committed to, or favour, these particular beliefs or values. But this has no logical connection with my role as an *educator*. Nobody would suppose that I should teach science, or history, or English literature in accordance with my own individual beliefs or values, however strongly I may feel about them. Indeed the more strongly I feel about them – as is likely to be the case with morality and religion – the more careful I should be to avoid stepping out of my role as educator.

2. This is perfectly consistent with a number of quite different points:

(a) It is often *difficult* for people who feel strongly about beliefs or values not to be partisan, and no doubt this applies to teachers as well as anyone else.

(b) When in the course of teaching a teacher is asked what his own beliefs or values are, nothing is to be gained (and something to be lost) by his refusing to tell. Indeed it may be quite helpful for him to use his own beliefs, like anyone else's, as subject-matter for discussion and investigation.

(c) No doubt in practice the teacher's own beliefs and values will influence his pupils to some extent; and this influence may go far enough to merit the term 'indoctrination'.

(d) There may be many cases in which teachers should not act as educators, but should deal with their pupils in other ways (force, indoctrination, conditioning, etc.).

3. But no one should conclude from this that teachers cannot or should not act as educators, at least for some (I would hope, most) of the time. It is all right to say 'You can't help your own beliefs affecting the pupils' or even 'You can't help indoctrinating', if all you mean is 'It is utopian to suppose that anyone can be completely neutral all the time.' But it is very far from all right if you imply that the teacher does not have a role – and that the most important role – as an educator: and since he does have that role, it is not sense to say that he 'indoctrinates' when he plays it.

For 'indoctrinate' only has meaning by contrast with other methods of dealing with people, one of which we refer to by the term 'educate'.

4. The point about the role of the educator as such, which I have been trying to sharpen throughout this book, has important practical implications. Teachers will not, I should guess, succeed in preserving neutrality in R.E. and other subjects if they adopt a merely negative attitude: that is, if they simply try to *avoid* indoctrinating or expressing their own viewpoints. They will succeed only if they have a clear conception of the *positive* role of the educator. The warmth and enthusiasm which each of us as an individual feels for his own particular beliefs and values must, for those of us who are teachers, be transmuted into warmth and enthusiasm for the *subject*, for education. It is this which we need to generate in our pupils: and if we have a real interest in generating it, we shall not need to worry too much about whether our own beliefs and values are creeping in. The teacher is required to have a stronger commitment to education than to his own particular views: if not, he is not earning his money.

Inevitably the remarks made in this chapter are fragmentary and unsatisfactory: and many teachers may feel that they are not as 'practical' as might be wished. I must defend myself, however, by pointing out that it is neither this Unit's intention nor its business to persuade teachers to adopt practical methods which have not been validated by research. The purpose of this book is to make clear the aims which teachers should have in mind: and of this chapter, to give *some* indication of the lines which a teacher who was clear about those aims would be most likely to follow.

At present there are not many educators in this field who have a clear grasp of the proper aims of religious education. But this tells us little about the merits of their educational *practice*, since educators do not always (or in this field perhaps even often) achieve their own aims. There are, no doubt, educators with the wrong aims who educate well, and others with the right aims who educate badly. Thus it may be that a teacher whose aims are avowedly indoctrinatory nevertheless teaches in a way that may satisfy the right criteria: and, conversely, that a teacher whose aims are appropriate to religious education teaches in a way (and with a personality) that does not satisfy the criteria at all.

Whilst therefore it is plainly important and beneficial that teachers should get clear about their aims, we cannot assert very much with confidence about the merits or demerits of existing systems. We do not even know, for instance, how far it may be desirable to initiate children into a particular clearly-articulated metaphysic (e.g. some simple form of Christianity) at an early age, and use this as a first stage on which to build a more intelligent and critical approach to religion in general: or whether children should be left free to invent or pick up their own metaphysic (or not do so), the teacher's job being regarded as solely concerned with giving the child emotional security and helping him assess and criticize what he feels. Of course intelligent guesses can be made: for instance that a programme which includes discussion and criticism is likely to be more effective than one in which the teacher simply lays down the law: that a context of teaching in which the teacher is in close contact with the child, knows how he feels, has his confidence, and can persuade him to talk about his own feelings, is likely to succeed more than a context in which the teacher is remote and tries to deal with religion as if it were something like mathematics. But so much depends on local conditions – the kind of school, the kind of children and the kind of teacher – that it will be the teachers themselves, at this stage, who are in the best position to turn these aims and indications into practice.[1]

One final warning must, however, be firmly issued. Such is the influence of educational fashion that the distinction between aims on the one hand, and methods, contexts and practical arrangements on the other is so often completely blurred. At the time of writing, for instance, there is a fashion for making religious education 'critical', 'child-centred', 'open-ended', 'liberal' and so forth. If this is a woolly way of making the point that the *aims* of anything we could respectably call religious *education* must include the aim of producing autonomous and rational adults, who can make reasonable choices in the sphere of religion and the emotions, then I have no quarrel with it. But if (as often seems to be the case) it is a woolly way of recommending certain *methods* as likely to achieve this aim, then the fashion is a very dangerous one. For it does not at all follow that the best way of producing autonomous and rational adults is to use 'open-ended' or 'liberal' methods

[1] Some further fragmentary suggestions which may well be relevant may be found in *I.M.E.*, pp. 409–13.

(whatever these are). It may well be that the best way – at least for certain stages of development – is to bring up children very strictly within the confines of one particular creed: that Sunday school and the ten commandments, learning psalms by heart and saying prayers by the bedside every night, is part of the most effective method of producing rational adults; that if we do not initiate children thoroughly into one particular religious faith, they will never really come to understand what it is to have a faith at all; that if we allow or encourage them to roam more or less at random through different religious outlooks and institutional practices, they will become insecure, anxious and in general incapable of making those rational appraisals which it is our aim to lead them towards. I do not say that I agree with this: but it is an empirical question which cannot be settled *a priori*.

I have discussed these problems elsewhere in connection with moral education,[1] and need not pursue them here. The prevailing fashion, which affects not only religious education but also the practice of education in most curricular subjects, may indeed have hit, *per accidens*, on at least some of those new methods and contexts which do in fact fulfil our aim: and certainly the history of the old-fashioned methods, in religious education at least, is far from impressive. But the time is now long past when we can afford to be at the mercy of such swings of fashion, moving in one decade towards 'liberal', 'democratic' and 'open-ended' methods, and in another talking anxiously about the importance of tough-minded discipline and accurate scholarship. The sensible teacher will do well to resist the influence of prevailing fashions of whatever kind.

---

[1] *I.M.E.*, Chapter 3.

12. 'R.E.', the State, and partisan belief

By putting religion in its proper perspective, we have already hinted at the kind of attitude-change that we require from those of all creeds and from those of none. Religious education, properly considered, is first and foremost a part of the education of the emotions. It is not, or not primarily, instruction in creeds, dogmas, sacred writings, history, literature, psychology, sociology or any of the other areas that have attached themselves to such emotions. Certainly it is not any attempt to *inculcate* particular religious (or anti-religious) beliefs; nor even any attempt to inculcate the religious or metaphysical attitude as a whole. In so far as particular religious bodies are concerned with education, therefore, they must be prepared to put the religious attitude, and still more their own particular beliefs, on the shelf, and devote their attention to the communal problem of how, in general, religious education is to be done.

This is a big demand; but little progress can be expected unless it is met. If 'religious education' is to stand for anything respectable at all, it cannot be the case that the aims of (say) Catholic religious education should differ from Protestant, or those of the education offered by convinced theists from that offered by convinced agnostics. Religious education must be put on all fours with other kinds of education; it must be based on a communally accepted method, derived from the criteria of rationality appropriate to the subject. Just as we may have widely differing beliefs about particular historical interpretations or particular works of literature, yet agree on a joint plan of education in history or in literary criticism, so we may continue to differ about our personal religious beliefs and practices, yet agree on a joint plan of religious education. Our coming to agree will depend on our understanding of the criteria of rationality appropriate to religion: hence this book. But it will also depend on the strength of our desire to *educate*, rather than to indoctrinate or (more feebly) to keep the pot lukewarm by giving our children some vaguely-conceived instruction in matters contingently connected with certain religions, but not central to religion as a whole.

In a society that has any pretences to be liberal, adults may, of course, practise whatever religion they choose, so long as it does not interfere with other people. But whether particular religious or anti-religious partisans should be permitted to indoctrinate their own or other people's children with their personal views is more questionable. In part, of course, this is a political question, in the sense that to allow or forbid this in a particular society might (a) be impracticable, or (b) if not impracticable, cause more trouble than it is worth. Political decisions have to be taken on the basis of accepting people as they are, along with their prejudices and other forms of unreason. But there is also a question to be asked about what the members of a society, as individuals, ought to think on this topic: and hence about what they would, if reasonable, decide.

I do not think there can be much doubt about the answer to this question. Children are not objects or personal possessions: they are people or potential adults. They have rights. Their central right – or, more precisely, that in virtue of which they have rights at all – is to be free: to be helped or educated, rather than indoctrinated or forced into one particular kind of religious or anti-religious belief. The beliefs of the child's parents, as of his society, are here irrelevant. Parents do not *own* children: and the relevant considerations apply here as much to beliefs that we may approve as to beliefs that we may not. If indoctrination is wrong, it is wrong for Christians, Buddhists, agnostics and atheists, as well as for the Nazis of the '30s and Chinese Communists of the '60s.

This does not, as has sometimes been supposed, lead us directly to the view that church schools should be closed: still less to the view that religious education should be abandoned by the state (as is generally the case in the U.S.A.). For it is not at all clear that those who might *prima facie* be thought partisan, because of their official commitments, are in fact really so. If we keep our eyes firmly fixed on the only important criterion, which is whether a child's freedom is respected and his education helped or hindered in this area, we shall not fail to note that this criterion is likely to cut across all partisan groups. There will be indoctrinating and non-indoctrinating Catholics, Protestants, agnostics, atheists, humanists, and so forth. What we must look at is not an educator's own commitment, but his desire and ability to educate rather than indoctrinate. When we have some reasonably effective means of assessing this, we shall be in a position to disqualify certain teachers and schools as breeders of indoctrination, and to allow and encourage others as creators of freedom and understanding. But it is not at all clear who those thus disqualified or encouraged will be. All we can say is that it very much behoves those who do have a strong personal commitment to search their minds and hearts.

None of this implies that the particular religious sects should shut up shop as partisan organizations. It is not at all disreputable to have particular views not shared by all other people, whether these views are in the field of religion, morals, politics, science or anything else. Nor is it disreputable to create and sustain organizations and institutions that cater for those of similar opinions and attitudes. The only disreputable thing is to use methods of persuasion, whether on the young or on adults, which are indoctrinatory rather than educational. It must not be thought, therefore, that our thesis implies anything derogatory to Christian or other institutions in so far as they cater for the needs of the faithful. On the contrary: it is plainly healthy and educationally desirable that there should be differences of opinion represented by different religious and non-religious organizations, and it is plainly desirable on other grounds that those who are convinced of the merits of a particular metaphysic should be allowed and encouraged to celebrate and express it in ritual and institutional contexts.

What is important is that the distinction between this and *education* should be preserved. The distinction is relevant to a great many contexts: a good topical example is the question of religious broadcasting on radio and television. One objective of such broadcasting will naturally be to provide adherents of particular sects with programmes that satisfy their particular commitments: here we would think in terms of church services, the meaning of Christian beliefs, the work of missionary organizations, and so forth. A quite different objective would be served by programmes *about* religion (as against programmes that serve the needs of a particular religion): and here we should rather think in the terms suggested above. In so far as people are interested in religion, or in so far as it is the business of radio and television to create such interest, those responsible for such programmes will have to take seriously the whole business of religious education. They will want to give hearers and viewers the feel of religion, and to raise (in whatever dramatic forms may be suitable for the various media) those issues which a person interested in religion would want to have raised and, so far as possible, settled. So long as the distinction is clearly grasped, the rest may be left to the imagination of producers and scriptwriters.

Given something that could respectably be called 'religious education', the much-canvassed question of whether 'R.E.' should be compulsory or not becomes transformed and easier to answer. For the question is only worrying if we conceive of R.E. as a means of inculcating some particular creed (and hence, not really as education at all). If it is genuinely education, however, there is absolutely no reason why any majority or minority group of parents or others should not welcome it, along with all other forms of education. For the topic-area, as we have argued, is a very important one for all children: important enough, in my view, to be compulsory.[1] It would be hard to maintain that the education of the religious and other emotions was not as necessary as, for instance, education in science or mathematics or foreign languages. As with all topics, there are problems about how much time to devote to it, in comparison with other school activities and subjects: but at least there will be no *special* problems about R.E.

Meanwhile, however, it remains true that the official policy of many countries is partisan. Acts of Parliament, or other authoritative edicts, are *de jure* or *de facto* in force, which enjoin upon teachers the promotion of particular religions or metaphysics; and to a greater or lesser extent, local educational authorities promulgate syllabuses and suggestions which toe the partisan line. This has numerous disadvantages. Even in a highly liberal society such as the U.K., conscientious teachers of R.E. find the official policy difficult to forget (though perhaps they should try harder); and those too cowardly or too lazy to teach the subject in an intelligent and rational way may always hide behind the official policy. Similarly, partisans on the other side (organized atheists, humanists, or Communists) who reasonably dislike oppression or indoctrination, but are apt unreasonably to suppose that 'religious education' must be the title of something evil or time-wasting, give more time to political pressure than to unprejudiced thought.

A tolerably sophisticated observer will not be surprised at (though

[1] Of course it is odd that R.E. should be the *only* compulsory subject. No doubt we should add others, so long as we are absolutely sure about their importance.

he cannot praise) the prevalence of this situation in politically immature countries. For reasons which sociologists have perhaps yet to understand fully, the rulers of non-liberal or quasi-totalitarian societies tend to combine their laudable desire for order and economic progress with a curious passion for imposing moral and metaphysical purity. At the time of writing, such countries as the U.S.S.R. and its satellites, China, Greece, Spain, Portugal and others too numerous to mention have not felt secure enough to relinquish the desire for control over the metaphysical outlooks and the moral beliefs of their citizens. One expects such societies to have a firm party line in these matters. Yet it is not clear that rulers of liberal societies do much better. The 'party line' in religion and morality is not so firm, and allows the individual much more scope: but they have not so far made the crucial move of positively encouraging forms of education designed to increase freedom and rationality, as opposed merely to allowing different partisan sects to flourish without penalty.

Hence it remains true, even in the U.K. (perhaps the most 'liberal' of modern societies), that politicians and state officials still view religious education as primarily a matter of political pressures and compromise. Political changes may be made if the churches are agreeable, if there is a consensus of 'educated opinion', if the humanists or other minority groups do not make too much political trouble: and so forth. I am not implying that governments should not take the will of the governed into full account: but to organize religious or moral education by such criteria is as absurd as to organize education in science, or history, or any other subject by reference to political pressures. No government can function if there is not some measure of public support: but it is every government's duty to give the public a lead in the direction of what is reasonable.

This is not to say, of course, that there are not genuine *political* problems about religious education, as about all forms of education. Politics is concerned, not just with finding the most coherent and rational solutions to problems, but also with finding solutions that are publicly acceptable in the sense that they represent the best compromise between a number of conflicting interests – indeed to many people the word 'politics' means not much more than the latter: and of course political and governmental authorities must take their decisions on the basis of what is acceptable rather than (or preferably as well as) what is rational. But there are two quite different types of consideration here: and we have the right to insist that they be clearly separated. Political authorities need *first* to be clear about rational solutions, for which they need to attend to the relevant experts: and only *then* to consider the practical possibilities and difficulties of putting these solutions into effect. The position at present seems to me to be that the authorities have absolutely no idea at all about what is rational: if they had, and could present it clearly, they might find that it was also publicly acceptable.

None of the above, however, touches on a question which often underlies discussions about 'religious education', even though (as I have argued) it is not properly raised under that title. This is the question of whether we ought not, in fact, to indoctrinate, inculcate, encourage or preserve a specific metaphysical outlook in our society. Thus there are those who feel, in this society, that we ought to do something called 'preserving Christian values', 'keeping Britain a Christian country', 'inculcating a Christian outlook on life', and so forth: and of course in other countries logically similar aims are put forward (usually with much more self-confidence) such as 'maintaining the socialist revolution', 'generating a spirit of nationalism', 'inculcating a solid Marxist basis of thought', etc. Such people might grant (at least on reflection) that one could not justify such programmes as *educational* in any proper sense: but they might still argue that it was good to carry them out.

Some of these people might feel that it was necessary to 'preserve Christian values', by indoctrinatory periods in the school timetable and other methods, simply because 'Christian values' are 'the right' ones. On this basis they might want to deny that Marxists, Nazis, etc. had a similar right to indoctrinate Russian and German children. But it may also be felt that it is necessary for every society to preserve some 'common morality', backed by a common metaphysic, and hence that other societies are entitled to inculcate different metaphysics. The argument here is not that one particular metaphysic is 'right', but rather that without *some* metaphysic society 'collapses' or 'disintegrates': that a common metaphysic is, as it were, a sociological necessity if we are to avoid results that everyone would grant to be disastrous.

I do not wish to attempt any lengthy contribution to the literature on this subject, since it is not strictly germane to the concept of education. I refer the reader to some of the most important works,[1]

[1] See B. Mitchell, *Law, Morality and Religion*, and the references therein.

and to the relevant passages of our first publication.[1] Here I wish only to make the following points:

1. It is granted that without the establishment of some norms ('ground rules') of behaviour disastrous social consequences may ensue, and that education itself may become in practice impossible. We are chiefly concerned here with social expectations and the institutionalization of conflicts: thus unless people have norms about truth-telling, keeping contracts and not damaging and killing each other it is hard to see how any society can operate at all. If this is what is meant by 'common morality', then it is plainly a *sine qua non*.

2. It is also granted that these norms may require to be established or maintained by a number of non-rational methods of dealing with people, including children (indoctrination, conditioning, force, social sanctions of various kinds, and so forth).

3. It may even be granted, as a bare empirical *possibility*, that in order to preserve these norms, and/or to preserve the individual members of society in a state of sufficient psychological security and integration, it may be necessary to inculcate belief in – to indoctrinate – specific *metaphysical outlooks*. Thus it is not logically impossible that many people would become hopelessly neurotic, or fail to do any work, if they were not indoctrinated to accept certain metaphysical views about God, or Marxism, or Arab destiny or whatever.

But:

4. It must on any view be to some extent *regrettable* (even if sometimes necessary) that these non-rational methods should be used: since the development of rationality is at least *one* desirable end, and the use of indoctrination militates against that end. Hence:

(i) The onus of proof is, in each case, on those that wish to claim the necessity of indoctrination or some other non-rational method.

(ii) We must be sure that we use only the minimum number of non-rational techniques necessary to do the job.

(iii) We must be sure that we select the content of what is to be indoctrinated with a view to the good of individuals as ends in themselves, and not because of our own personal preferences for certain beliefs or values (see pp. 149–51).

[1] *I.M.E.*, pp. 142–76.

(iv) In any case, we must draw a sharp distinction in both theory and practice between these non-educational contexts, and other contexts in which we are out to educate rather than to achieve other ends.

A person who wants to 'preserve' or 'inculcate' Christian (Marxist, Mohammedan, etc.) values may of course simply *mean* that he wants to preserve the 'common morality', the essential 'ground rules', mentioned in 1. above. In that case I have no quarrel with him. But he is likely to mean more than this; and in that case he is obliged to build up an argument on the lines given above. That is, he is obliged to show that the inculcation of these specific (and questionable) values, of the metaphysical outlook that sponsors them, and of the behaviour-patterns that are characteristic of them, is in fact necessary for the preservation of the 'common morality', the 'ground rules' without which we cannot (so to speak) do business at all. Showing that all this is necessary involves showing that it cannot be done by other methods which involve less indoctrination. In building up such an argument he is bound to rely on empirical evidence from history, sociology, psychology, anthropology and other such disciplines. The onus of proof, he will remember, is on him.

I do not feel it is very likely that he will be able to establish anything like a substantial case; and it would perhaps be more worth his while to consider whether the truth lies elsewhere. There are not a few people for whom some such metaphysic is, in fact, a psychological necessity – or who at least feel it to be so. For such people it seems as if to abandon the metaphysic would be to abandon all motivation, even all reason, for behaving in ways which we all know to be sensible – telling the truth, not killing our fellows, and so forth. The metaphysic sustains and supports them, not only in matters of interpersonal morality but also in their private lives: it is essential for their happiness, their integration, perhaps even their sanity. They are thus tempted to extrapolate from their own experience, and claim that what is true (or what they think to be true) for them is true for everyone else also: that the morality of other people, if not underpinned by the metaphysic which appeals to them personally, is at worst non-existent and at best insecure and unreliable.

That these people should recognize themselves in some such

terms seems to me very important, because by doing so they will at least be able to *face* the question of whether such metaphysics are essential for others as an *open* and *empirical* question. Is it saying his prayers and going to church and believing in Jesus that really makes the child able and willing to keep the ground rules, or is it more to do with having an affectionate and reliable mother and a kind but firm father? Is it to do with reading the Bible, or being able to communicate in general with other people? To these (very-over-simplified) questions we may return answers in the shape of informed guesses, or – after a good deal more work – answers backed by proper research. But we shall not even begin to do either unless we can unfreeze ourselves from postures that may be inevitable for us, but are both uncomfortable and dangerous for our children.

Liberal governments, at least, fail here not (I believe) because of any desire to act illiberally, but rather through mere ignorance and incompetence in educating themselves. They are aware of the importance of economic and scientific issues, and know fairly well how to gain and understand the advice of the relevant economic and scientific experts. The same cannot be said for issues of a moral or religious nature. Few politicians and officials are aware of the nature of such issues, of the expertises required for settling them, or of who the experts actually are. Their own training has not succeeded in making these matters plain to them; the experts themselves are not very good at communicating effectively on their own; and there is no adequate mechanism for communication between experts and official decision-makers. Until something is done to remedy this, I do not think it likely that much progress will be made in this particular area.

Fortunately, although this is saddening, it does not matter as much as we might think. Progress – slower perhaps, but just as solid – can be made, in most liberal countries, without having to convince governments. Conceptual clarity, new ideas, and validation by research can spread quietly through the educational system. Hard-working politicians, who have little time for educating themselves or reading books, may be left to catch up in due course; and one may hope that there will always be some who interpret 'politics' in a sufficiently wide sense to understand, accelerate and perhaps contribute to such progress. Meanwhile there is plenty of work to do.

APPENDIX I

'God' and 'making sense of the world'

Some of the notions here considered have, in my view, generally confused rather than clarified the problems of religious education, with which we are centrally concerned: but since they seem always to enter into religious discussions, and since many people in our culture seem to feel lost without them, I append the following note.

A. GOD, GOD AND GODS

Discussions about 'the existence of God' are common in theology and philosophy: but the disputants have not always distinguished clearly between different kinds of enquiry. The differences are often marked by different uses of the word 'god' or 'God'; but it is more important for our purposes to distinguish the kinds of enquiry themselves.

The crucial distinction is between enquiries (1) about the existence of some *worshipful* entity or entities, and (2) about merely the *existence* of some entity or entities. We may distinguish further:

1 (a) An enquiry in which we talk of '*the* gods', or mention a god by name ('Poseidon'), or spell 'God' with a capital letter. Here it is understood that there are limits, even if flexible ones, set on the kind of god that is under discussion. Thus most modern discussions about the 'existence of God' are about a god which at least some Christians would recognize and accept as their own: or if not Christians, at least monotheists or believers in the 'higher' religions. Establishing the existence of Poseidon, Baal, or a *lar* would be insufficient or inappropriate: insufficient if the entity failed (as it were) to cover enough ground; and inappropriate if it covered the wrong ground. Poseidon is only one god, and this is not enough for God; Baal, even if he were all-powerful, would lack the appropriate attributes (goodness, justice, benevolence, etc.).

1 (b) A range of enquiries where the limits are looser: 'Is there *a* God?', and 'Are there gods?' represent progressively looser con-

cepts of god. The capital 'G' in the first question would normally suggest something like a monotheistic or Christian-type god; but not to the extent that is suggested by 'God' in (a) above, where 'God' (without any article) is used in some ways like a proper name. The small 'g' in 'Is there a god?' takes us still further away from the monotheists' God; and 'Are there any gods?' takes us further yet.

Quite different are the following:

2. Enquiries where 'god' is used in what we may call a sociologists' sense (though we might equally well call it a historians', or psychologists'): i.e. where we can speak of 'the gods of Greece' without implying that they are real, i.e. worshipful, gods.[1] Totem poles, ancestors, stocks and stones, and psychological projections (e.g. of father-figures) are gods in this sense: that is, they may be *objects* of worship, prayer, etc.,[2] without necessarily being in our view *worthy* of worship or prayer.

3. Enquiries where 'god' is used in a way which does not imply that they are worshipful *or* that they are worshipped. Not all people who believe in a god or gods are religious: for their gods may not be such entities as would call for characteristically religious feelings, attitudes or activities (e.g. the Epicureans' gods). For the Epicureans (and no doubt for others also) 'Do the goes exist?' is a kind of scientific or empirical question.

The status and importance of a belief in God, a God, a god, or gods can only be appreciated by insisting on these distinctions. To ask about 'the existence of God' is most naturally understood as a 1 (a)-type question: an enquiry about the merits of a *particular kind* of religious belief. One can have other kinds of religious belief without having *this* kind or believing in *this* god, i.e. God. But as we move into 1 (b)-type enquiries, and ask whether there is *a* God, or god, or gods, it becomes progressively more difficult to retain at first anything like a monotheistic religion and later anything like a theistic religion at all.

It is thus an obvious point, but worth stressing – especially for those whose thoughts move entirely within a particular culture or

[1] Compare the 'sociologist's sense' of morality, meaning (roughly) the *mores* of a particular society. See *I.M.E.*, pp. 44–5.

[2] This is the most natural interpretation of 'false gods': 'As for the gods of the heathen, they are but idols: but it is the Lord that made the heavens.'

historical period – that attributes which we commonly write into the concept of God were not thought to be necessary by those of other cultures and ages. Attributes referred to in our dictionary definitions, such as 'the supreme being', 'the creator of the world', and so forth, rarely apply to polytheistic religions; and even such attributes as goodness, benevolence, justice and other moral concepts are not essential – people have believed in evil and unjust gods who ought if possible to be avoided, placated or thwarted; and even such attributes as immortality or super-human power are not absolutely essential – Cronos was killed, and *lares et penates* are not in general more powerful than men (even though they may have certain powers that men do not have).

The difficulty of providing exact translations for the Latin *deus* and *divus* (e.g. in reference to the deification of Roman emperors), or the classical Greek *theos* and *theios*, is only one instance of this general point; and the closeness of the noun and the adjective in each of these pairs suggests the need to remember how tightly our own 'God' is still tied to a Jehovah-type, creator and controller image. The tie is tight enough, at least, for not a few people to find it more natural to express their theological points by referring to 'the death of God' (i.e. our particular God) rather than to retain the word 'God' whilst trying to change our picture of God's nature. Our God is still (so to speak) very much a transcendent being, for which we need a noun.

'Worshipping God' is thus not tautological, and the accusative is not the cognate accusative of 'playing a game' or 'dreaming a dream'. For 'God' usually refers to a particular kind of god which a man *might* (logically) *not* worship: so that 'I worship God' (*sc.* rather than Dagon) is informative in the same way as 'I play chess' (*sc.* rather than draughts). Nor is 'worshipping a god' tautological. For there are other things one can worship besides gods (the sun, one's wife, etc.). We have to resist the temptation to think that all forms of religion involve hypostatizing some entity or entities which are then called 'God' or 'gods'. If a man is asked what the object of his worship is, and replies 'a god', he has not told us much: but he has told us something – namely, that he has hypostatized. If he says 'God', and the context makes it plain that this means (say) the Christian God, then of course he tells us much more. For we can unpack 'God' in recognized ways: the concept will include dispensing love and justice (but perhaps for many

o

believers in this century not eternal punishment), being the creator, being like Jesus, and so forth.

But if enquiry about 'the existence of God' is, in our culture and language, enquiry about a particular kind of religious belief, it is not therefore enquiry about a particular belief *within* that kind. The belief that (the Christian) God exists is neither just one Christian belief amongst many, of a logically similar status to other beliefs (e.g. about hell, salvation, the virgin birth, etc.); nor yet is it to be taken as a kind of major premiss or corner-stone belief, from which other beliefs can be derived. To acquire such a belief is not so much to have accepted the most important belief out of a collection of beliefs owned by one kind of religion, but rather to have gained a general licence to start acquiring beliefs from that collection. It is more like buying a ticket for a particular play, or sitting down in the theatre to accept the world which that play portrays, than holding any specific belief about what happens on the stage.

We need to distinguish these from (2)-types of enquiry, only to avoid the muddle introduced by those who have said, in effect: 'It is silly to discuss whether there is a god or gods, for "god" is simply a name for what human beings worship or prize most highly. Everybody prizes something highly – everyone has some religion – so of course there are gods: the only thing worth talking about is what sort of gods they are.' The basic point behind this thesis is of course important: but it is confused on these counts: (i) because there are uses of 'god' (as in 1(a) and (b)) which relate not to *actual* but to *proper* objects of worship; (ii) because, not everything worshipped is a god: (iii) because although everybody perhaps prizes something highly, not everybody *worships* or has a religion: (iv) because there are cases of god and gods that are not worshipped. The (2)-type use of 'god' is more suited to psychological or sociological enquiry about religious belief than to an investigation of its rationale.

Similarly, a (3)-type enquiry is not *pro tanto* a religious enquiry at all. For if by 'god' or 'the gods' we refer to alleged entities that are neither worshipful (as in 1(a) and 1(b)), nor are actually worshipped (as in 2), then an enquiry about the existence of gods in this sense will be logically parallel with an enquiry about the existence of Martians, super-beings from another galaxy, etc. – that is, a scientific enquiry. Of course we may *first* conduct an enquiry into the bare existence of entities, and *then* an enquiry into whether they are worshipful: indeed, some such procedure is suggested in the main text (Chapter 4). But if these enquiries are not to get muddled, we must remain alert to the different senses of 'god' as outlined above.

B. 'MAKING SENSE'[1]

There are still many who regard the notion of God as necessary in order to 'make sense' either of certain events or phenomena in the world, or of the world as a whole.

1. First, some people still bring in God because they are unable to understand (or perhaps – see 3 below – it would be better to say, to *accept* or learn to live with) certain events or phenomena: the origins or patterns of the physical universe, a flood, the illness of a loved one, a sudden cure, a psychological conversion, and so forth. In this context God is often thought to give some kind of *explanation*; but it is fairly clear from what we have already said that this cannot be an explanation in those senses of the word to which we are normally accustomed. For (1) a purely causal or scientific explanation would make God into a kind of scientific cause: and (2) an explanation in terms of intentions or purposes would make him into a kind of super-being, more powerful than but logically no different from any other rational being in the universe.

Neither of these beliefs would be specifically *religious*. It would be important and interesting to know (1) that there was some force in the universe which accounted for certain phenomena, or (2) that apparently random happenings in fact occurred because of the will and intentions of a super-being. But in the former case we shall simply have discovered a new area of scientific enquiry, and in the latter simply have added to our stock of rational beings in the universe. If these beliefs have a religious function, it is not in virtue of their role as *explanations*.

2. Another way in which people bring in God to 'make sense' is by casting him in the role of a sponsor of moral values. An example, still regrettably topical, is the Christian (or perhaps what used to be the Christian) belief that certain facts about God oblige us in certain moral directions. The implication is sometimes that God's power, sometimes that his status as our maker and preserver, makes treasonable for us to obey him or gives him a moral claim on us. One

---

[1] See on this topic Karl Britton's excellent *Philosophy and the Meaning of Life*.

is tempted to believe that it is only the religious context, and the use of the word 'God', which makes this seem plausible. Closely connected with these views, and by no means confined to the Christian religion, are the innumerable instances where the use of such words and phrases as 'designed to . . .', 'meant to . . .', 'the purpose of . . .', etc. indicate the belief (conscious or unconscious) that *the way in which the universe is set up gives us moral values ready-made.*

A quick way of unbewitching oneself is to imagine the sudden discovery that the world as we know it is in fact the creation of a super-being from another galaxy. This super-being is of immense power, and is responsible for the creation and preservation of our world and ourselves: also he has certain designs, intentions and purposes for us and for various aspects of our lives. Will anyone now say that his power alone or his status obliges us morally? And will it not be admitted that the question of whether we should obey or thwart him in this or that respect is a real question, and a question which only we can (logically) decide for ourselves, by our own moral thinking?[1]

Such criticism, however, could hardly be taken as criticism of most actual religious or metaphysical outlooks: for, as has been said in Chapter 5, such an outlook in practice will contain built-in values and attitudes. To most Christians, I would guess, the question 'Why should we do the will of God?' appears logically odd or unreal: and rightly, because the concept of God in Christianity already has a certain emotional investment attached to it. If the investment were not made, we would not be talking about the Christian God but about something else. Here again criticism must be directed at the first steps: that is, at the belief that a certain religious object justifies certain emotions and attitudes – at the belief in God itself.

We may legitimately wonder, therefore, whether religious believers really want to *derive* their morality *from* their religion. A better description of how they actually think might be to say that their moral ideals *take the form of* religious beliefs. In practice,

---

[1] Peter Geach (*God and the Soul*, Routledge 1969, p. 126) says it is an 'insane question', but I am not clear what this means. To go against the will of an omnipotent being might be insane *behaviour*, but the question 'Why should we do what he wants?' seems not only sane but, for Geach, easily answerable in terms of personal expediency. Geach is content to describe his view as 'plain power-worship'. With an author of such clarity and honesty, at least we know where we are.

such phrases as 'the will of God', 'the Christian life', 'what Jesus wants of us' and so forth are used to describe moral ideals: these phrases have a descriptive content (given by tradition or some common understanding or interpretation of a tradition), and at the same time an evaluative element. (The model case here is the phrase 'natural law', as traditionally understood.) This blend of fact and value is such that (a) not just anything can count as 'the will of God', whilst at the same time (b) it will not usually make sense – for most uses of the phrase anyway – to ask the question 'Why should we do the will of God?' By such devices believers have it both ways: the position is open to attack only by insisting on some form of the fact-value distinction. Thus we can ask 'Can one identify "the will of God" independently of any particular value-judgements or moral beliefs?' or, more precisely, 'To verify whether X is the will of God, do we need (a) to know or believe that X is good, or only (b) to know or believe something factual (e.g. that X is stated to be the will of God in the Bible, that saints and fathers of the church have taken X to be the will of God, etc.)?' There are then two alternatives: (a) in order to know that X is the will of God, we have to know independently that X is good; and in that case we must have other criteria for determining that X is good: (b) in order to know that X is the will of God, we have only to know something factual (it says so in the Bible, etc.); in that case, the question can arise of why it is our moral duty to do the (factually defined) will of God: and we shall have to have moral criteria to answer this question. In both cases these other criteria are logically antecedent to the will of God.

Thus Professor Basil Mitchell, in an illuminating parable[1] about the authority of theology or religious belief: ' "We have reasons to believe", he will say, "that our King is very wise and that is why we accept his authority. . . . We have need, of course, to interpret the King's commands, so as to apply them intelligently. . . ." '. But behind this lie antecedent criteria (a) for believing that the King is very wise, (b) for 'applying' his commands 'intelligently'. And so with all cases of 'authority'[2]: where 'authority' doesn't just refer to some kind of psychological pull, it must refer to a sphere of discourse (history, morals, mathematics, etc.) where the person only *is* an authority because he is good at the rules and procedures

[1] *Law, Morality and Religion*, p. 118–19.
[2] See *I.M.E.*, pp. 100–101.

governing the sphere of discourse, which are logically antecedent to the authority of the person.

3. Both 1. and 2. have been fully criticized elsewhere, and this is not the place to spend more time on them. I am convinced, however, that underlying both these temptations is a feeling of a much more general kind, of which 1. and 2. are only the most natural symptoms. This feeling is describable, and has often been described, in such phrases and questions as 'A sense of the contingent',[1] 'Why should this happen to me?', 'Is life meaningful?', 'Why is everything as it is?' and so forth. It is a desire to escape from what some choose to call the randomness, arbitrariness, or meaninglessness of life: its lack of purpose, justice, or general rationale. This desire to 'make sense' of life, or of certain elements in life, is neither irrational nor absurd, and is not necessarily connected with naïve attempts to misuse religion in the ways described above.

Various writers have long since pointed out some of the difficulties involved in giving meaning to such questions, and it would be a naïve person indeed who regarded them as logically parallel to ordinary questions of the same grammatical form, e.g. 'What is a hammer for? What is this train's destination? What is the meaning of this inscription?', etc.[2] This is not to say that the questions are meaningless; or that they are not, in *one* sense, 'serious': but there are obvious cases where nobody would be tempted into taking the words with that *kind* of seriousness we give to some other cases. In *The Wizard of Oz* Judy Garland sings sadly 'Somewhere over the rainbow bluebirds fly: birds fly over the rainbow, why, o why, can't I?'. Nobody here feels tempted to talk about human anatomy, Garland's power-weight ratio, etc.: we all immediately recognize it as something more like a lament than a question. We might say, it is a serious *lament* but not a serious *question*. Often again it depends on the context. If waking up on a black Monday morning and thinking of having to start a grim week's work I say 'Oh, my God, what's it all for?' I don't necessarily welcome a metaphysical answer. I know I am just groaning. But if I am being earnest, or at a conference, or (in an old-fashioned sense) philosophizing, I very well may want, and (apparently) come to believe, an 'answer'.

[1] See I. C. Crombie's essay in *New Essays in Philosophical Theology* (ed. A. Flew and A. C. MacIntyre).

[2] See S. Hampshire, *Spinoza* (Penguin 1951), Chapter 6; also *The Nature of Metaphysics*, ed. D. F. Pears (Macmillan 1962), particularly pp. 1-39 and 142 ff.

'Making sense', in the more specifically religious connotation of the phrase, is not like (1) finding a scientific explanation of brute facts, nor (2) solving a puzzle, or working out the rules of a game which someone else has made up. Many such phrases, like 'puzzled', 'at a loss', 'not understanding', or 'feeling worried', refer to something more like the psychological notions of 'adjustment', 'being in control', 'acceptance', or 'coming to terms with life'. Thus one may 'not understand' or 'feel baffled' by a painting, or a piece of music, without there being any possibility of intellectual *explanation*: the painting and the music are not brute facts to be explained by the scientist, or puzzles set by the artist which have to be solved, as are genuine picture-puzzles. The person who 'does not understand' a work of art fails to appreciate it: and whatever else may be involved in the notion of appreciation, there is certainly the element of coming to terms with it, becoming familiar with it, accepting it, or (as we might say) bringing it into one's universe. It becomes something which we can deal with, assess, and relate to.

This kind of 'making sense' is relevant to other departments of life as well as to art, and to life as a whole as well as to particular departments or aspects of it. Much has been written about it under such fashionable headings as 'existentialism', 'alienation', 'a sense of belonging', 'structuring one's universe', and so forth. Various descriptions, explanations, and remedies have been advanced: and religion appears most naturally in this context as a *remedy*, rather than as (in the strict sense) an *answer*. It offers a way of structuring the world. Most religions offer us a picture of an already structured universe, created not by ourselves but by a God who has thereby, as it were, placed us in our proper or natural positions. This placement, which relieves the individual of much of the burden of choice, may be more or less detailed. It may not always justify the current social structure, so that we know that our social roles are ordained: but it is almost certain to justify or appear to justify particular ideals or moral codes: and at the very least it will give us the bare but much-desired sense of belonging or being placed, the notion that we are not alone in the world, the idea that something at least has been or is being done *for* us, so that not everything has to be done *by* us.

Another feature common to many metaphysical outlooks is the *subordination of the individual*. I intend 'subordination' here in a literal sense. The human person is conceived as being (in some sense) lower in the universal order than some other entity. One uses the word 'entity' with some discomfort: for what is placed over and above the human individual need not be anything so (apparently) definite and (so to speak) self-contained as a God. It may be 'the will of the Party', 'the spirit of Germany', 'art', 'duty' or indeed almost anything – for the element of subordination comes out in the way in which a person uses such words, and the part such concepts play, *in his life*, and cannot be directly derived merely from the fact that they figure in his overtly stated metaphysics. Nevertheless, this feature finds at least one natural home in the traditional hierocratic picture presented by Christianity.

Here we would naturally be interested to know how far, or in what senses and ways, the desire to be 'placed', to 'make sense' of the world, is rational or irrational. One might start by remembering the infant's (and indeed the adult's) need for security and for a solid framework within which to live: and the description offered by many psychologists of the secure and happy person as one who can work towards long-term aims, and embrace a large part of the chances and changes of life within some general pattern or ideal. This would be a general question of the merits of having *some holistic* metaphysic, as against (a) questions about the merits of one holistic metaphysic as against another, and (b) questions about the merits of a metaphysic that did not involve 'the whole of life' in the way described. We should want to ask, for instance, how far it was necessary for a man who was otherwise emotionally secure, and able to face a large part of life without anxiety, to formulate a conscious holistic metaphysic at all: might he not just *feel* secure in the world, without having consciously to use some *picture* (whether religious or otherwise) which sketched out his secure placement in the world for him? These, again, are questions to which psychological knowledge is highly relevant, even though we might hope to establish some general criteria by which to make use of such knowledge.

Closely connected with this is a conception of God which is peculiar to certain very sophisticated versions of the 'higher religions', and which has been expounded by several contemporary philosophers.[1] For instance: '. . . the man who loves God cannot be touched by the world, by how things are. Socrates wanted to

[1] The reader will most quickly appreciate the line of thought to which I am referring by looking at D. Z. Phillips' 'From World to God', in *P.A.S.*, Supplementary Volume, 1967, and taking up the references therein. See also J. R. Bambrough, *Reason, Truth and God*.

say that all is well whatever is the case. Kierkegaard wanted to say that whatever is the case, eternal love cannot suffer defeat. Wittgenstein wanted to say that he had an experience of feeling absolutely safe, and that nothing could harm him',[1] '. . . perhaps a formulation less adequate than most is to be found in the Psalms: "The earth is weak and all the inhabiters thereof: I bear up the pillars of it",'[2] and so on.[3] With this line of thought we can, for our purposes, take a fairly short way. What is here described are, indeed, recognizable feelings: nor are the remarks that express them wholly incomprehensible to us. But not everybody ties these feelings on to the concept of a *God* or even on to any kind of *religion*. There are people, both sane and not so sane, who have precisely these feelings: the form of expression they use may well depend on the particular culture or social forms of thought in which they have been brought up, or to which they are attracted.

However important such expositions may be, therefore, we may reasonably conclude that they are not expositions of anything that is central to religion in general, or even what is commonly believed by adherents of particular religions. Moreover, there are strong indications that these feelings and remarks fit in well with our general thesis, which is to establish a connection between religion and the emotions. Norman Malcolm, another exponent of the view we are considering, very properly quotes Kierkegaard: 'There is only one proof of the truth of Christianity and that, quite rightly, is from the emotions, when the dread of sin and a heavy conscience torture a man into crossing the narrow line between despair bordering upon madness – and Christendom'.[4] This is but one remark of the many which suggest strongly that we have here the case of a particular religion or metaphysic, dependent on particular emotions and attitudes whose rationality needs to be investigated.

---

[1] D. Z. Phillips, op. cit., pp. 149–50.

[2] R. M. Hare, *New Essays in Philosophical Theology* (ed. A. Flew and A. C. MacIntyre), p. 101, S.C.M. paperback edition.

[3] See also Cora Diamond's 'Secondary Sense', *P.A.S.* (1966–67), p. 189–90, particularly the references to Wittgenstein's lecture on ethics.

[4] p. 60 of Malcolm's essay in D. Z. Phillip's *Religion and Understanding*.

APPENDIX II

The function of awe and religion

In the main text we have been concerned with religious *education*: that is, with the principles by which we can detect and try to remove irrationalities in the sphere of religion. I have expressed no views as to whether religion in general, or the awe and worship that are at the conceptual heart of religion, is necessary or desirable: nor, strictly speaking, is this an essential prerequisite for the educator, whose function is neutral with respect to the desirability or otherwise of religion. Nevertheless, the question is plainly not irrelevant to religious education. For if we were clearer about the answer it would give us some help in assessing how far our educational methods had succeeded: just as, if we knew what actual moral principles were reasonable, we could get some guidance about the success of our moral education by seeing whether our children came to adopt those principles – even though we did not set out to inculcate them. Chiefly for this reason I append the following tentative note.

Arguments about the objects of religion ought to be of this form: 'What phenomena will the reasonable man find awesome, adopt an attitude of reverence towards, and worship?', or again 'What reasons are there for counting certain phenomena as awesome, revering and worshipping them?' The two answers normally given are (i) 'None: there are no reasons, for awe is of no use; it is simply something which people feel when they can't understand or explain or defend themselves against the world or control nature'; and (ii) 'Whatever things we think to be morally valuable, those we should be in awe of, because this will help us to maintain a proper morality'. Both these answers attempt to distort the notion of awe: the one regards it as otiose, the other as a means to an end. Neither finds a place for awe in its own right: and consequently both accounts of religious belief tend to distort.

Many writers have tried to say something about the persistence of the religious emotions in human beings, and the dangers which beset any attempt to deny such emotions or to overthrow religion.

This may involve two distinct, if connected, assertions: (1) that the religious emotions are inevitable, (2) that they are desirable. The difficulty is to decide in how strong a sense to take 'inevitable' and 'desirable'. For even those temperamentally most opposed to religion might agree (1) that *for men as they are* (emotionally insecure, lacking enough control over the world, etc.) the religious emotions are inevitable, and even (2) that *for men as they are* they may be desirable (the alternative perhaps being mental breakdown or social chaos). But they would deny that this showed either the inevitability or the desirability of the religious emotions in any absolute sense: that is, they would hope that improvements in science, politics, child-rearing, psychiatry, or perhaps even genetics would render the religious emotions, and consequently religion itself, otiose.

Perhaps a parallel will help to make this issue clearer. Somebody might want to say that romantic love, or fear of the unknown, were 'basic' or 'persistent' or 'ineradicable' parts of 'human nature'. Our first question would be whether this was so in a very strong sense, i.e. whether one could conceive of a human being who never had such feelings (either consciously or unconsciously), even granted all the changes that might be made by advances in biology or other sciences, or by new kinds of child-rearing, social systems, etc. To ask this would be to ask whether these feelings were *conceptually connected* with what we understood by 'a human being': and by 'human being' here we would not refer solely to bipeds on this planet, but to any creature possessed of the minimum requirements for consciousness or intelligence. (For human beings might change their shape or place of residence.) If we arrived at the conclusion that there was no conceptual connection, we might then go on to ask (a) since these feelings are not logically ineradicable, how deeply-rooted they are in human beings: that is, how academic or futuristic it would be to say that they *could* be eradicated: and also (b) whether they are feelings which, in any case, it is sometimes profitable for human beings to have (perhaps romantic love keeps families together, and fear of the unknown generates prudence).

On the other hand, we might be considering, not love and fear as directed towards particular objects or involving certain kinds of beliefs (as romantic love and fear of the unknown do), but just love and fear in general. Here we might well maintain that the concept of a conscious, intelligent creature without such feelings was incoherent. Thus we could argue (more fully than I am arguing here) that any such being would have desires and purposes, and make choices. He would have certain criteria of choice, in reference to which he would call some things in his environment 'good' and others 'bad'. He would also have a sense of time. Hence he would have (i) a feeling about the good things in his possession or out of it, which we may call 'love': and (ii) a feeling about possible bad things coming to him in the future, which we may call 'fear'. Many other emotions, for instance hope (the inverse of fear), might be shown to be conceptually necessary in this way. If we could make this argument stick, we should then be in a position to regard as logically absurd any programme intended to 'banish fear' or 'take away love' from human life.

This notion of 'conceptual inevitability' needs a good deal more elucidation than I can give it here. In particular one distinction needs to be made, between (a) feelings which a creature *will certainly* (for conceptual reasons) have in any environment, and (b) feelings which it will always be conceptually *possible* for him to have in any environment. For instance, since there are conceptual reasons for saying that there is always the chance of a bad thing happening to any creature, fear seems to come under (a): any creature with reason, imagination, etc. will consider this chance and *eo ipso* feel fear or apprehension. On the other hand, it may be that the creature's environment is so well organized that all the things he counts as 'good' are in his own possession, so that *in fact* he never feels jealous or envious of another creature; although since this empirical situation might change, it is always conceptually possible (and of course empirically very probable) that he should feel jealous or envious. Jealousy and envy would therefore come under (b). In the same way, what is felt for bad things – hate, dislike, distaste, disgust, etc. – will certainly be felt, just because there will always be 'bad' things (since the creature exercises purposive choice). But we cannot say that he will certainly feel regret, since it is always conceptually possible that he never makes a mistake (though of course by the same token it is always conceptually possible that he may).

Both (a) and (b), however, seem to me different from any question of (c) empirical inevitability, even if we take this in a very deep sense. Thus the question of in what sense such things as anger, frustration and aggression are inevitable for human beings might be answered in any of these three ways. We might say (a) that for any creature in any environment there will be a delay between a desire and its fulfilment, and that what is felt during this delay precisely is what we mean by 'frustration' or 'anger': i.e. that we can get the concept 'frustration' out of the concept 'desire' plus other things conceptually necessary to any environment, such as that actions take time. Or we could say (b) that what we mean by 'anger' and 'frustration' occur only when the delay is too long, or when there is a very real chance that the object of desire may not be attained: that this is conceptually possible in any environment, but that it *need* not ever (for conceptual reasons) be the case. Or we can argue (c) that with human beings as they are, particularly at certain phases of development (notoriously in early childhood), and with the world as it is, anger and frustration will inevitably arise. I should incline to the third (see my *Logic and Sexual Morality*, Ch. 9):[1] but the position is far from clear.

(c) of course entails (b): what is empirically inevitable is conceptually possible. But not *vice versa*: it may be practicable so to arrange things that the conceptually possible emotion is never instantiated in practice. So the categories should look like this:

I. Conceptually inevitable (and therefore of course empirically inevitable).
II. Conceptually possible and (i) empirically inevitable, (ii) not empirically inevitable.

And there will be further questions to be asked about what is to count as 'empirically inevitable', or how tightly we are to screw up the concept. For we must allow a sense of 'human nature' (what is *given*) which is not tied simply to conceptual inevitability: we must allow this at least for practical purposes, even though the content of the concept will vary from one practical context of enquiry to another.

There are, then, three sorts of arguments which we may bring to bear:

(1) That the religious emotions are conceptually inevitable for human beings;
(2) That they are, in a very deep sense, empirically inevitable;
(3) That they are in any case desirable.

[1] Penguin 1966.

I think that all these are true: and though I cannot argue for them at length here, some of what follows may perhaps establish at least a prima facie case for one or more of them. It is possibly worth noting that either (1) or (3) would be sufficient to demolish any programme designed to get rid of the religious emotions; and (2) would be sufficient to demolish any such programme for the foreseeable future.

Any rational creature has to develop his rationality from scratch: he has to grow, if not physically, at least in the sense of coming more and more into contact with his environment, and trying to make sense of it both intellectually and emotionally. Inevitably during the period of growth there will be certain things in the world that strike him with particular force, in the face of which he feels particularly passive, receptive and humble. What a human child feels for its parents, for thunder and lightning, the dark and many other objects can be regarded as only one instance of the general truth that any growing creature is acted upon emotionally, and sometimes with great force, by certain features of his environment. Before these features he will feel small. This feeling may be coupled with, or replaced by, such other feelings as fear, wonder, hatred, or love: but it exists in its own right, and may indeed be regarded as more primitive (both conceptually and developmentally) than they.

Even when such a person has (so to speak) come to terms with his environment, he will still relate emotionally to that environment and to new features in it: he will still be able to admire, feel respect towards, or be powerfully impressed by certain things. These may vary. Like John Dewey, he may be impressed by certain methods of enquiry: like Dubedat in Shaw's *Doctor's Dilemma*, he may be a worshipper of beauty: like Hitler, he may be emotionally enthralled by the destiny of a nation. Certainly a person – perhaps particularly in an environment made secure by science and a well-organized social and political system – may at least seem never to feel anything that we could call awe, nor even any very high degree of admiration, respect, reverence or wonder. (And certainly he may never (a) carry this feeling over into the activity of worship, nor (b) have available any social or institutionalized forms, which would enable us to speak of his having a *religion*.) But there will always be the conceptual possibility, even if there is not the conceptual necessity, of his feeling awe and other religious emotions.

Moreover, the fact that in his time of growth or childhood he could hardly have escaped being impressed in the way, and to the degree, that we describe under the term 'awe', may be more relevant than we suppose to his life as an adult. It is quite possible (as we have seen) for a person to feel awe (and other feelings) *unconsciously*, and without admitting to himself that awe is what he feels. Here again the objects of his awe may vary: his boss, worldly success, his wife, his conscience, death, illness, political power and so forth. Particularly in our culture, where awe is not fashionable, it is more than likely that such a person will deny what his behaviour (and perhaps a little psychoanalysis) might reveal. Indeed it seems very unlikely, and perhaps might be argued to be conceptually impossible, that a person could entirely *grow out of* awe, in the way in which a person can grow out of *particular objects of* awe, fear or any other emotion. Either the objects of awe will change, or (as must often happen) the awe together with its original objects will go underground, to reappear in his adult behaviour, even though he may deny it.

Finally, even if no case for any kind of inevitability could be established, there remains a case for awe as a desideratum. It will be granted that there are things, even if we are not clear about exactly which things, that are of overwhelming importance not only to the emotional life of human beings but to their practical decisions and choices. What is of overwhelming importance should, at least initially, be felt as overwhelming: it is desirable that we should, on occasion, be able to feel passive, humble, 'in the presence of something greater than ourselves'. To say this is to say nothing about the existence of magical forces or Jehovah-like personal deities, nor to deny the subsequent necessity for intelligent and critical thought: it is simply to say that the degree of reverence, admiration, 'feeling small' and receptivity which the word 'awe' suggests is often an appropriate emotion, without which we might tend to deny or turn away from the full force and importance of the object.

In considering how one might determine – for it is not the business of the philosopher or educator as such actually to determine – which objects are appropriate objects of awe, one may be tempted to think too many criteria to be relevant. There is, first, the *social* appropriateness, conceived largely in terms of what 'we' (meaning usually a particular culture) consider appropriate: but of course a whole culture, even the whole race of men, might be wrong.

Secondly, there are reasons given for the appropriateness of awe which do not actually justify *awe* as against some other feeling or attitude. Thus one might suppose it to be of the highest importance that a man should keep his mind firmly fixed on his duty to his neighbour, and on the criteria of rationality which may help him to live a happy and useful life: and we may even think it right to set up hero-figures (Socrates? Kant? J. S. Mill?) whose lives and teachings stress the importance of these things. But why should a man be in *awe* either of the things or the figures, rather than just respect them, look up to them, or (as we have already said) keep his mind firmly fixed on them? To say that most men will not do this unless they are actually in awe of them is only an *ad hoc* or *ad tempus* argument for awe.

I should myself be inclined to look elsewhere for appropriate objects of awe. First, there are powerful forces in human life towards all of which we cannot (logically) always feel wholly detached or autonomous. Thus, whilst it may be possible for human beings to remain detached from, unawed by, and in some sense quite at home with the world of material objects, it is not possible that they should always be in this state of mind with regard to their own emotions. Not only psychologists like Freud and Jung, but the great tragic writers and novelists also, have clearly shown the way in which our emotions, and hence phenomena in the outside world which have emotional significance for us, are not always amenable to conscious control in the way that material objects may be, but may always irrupt into our lives, sometimes with devastating results. These emotions, and whatever things in the external world symbolize and echo them for us, imply a degree of non-freedom that will persist so long as human beings remain human.

Of course a man may deny or refuse to face these emotions, turn away from those things that evoke and symbolize them, and (perhaps unconsciously) reject that part of his personality which he cannot regard with detachment: just as a man may not ever make an approach to, or be moved by, works of art. But the pseudo-liberal ideal of a fully controlled, wholly free human being is not logically coherent; and any attempt to realize such an ideal too quickly, as opposed to a willingness to work (endlessly) towards it, must result in a shrunken and jejune view of human personality. The necessity for awe, then, arises from the acknowledgement that there are forces – emotional forces if not material ones – which are (a) an inevitable part of human existence, and (b) in themselves over-whelming, impressive, and awesome.

Both the necessity for awe (rather than respect, understanding, etc.) and the preservation of autonomous judgement can be main-tained by noting that awe, when combined with formalized worship, which (as we put it earlier) celebrates and in a sense institutionalizes the awe, is not so much a mode of avoiding autonomous control and critical judgement, but an essential preliminary to it. At least this is true if, as I have suggested, the awesome objects are to be connected with those human emotions which are both inevitable and crucial for human life. Thus, in dealing with the material world, nothing is lost if we have only an attitude of respect for the facts: we need only this, combined with the autonomous activities of criticism and assessment themselves, to gain all we want. At best, awe felt for material objects would merely add something to the range of human feeling. But an initial feeling of awe is, I suggest, an essential first step in being able to acknowledge and subsequently to face emotions which by their nature are bound to move us powerfully. We need to feel these first *as* mighty forces, if we are subsequently to have the kind of understanding of and control over them that we wish. And to keep us permanently in touch with this feeling, we need formalized worship.

The other great (or potentially great) force in human affairs, to which awe might appropriately be directed, is the human reason. But the justification for the appropriateness of awe here is somewhat different. Awe felt for the emotions was justified as an essential first step of *recognition*, leading eventually to a proper understanding and control; to feel in awe of and worship the powers of the human reason is precisely to *be* concerned with that understanding and control. In the former case we contrast humanity with emotionless robots or calculating machines: in the latter we contrast humanity with non-rational animals or plants. The difference appears in the different senses in which we call either 'important'. All our strong feelings are 'important' in the sense that they figure (for good or ill) largely in our lives: they have to be recognized, understood, and taken account of – as Hippolytus failed to take account of Aphrodite. The principles of rationality may be, and potentially certainly are, 'important' in this sense: but they are also 'important' in the quite different sense that we ought to *follow*, *obey*, or *submit to* them – just as Hippolytus ought to have followed Wisdom or Prudence.

P

These two elements are easily detectable in the history of religious practice. The so-called 'higher' religions have been very much concerned with law and reason – somewhat, it may be argued, at the expense of suppressing certain emotions: and conversely, one might suppose that the more polytheistic or pantheistic religions, while encouraging awe and recognition of human emotion, failed to provide any effective *ideal* to worship. In our culture, and perhaps most technologically advanced cultures, men are apt to stress what they at least take to be the rational – the rule-giving, the ordaining, the action-guiding, the choice-determining. In the mouths of many such, 'worship' partly means 'think good' or 'attach a moral value to'. It is this preference, historically, which has squeezed some religion dry of its more Dionysiac elements for the sake of Apollo: and, in some cultures, replaced or tried to replace religion by other outlooks (such as Marxism) which seemed to be more effective for the encouragement of control, order, and moral virtue.

It is truistic to point out that both are of equal importance. This is not to say that both compete for the same job: there is no question of some mythical conflict of 'reason versus emotion'; for the *kind* of 'importance', as we have just pointed out, is different. We require a religion that does justice to, and in which we can worship and celebrate, the immense and inevitable force of emotion, both as felt within ourselves and as symbolized in the external world: and we require a religion that does justice to, and in which we can worship and follow, the principles of rationality. Without the former any religion is sterile, self-defeating and easily overthrown: for one cannot be fully rational without awe and recognition of emotion, and a too severely repressed emotion will have its way somehow. Without the latter any religion is pointless: for there is no merit in awe and recognition of emotion unless it leads to improved control and understanding, which requires the principles of rationality.

I do not pretend to know what such a religion would look like, because it seems to me that not much serious work has been done on the problem of working out such a religion. To many, whose views on religion are coloured by past and present religious practice, the whole business of 'working out' a religion will seem self-contradictory. Others, whose orientation is more psychological, may regard it with more favour.[1] Plainly there are vast numbers of

[1] See for instance R. B. Cattell's suggestions commented on by J. C. Flugel in *Man, Morals and Society* (pp. 335 ff.).

empirical questions which need to be asked and answered, both about the content of such a religion and about its outward forms and ritual, before even a tolerably clear sketch could be made; and I shall not pursue this task here. But, if what I have said above is at all on the right lines, it is a task that very much needs pursuing.

This should not convey the impression that psychological understanding and control can *take over* from what survives of religion in our culture, in the way that scientific understanding and control has already robbed religion – or what passed as religion – of a large part of itself. If we are concerned with control and understanding in this sense, the obvious candidate to take over from religion (at least in a culture which is economically and materially secure) is psychiatry. Where we are interested in education, perhaps particularly where our religion is wrong, inappropriate, irrational (or whatever word we may find we want to use), we may indeed advocate methods not wholly disconnected from the methods of psychiatry. But religion is not itself a form of education: it is essentially a social form whose proper function is to keep alive a certain kind of awareness of certain appropriate objects. Sound religion will survive psychiatry: just as good art will survive it, just as other rational emotions and expressions of emotion will survive it. Only psychiatrists who suppose that all religion must be irrational would feel disposed to deny this. No doubt much religion is in practice irrational: but this does not tell against religion as such.

The notion of building ourselves a religion, of using our autonomy in the field of religious belief and worship (as we have begun to use it in the field of morality and as we have used it for some centuries in the field of science) demands more psychological maturity than most people at present enjoy. Many arguments about religion are in practice fruitless, because in practice most believers have wrenched and distorted the religious form of life and discourse into a shape which is designed to insulate them from understanding and assessing the merits and purposes of that form of life and discourse as a whole. To such people, some of the most crucial features in the religious mode are ultimate, unquestionable, 'beyond the scope of reason'. Much of their thought, when their backs are against the wall, is of the form 'You may say what you like, but somehow I just know . . .' or 'I just feel certain . . .' or 'it's true for me, anyway'. We are reminded of naïve intuitionism in moral thinking, or the insulated certainty of infatuated lovers. Because of this attitude, non-believers (and certain philosophers after the style of Kierkegaard and Wittgenstein) have simply assumed that this insulation is part of the essence of religious belief. Psychologically, this may have been often or even always the case: logically, as I have tried to argue, it is not; and the distinction is of immense practical importance for the future.

It seems to me (to speak personally) that any open-minded, sensitive and serious person must feel the tension of two forces. On the one hand, it will be strange if there are not *some* elements or features of religious practice which make a strong appeal to him: this may be the words of the Church of England collects, or of the Bible; the emotive force of a Bach chorale or a Gregorian chant; the Sunday evening service at his old school; the *numen* of a cathedral or a country church – anything, depending on his cultural background and psychological disposition. On the other, it will also be strange if he does not feel the need to make some kind of sense of these feelings – to consider their appropriateness, to wonder whether any or all of them are really 'religious' or whether they could not be evoked and catered for in other ways, to ask questions about the form of life as a whole and its virtues for other people besides himself (including his children). In order to answer these questions, he must be able to stand, at different times, both inside and outside the religious form of life. Only such people, in my view, are likely to make much contribution either to the philosophy of religion or to the religious health of themselves and their fellow-men.

APPENDIX III

'Outlooks' and other people's interests

In this book I have been specifically concerned with religion and the emotions, particularly with the ways in which emotions can be reasonable or unreasonable. I have said nothing about the component PHIL (concern for the interests of other people as equals), which in our first publication was shown to be particularly relevant to moral education in general;[1] and I add this Note chiefly in order to explain the relevance of PHIL to what we have described as 'ideals' or (to use a more general term) 'outlooks'.[2]

PHIL, in our shorthand language, is used to refer to an attitude. A person shows PHIL if he is concerned for other people, acknowledges their rights as equals, grants their desires and interests the same weight as his own, and so on. This would normally involve at least (a) the *belief* that other people counted in this way, (b) a *feeling* of concern in relation to other people, and (c) appropriate *action* taken as a result of this belief and feeling. We are dealing, then, with a *particular* attitude or outlook which could be contrasted with very different attitudes or outlooks: and all these could be subjected to the same criteria of rationality for the education of the emotions, the criteria I have outlined in our final taxonomy in Chapter 10.

So far as the main purposes of this book go, then, it is not my intention to defend either PHIL or any other particular attitude or outlook at the bar of rationality. For the criteria of rationality with which we have been concerned would operate even if there were no question of other people's interests at all – if, for instance, a man were to guide his life by some outlook while living on a desert island. Nevertheless, in practice most people do not live on desert islands, so that the question of the rationality of the particular attitude PHIL is of considerable importance. Some of the problems

[1] See *I.M.E.*, pp. 76–83.
[2] See Chapter 2.

here have been discussed at length by various philosophers.[1] They
are extremely complicated, and I can do no more here than sketch
out the lines on which I think one conceptual argument[2] might be
constructed.[3]

A

1. First, it is primarily a minimal interpretation of PHIL that I wish
to defend. This interpretation is such that to defend it is not to
defend what would normally be called an unselfish or altruistic way
of life for individuals or social groups: e.g. a co-operative rather
than a competitive or *laissez-faire* economy, or a life of self-sacrifice
rather than a life of buccaneering. It is rather to defend that notion
of justice or equality or status which I take to underlie agreements,
contracts and common policies of all kinds, whatever their content
may be. Any social group can agree to arrange its life on the basis
of a harshly competitive game, or on the basis of constant mutual
co-operation. What I am concerned with here is whether there is a
PHIL-type agreement in the first place: that is, an agreement in
which all the individuals of the group have an equal *voice*. Whether
the content of the agreement is reasonable or unreasonable is a
different question.

2. We are talking, then, about respect for the outlooks and aims of
others, however lunatic, weak-kneed, fanatical or irrational they
may appear; about what Professor Hare says the 'liberal' does – that
is, 'he acknowledges, as part of his ideal, the ideal of toleration –
that is to say a readiness to respect other people's ideals as if they
were his own'.[4] 'Respect' does not here mean anything like 'think
wise', 'approve of', or 'admire'. It means rather 'allow equal weight
to'. The model case, or at least a model case, of 'respect' in this sense
is during a discussion between people each of whom is prepared

---

[1] See in particular R. M. Hare, *Freedom and Reason*, Chapter 9: and references
given in *I.M.E.*, pp. 102–8: also R. M. Hare's remarks in *Jowett Papers*, ed.
B. Y. Khanbhai *et al.* (Blackwell 1970), pp. 50–52.

[2] Some points in what follows are worked out in greater detail in Mr T.
Nagel's *The Possibility of Altruism*, which I am grateful for having seen before
publication.

[3] Other arguments, both conceptual and empirical, may also be possible,
some of which are mentioned in *I.M.E.*, pp. 102–8.

[4] op. cit., p. 177.

to listen to and take seriously what the other person has to say. Here I may think your views foolish in this extreme, but I respect you as a person who, like myself, *has* views, and is entitled to a fair hearing. If I can convince you, by the light of some criterion that we both accept, that your views are foolish, well and good: but the discussion starts with the presumption that both views are of equal status, that both deserve attention, and that (in this sense) both have equal weight or importance. But of course there are plenty of other cases. I may want to go to Italy for a holiday, and my friend to Spain: I may subscribe to an ideal of extreme tidiness in my flat, whereas my wife may prefer a way of life which is in this respect less stringent: I may prefer a multi-racial society, my neighbour a racially segregated one. In all these cases we commonly suppose, not that each want or ideal is necessarily as reasonable as its opposite, but that each has as much right to be considered: and we further suppose that, if one party is not persuaded that the other's view is in fact more reasonable or wiser, some sort of bargain or compromise should be made. We do not suppose, at least in many cases, that either party is entitled simply to *override* the other.

3. 'To have ... an ideal is, at least, to want something (e.g. .... to want a society free from Jews).'[1] The force of this does not depend only on the implication of wanting inherent in such words as 'ideal', 'values', etc. If something is to be seriously called *my* ideal, as opposed simply to an ideal of which I happen to be aware, it must be backed by some kind of will or (in a broad sense)[2] desire on my part. I must want or wish it to be realized, prescribe it for myself and perhaps for others, show some pleasure when it looks like being realized, be willing to work or vote for it, and so forth. If there are no such signs to be noticed in me, no indication that I *want* anything, we should have no reasons for saying that this was *my* ideal rather than that it was an ideal that I merely had in mind or was familiar with. This remains true even if it seems more apt to talk of a man's 'ultimate values', standards, criteria, principles, 'preferred society', 'desired way of life', etc., rather than of his 'ideal'. In so far as any of these are his, they are something that he wants to use or to realize in action.

---

[1] R. M. Hare, op. cit., p. 169.
[2] See Chapter 6, p. 83.

4. Next, a person who wants something always has at least *one* reason for trying to get it. This reason is that he thinks that getting what he wants will in some way benefit or advantage him or someone else (make him happier, satisfy him, be good for him).[1] The logical fact that he has a reason for trying to get what he wants is conceptually distinct from the psychological fact that he may also have some impulse or motivating force which drives him towards getting what he wants. A man's behaviour may be *explained* or predicted in terms of such impulses, even when the man has no reason or *justification* for following them (because he does not think that following them will do him any good). Reasons, in this sense, are interpersonal. My being hungry may explain my grabbing food: but my being hungry can only justify my grabbing food if 'being hungry' in general is a justification of 'grabbing food' in general: that is, if I can represent myself as one case or instance of a general principle of justification – if I or anyone else so placed *ought* to grab food when hungry.[2]

5. I now want to envisage a case (surely very common) where this turns out to be a man's *only* reason for trying to get something – in this context, trying to realize an ideal (set of principles, standards, criteria, values, etc.) in the empirical world. We build up this case by pressing a person until we arrive at what we may call his 'ultimate' ideal. As we saw in Chapter 5, a man may of course have reasons *within* the framework of an ideal. X may be asked by Y why he intends to fight the duel, and answer in terms of 'not backing down', 'behaving like a gentleman (or a gunfighter)', and so on. These reasons may not be acceptable to Y, who will continue to press his questions: and eventually it will transpire that X follows an ideal of 'honour' which he does not attempt to defend by any external reasons: it is just that this is the kind of life or society he finds satisfying, in the same way that Y may find it more satisfying to apologize instead of fighting, and subscribe to some more Epicurean ideal for which, again, he has no external justification. Of course this impasse may not occur: X and Y may find and be prepared to use common ground at some higher level ('the survival of society', for

---

[1] ibid.

[2] There is of course much more to be said about this, perhaps particularly that reasons or justifications can figure in explanations (when X does what he ought to do because he sees that he ought to do it).

instance) or one of the two may, under questioning, come to regard his ideal as something which he only wanted compulsively: that is, he may become more 'emotionally educated' and no longer *endorse* these wants, or come to want different things. But there may be an impasse of the kind described.

6. The logical nature of this impasse is important for our argument. I am envisaging a situation in which neither X and Y can quote any reasons which are acceptable to the other party: where it appears that they have no stock of reasons in common. It is not too mis-leading to say here that X and Y are driven back on their 'ultimate values'. We must remember, of course, that these 'values' may take the form of ideals, principles, rules, standards, and so forth. If X and Y are sophisticated, the impasse may consist of a clash between second-order views about what should count as a reason ('whatever is relevant to honour' as against 'whatever makes for comfort'). But in all these cases, it seems that X and Y can no longer *argue* interpersonally for their respective views: that they have run out of reasons accepted as valid by both.

7. Yet there is still a sense in which either X or Y may say that his ideal (set of principles, stock of reasons, etc.) is desirable, or good, or right, or that it ought to be followed. Such words and phrases, of course, imply the existence of some kind of rule, criterion, or reason: and there is still one kind of reason left. This, as we saw, is simply that X and Y both *want* their 'ultimate values' to be realized; that they both think that this realization would be in some way satisfying. Each would, perhaps, be happier, or less guilt-ridden, or less dissatisfied. Left to themselves – that is, if the empirical world allowed both X and Y to practise their ideals without conflict – each would be justified in doing so, and it would be reasonable (not just understandable) that they should. Of course X or Y may need to be pressed very hard to arrive at this point. X may say that his justification is not as general as 'anybody's getting satisfaction', but limited to (say) 'gunfighters getting satis-faction'. This, he claims, is still a justification: it is merely an accident that he himself is a gunfighter (if indeed he is). But once again the question arises for X of what reason he has for adopting this principle. The principle is *part* of X's 'ultimate values', and not shared by Y. Y will ask him why *that* should count as a reason: and X's answer can only be that he, X, *wants* to go in for that sort

of reason. But now Y wants to go in for another sort of reason, so that once again they are on equal terms.

8. One might think that X could claim that what he or anyone else wants or thinks will bring satisfaction to him is quite irrelevant, even at this stage of the argument. His own set of reasons are hermetically sealed: he *ends* by saying something like 'because it's honourable' and refuses to go further. He says to Y: 'Well, there is my ideal, my stock of reasons: it's too bad that it touches yours at no point. You can take it or leave it: but at any rate I shall pursue it.' But to this Y can reply: 'But you have no *reason* to pursue it, if you refuse to use the last-ditch reason that you think it will satisfy you. You can't intelligibly claim that your ideal is *right*, or that you *ought* to pursue it, since these words imply some higher rule, standard or criterion which *ex hypothesi* you deny. Either you grant that its being your ideal, something wanted and thought satisfying by you, *is* a reason for its being realized – and I am fully prepared to grant this, noting only that there is equal reason for my ideal being realized, since that also is a case of something wanted by somebody: or else you regard what you and anyone else wants as irrelevant, in which case you have no reason at all. Each of us prefers his own ideal: but why should your preferences prevail, just because they are yours? If I cannot convince you that my type of reasons is logically appropriate, I am prepared to grant equal weight or validity to your type: and must you not grant the same? For now each of us has run out of other reasons: we are left only with our own wants. If you don't even count wanting as a reason, then neither of us has any reason at all; if you do count wanting as a reason, my wants and yours – and the wants of any creature that can be said to *have* wants and satisfy them – are equally cases of wanting, and have equal validity: so that neither of us is rationally entitled to override the other – we must go on arguing, or make some kind of compromise.'

9. Hare quotes[1] the case of three people dividing chocolate: they all have an equal liking for chocolate, and no other considerations are thought to be relevant: and 'it seems to us obvious that the just way to divide the chocolate is equally'. This is intelligible only on the assumption that 'liking' provides a reason; and so of course

---

[1] op. cit., pp. 118–19.

it does. But this argument can be pushed to cover ideals. If we say that X's ultimate ideal or outlook is x, Y's y, Z's z and so forth, then the *only* reason X can give for having *his* ideal realized is that one person wants it (X), the only reason Y can give is that one person wants it (Y), etc. These reasons are equipollent: and a moment's reflection by Y and Z will show each that each has no more right, reason, or justification for having his ideal realized than any other of the three. One man's good, we might briefly say, is as important as another's: for this sort of reason for a man's claiming something as good connects with the satisfaction of wants in general, and not just with *his* satisfaction.

10. Given the above considerations, it becomes easy to see the merits of PHIL-type ideals in a wider sense: that is, of ideals which either do not conflict with other people's wants and interests, or which themselves include the satisfaction of other people's wants and interests – for instance, the Christian ideal of love. It is a step forward, indeed, if our ideals are merely not mutually exclusive: if X's ideal can be realized without inhibiting the realization of Y's. For this allows full satisfaction both to X and Y, whereas conflicting ideals necessitate a compromise in which both parties inevitably suffer in the cause of rationality. But it is a much bigger step forward if X's ideal consists or partly consists of helping Y to realize his ideal, and *vice versa*: for this does not only avoid conflict, but by mutual co-operation furthers the ideals of both and hence the satisfaction of both.

11. What this last point shows, however, is simply that *if* X and Y had that sort of ideal it would be mutually beneficial. However, to have an ideal is at least partly to want something and find satisfaction in it: and this involves X and Y being a certain kind of *person* – the kind of person who finds satisfaction in helping another man, rather than who merely thinks that he ought to find satisfaction in this way. The position here is quite different from the position as regards the minimal PHIL that we have spent most of our time discussing. If X and Y have conflicting ideals, reason demands that they should reach a compromise, even though both of them accept some loss of satisfaction thereby. The demands of reason here need not involve that they should *change* their ideals or their feelings, since at that particular time (for the purposes of that particular deal) this may be impossible. Reason also demands that they should be

the sort of people that have mutually co-operative PHIL-type ideals: and no doubt they should keep on trying to be that sort of person. But until they are, they should not pretend that they are. If in fact X and Y get more satisfaction by pursuing their own ideals independently and in private, for instance, it is no use their trying to act as if this were not so – unless of course this is a good way of changing themselves as people, or of coming really to hold PHIL-type ideals.

B

The foregoing is one argument for the rationality of PHIL. But since we are concerned with practical education as well as philosophical argument, various points must be added.

First, I do not suppose that very many people will acquire more PHIL by having this argument pointed out to them, or that arguments of this type are in any simple sense valuable to the practising teacher. There are, no doubt, some people who are genuinely uncertain about whether other people's interests ought to be taken into account: and perhaps rather more people who are genuinely uncertain about the proper range of 'other people' (do children count? Martians? lunatics?). But there are, I would guess, far more who are not in serious doubt about the importance of other people's interests: who take this importance for granted, or even regard it as a defining characteristic of morality. It would be absurd to represent the world as only waiting for a watertight academic argument before immediately devoting itself to love and altruism.

In our view PHIL is the attitude that a rational person would have towards other people: that is, an attitude that would naturally accrue from an adequate supply of EMP, GIG and KRAT. Such a person would (with or without the assistance of academic arguments) recognize the existence of other people and understand their feelings: he would know that they were his equals, and have enough motivation to accord them their rights. Now it is, I suppose, conceivable that certain men might lack the intellectual or perceptual ability to appreciate that other men were men like themselves: and of course it is very common for men to talk as if some classes of other men (negroes, Jews, women, slaves), whilst human, somehow did not really count as important, as if their interests could be overridden. Hence I do not want to deny the twin possibilities

(1) that someone, for lack of GIG, really might not know that some entity *was* a person, or (2) that someone, for lack of EMP, might fail to realize that some human being had interests, desires, feelings and intentions in the same way that other human beings did.

Nevertheless, I should still guess that the major obstacles were not the lack of *knowledge* of the 'hard' facts, or the *ability* to know what other people felt (GIG and EMP). I would guess that the obstacles lie rather in the direction of KRAT(1) and (2): that is, in bringing this knowledge and ability to bear in specific cases, thinking seriously and responsibly about such cases, and being able to act and feel appropriately as a result of such thinking. I know, of course, that some writers (and many illiterates) appear to hold, as a serious theory, that certain classes of human beings do not count: though perhaps such theories are less common than they seem. (For instance, to hold that women and 'people with slavish dispositions', as Aristotle calls them, should be in inferior positions is not to hold that their wants and interests are unimportant: it might be the case that both their wants and interests are best served by keeping them in such positions, *if* – of course a big if – the psychological facts are as writers like Aristotle, Nietzsche and others maintain.)

How 'serious' these theories are is an open question. Not many of them convey the air of rational conclusions rationally arrived at; and quite a few look more like rationalizations arrived at, whether consciously or unconsciously, *ad hoc*: as for instance Nazi theories about Aryans and non-Aryans. A Nazi who was, in the relevant sense, 'serious', would be likely to be convinced by what Professor Hare has to say to him in Chapter 9 of his *Freedom and Reason*, or perhaps by the kind of argument we have outlined in 1 above. But, as anyone who has ever argued with such people knows, Nazis are not in this sense 'serious'. They would twist words, go round in circles, stop arguing and start shouting or hitting. The same applies, of course, to many people besides Nazis. Naturally such people are 'serious' in a quite different sense: that is, their emotions are strong, they feel passionately, and so forth. But they are not *intellectually* serious: and they are not likely to be much helped by intellectual argument.

This is not at all to say that such intellectual arguments are not worth deploying: if only because we cannot simply assume that those who disagree with us are 'not serious'. Further, the deployment

APPENDIX IV

'Insight'

Each of the components mentioned in our final taxonomy – GIG, EMP and KRAT – would justify a lengthy discussion, both from the conceptual point of view and from the point of view of practical education. This would be too great a task to undertake here: but I want to consider briefly in this note one particular ability (a kind of EMP). The chief justification for doing so is, perhaps, that there are a number of conceptual points about this ability and its development which need to be cleared up: but I must confess also to two strongly held opinions. First, I believe that this ability is of particular practical importance for the education of the emotions and for moral education, and that lack of it causes a large part of our practical difficulties. I do not think that teachers, parents and other educators will achieve very much in this field without a proper understanding of the ability, and a whole-hearted attempt to develop it in children and adolescents. Secondly, I believe that for the most part this understanding is not there, and that the attempt is not made. In consequence there seems to me to be an appallingly dangerous gap, which must be filled.

I shall call this ability 'insight', a term used constantly in works on psychiatry, psychology and the social sciences, though it is not often clear what is meant. The word suggests something more specific than merely awareness of knowledge in the particular field of one's own or other people's feelings. If I see somebody fuming and shouting and shaking his fist, we should hardly say that it was by exercising *insight* that I come to know that he is angry. A more sensible use for 'insight', and one which seems to correspond more to the instances of insight quoted at least in psychoanalytic literature, is to regard it as the ability to detect *unconscious* or *hidden* feelings, beliefs, etc. in oneself and other people. Here we shall be chiefly concerned with the former: that is, insight into one's own hidden feelings (a special kind of AUTEMP as opposed to ALLEMP).

It is well known, not only to psychotherapists, but to the human race generally, that insight into one's own irrational beliefs or feelings is often not sufficient to remove them. I may know that I unconsciously fear disaster or punishment; and I may even know (if the example may be granted) that I unconsciously believe that, by touching every lamp-post in the street or arranging my possessions with unreasonable meticulousness, this disaster or punishment can be averted: and I may know that both the fear and the belief are irrational. Yet I may still go on, and in one sense want to go on, behaving as I have done. With conscious fears and beliefs the case is different. I may fear to travel in a car because I believe that X is driving and that X is a bad driver: but once I learn either that X is not driving or that X is in fact a very safe driver, my fear is likely to disappear. If it did *not* disappear, indeed, we should suspect some cause or (perhaps unconscious) reason other than this straightforward fear and belief. Insight alone does not cure: or, in less clinical language, awareness of our secret faults does not by itself produce moral or spiritual improvement. We may 'repent' in the sense of coming to recognize that our fears, desires, beliefs, etc. are inappropriate or irrational: but we shall not necessarily 'repent' in the sense of changing those fears, desires, etc. This is a phenomenon sufficiently familiar to everybody.

Nevertheless, the importance of insight into one's own irrationalities is very considerable, even if no change of feeling results. It derives from the change of *attitude* which such insight, if it results in new beliefs sincerely held, even only at the conscious level, will necessarily bring. A man who comes to believe that his anger is unreasonable, and is prepared to admit this to other people (itself a fair test of the sincerity of his new belief), places himself in a new and far more satisfactory position both *vis-à-vis* his fellow men and as regards his own ultimate chances of improvement. For (a) he can say to his fellow men, in effect, 'Look, I'm very sorry about this, but I have an unreasonably bad temper at times: it's not you I'm really angry with then – I'm still fighting some unconscious battle with my father. I know this is a nuisance, but my conscious self disowns it: please regard me as ill or slightly mad on these occasions – in any case, I shall certainly not try to justify my anger any longer. If I go really crazy, I give you full permission to restrain me or lock me up; and if I ever have to be particularly diplomatic and tactful in my job, I'll try to get somebody else to deputize for me: I'll try to improve my temper', and so forth.[1] This changes his whole public *status*, in respect of these occasions; other men may find this tiresome, but they can no longer morally resent it.[2] Further (b), he now knows that he *is* unreasonable (it's not the fault of stupid friends, the weather, rheumatism, the Labour Government, etc.), and hence has a chance of cure. He can strive to acquire the grace of God, or go to a psychoanalyst, or induce the habit of counting up to ten before he speaks, or whatever.

Both insight (as we have defined it) and other less complex cases of the ability to identify one's own feelings, involve more than (a) the mere awareness *that* one is angry, frightened, etc.: more too than (b) knowledge of some early conditioning-experience which has set up a recurring behaviour-pattern. It is comparatively easy to identify one's emotions in so far as this is just a matter of identifying symptoms or actions: a man may find himself choking or snarling or clenching his fist, and readily perceive – if he stops to attend to himself at all – that he is angry. But for a full awareness of his emotion he needs also to know the *target* of his anger, and what

---

[1] A well-known example here is *Julius Caesar*, IV, 3:

BRUTUS: When I spoke that, I was ill-tempered too.
CASSIUS: Do you confess so much? Give me your hand.
BRUTUS: And my heart too.
CASSIUS: O, Brutus –
BRUTUS: What's the matter?
CASSIUS: Have you not love enough to bear with me
When that rash humour which my mother gave me
Makes me forgetful?
BRUTUS: Yes, Cassius: and from henceforth
When you are over-earnest with your Brutus
He'll think your mother chides, and leave you so.

[2] I incline to think that this is as significant, at least in a great many human situations, as what another person may or may not *do*. For, firstly, the self-confessed unreliability of the other person allows one to readjust one's expectations and take precautions; secondly and more importantly, one is no longer *at war* with him, so to speak: both parties are on the same side, in that they are in moral agreement. For instance, what is annoying about a person habitually being late is not chiefly that he *is* late (which often hardly matters), but rather (i) that one tends to assume that he will be on time, and is therefore often disappointed, and (ii) that he doesn't seem to be aware that being late is a form of contract-breaking – he doesn't realize that he is behaving unreasonably and immorally, or why he is behaving thus. He is not *repentant*. (See also P. F. Strawson, *Freedom and Resentment* (O.U.P. 1962.)).

Q

it is that he (consciously or unconsciously) *believes*: and this is usually much more difficult. The reason why it is more difficult is important: it is that often he has to bring the belief to consciousness, and that this involves a much more sophisticated process than merely noticing that he is (say) choking or clenching his fist. It entails the self-discovery of the hidden belief that generates his anger, of *why* he is angry: a more difficult matter than simply realizing *that* he is.

In *The Kreutzer Sonata*, Tolstoy describes his unhappy marriage. He realizes in retrospect that he felt obstinate and angry and unwilling to yield a point to his wife *because* it would mean 'yielding to her, and that I could not do'. But at the time (we may assume) Tolstoy did not say 'I am angry because I do not want to yield to her': still less did he go further and try to discover why 'yielding to her' was something that he believed to be intolerable. Had he done so, it is likely that the anger would have diminished, if not vanished: or at least, that he would have been able to deal with it in some more satisfactory way: for the mere process of *saying to himself*, for instance, 'I feel angry because I feel threatened', or '. . . because I feel smothered' (possible unconscious reasons why 'yielding to her' is 'intolerable') would show him the inappropriateness of anger to the situation. For the threats and the smothering are not real. To put it another way, it is only in one sense of 'mean' that to yield the point 'meant' yielding to her: that is, yielding the point was for Tolstoy a *symbol* of being threatened or smothered, a psychological equivalent. But of course in another sense of 'mean', 'yielding the point' means nothing of the kind: there is no logical equivalent. To be able to *say* (as Tolstoy could retrospectively) that yielding the point meant yielding to her is to be well on the road to realizing that this 'meaning' is Tolstoy's own, and does not derive from anything in the real world.

Tolstoy's description is remarkable, in a pre–Freudian author, for its conceptual (as well as intuitive) grasp of the nature of the situation.

To live like that would have been awful had we *understood our position*: but we neither understood nor saw it. Both salvation and punishment for man lie in the fact that if he lives wrongly he can befog himself so as *not to see* the misery of his position. And this we did. She *tried to forget* herself in intense and always hurried occupation with household affairs. . . . Thus we lived in a perpetual fog, *not seeing the con-*

dition we were in. And if what did happen had not happened, I should have gone on living so to old age and should have thought, when dying, that I had led a good life.

In the same passage: 'Charcot would certainly have said that my wife was hysterical and that I was abnormal, and he would no doubt have tried to *cure* me. But there was nothing to *cure*.' To this is attached, in the copies circulated in Russia when the book was banned:

> All this mental illness of ours occurred simply because we lived immorally. We suffered from our immoral life, and to smother our suffering we committed various abnormal acts – just what those doctors call 'indications of mental disease' – hysterics. It cannot be cured by any suggestions or bromides, but *it is necessary to recognize* what the pain comes from.

The recognition of which Tolstoy speaks, and which Freud and his followers more fully describe, is on our interpretation a *conceptual* necessity. The 'patient' who 'suffers' from the 'disease' has to *relearn*: he has to face the situation, recognize it for what it is, and learn a better (more reasonable) way of dealing with it, if he is to be 'cured'. The 'symptoms' – that is, particular items in his behaviour or feelings that derive from his earlier mislearning – may of course be removed by other means: he could leave his wife, take drugs, remain permanently in a drunken stupor, or (perhaps) work so hard that he could avoid facing the real situation. But this would not make an unhappy marriage happy: it would, *pro tanto*, only abolish rather than solve the problem of how to live happily with one's wife.

How, in general, can a man acquire this kind of knowledge? This is a vast question: but we may at least notice an important distinction between (a) coming to know what one feels by some inductive or quasi-scientific process, and (b) coming to know what one feels by a process of more direct observation, which involves something like *recreating*, and hence consciously entertaining, the feelings and the beliefs that go with them. We are sometimes tempted to say that a person does not 'really' know what he feels unless he does (b): but this is a mistake. In the normal sense of 'know', a man can come to know what he feels by either process. (The temptation here is analogous to the temptation to say that A can never 'really know' that B feels such-and-such, because A doesn't feel it himself: and perhaps also that a blind man cannot 'really know' that the sky is blue, because he can't see that it is. The error here arises from assimilating 'know' to words like 'see' or 'feel', as if knowing always implied some kind of direct perception or acquaintance.) Nevertheless, there are important differences in the two processes.

To extend our previous example, suppose I get angry with my wife on certain occasions: suppose I notice this, and wonder why. I might start by saying that it's 'because she's so stupid': my friend, however, points out that there are plenty of other occasions on which my wife is just as stupid (or just as sensible), but when I do not get angry at all. By narrowing down and isolating the relevant factors, he may be able to demonstrate that it is probably an unconscious feeling of being threatened or not being loved that makes me get angry. Or I myself might coolly note a few facts about my behaviour, and correlate them with some well-established psychoanalytic theory (if any such theory can be regarded as well-established). I could say, in principle, something like 'Well, I am a youngest child, spoilt by my parents, and I often get angry with my wife, so probably I unconsciously expect my wife to love me like a mother, and I get angry because (if she doesn't agree with me all the time) I unconsciously think she doesn't love me', etc., etc. (spelt out at greater length). All this knowledge would be (so to speak) theoretical; that is, not accompanied by a re-living of the relevant feelings, and hence not likely to bring about any changes in my feelings. But it would still result in knowledge, even if it is unlikely that I could ever acquire any *detailed* knowledge by this method (for reasons given below). Here the first method ((a) above) would have been used.

This is a conclusion I can also come to, however, by a quite different process: my friend, acting as an amateur analyst, might say 'What do you mean, "stupid"?' and I might reply 'Well, she doesn't see what I mean – sometimes I don't think she even *tries* to see', and so on – gradually working my way round to recreating the anger in myself, but this time giving it a fuller conceptual description. (One might say that here I *remember the anger*, as opposed to simply remembering *that* I was angry.) On the original occasion when I was angry with her, I may not have conceptualized any reasons at all; then I move to saying 'it's because she's so stupid'; then I move to saying 'it's because she doesn't even try to understand me'; and finally I might realize that her behaviour (perhaps through no fault of her own) is taken by me as a sign of her not loving me. Here I shall have used method (b).

This is not to say that reaching the conclusion (that I am angry because I feel unloved) is, in (b), a matter of using some magical power of introspection. It is a matter of being more honest with myself, of taking time off to examine my feelings and beliefs more precisely, and above all of having a context of communication in which I am encouraged both to recreate the feeling and to conceptualize it more fully. This is usually impossible in everyday life, just because everything happens so quickly: my wife says something, and before we know where we are a whole system of unconscious beliefs and emotions has been brought into play, so that we find ourselves quarrelling. The only thing to do here is to retrace one's steps (in more complex cases, this may involve retracing them back to one's childhood), so that I have time to appreciate just what I believe and feel at each stage.

We gave reasons above (p. 229) for saying that even the 'theoretical' knowledge acquired by method (a) is extremely valuable: but it is not hard to see the advantages of using (b). The point here is not (what is false) that (b) results in a *logically* superior kind of knowledge: nor only (what is true) that (b) is more likely to result in a change of feelings than (a). It is also that (b) is greatly superior to (a) *as a method of collecting evidence*. Though prolonged and careful observation, either on my own account or by another person, may produce the knowledge required, the complexities of human belief and emotion are such that we need more, and more detailed, evidence than we are likely to get by this method. We need to play the tape-recording again at a slower speed, so to speak, in order that each individual note and nuance may emerge more clearly: and we also need the person's own explications, glosses, and annotations on what has been recorded.

This brief and bird's-eye view of the *a priori* merits of method (b) as a means of acquiring insight should naturally indicate to educators the kind of context that will be required if method (b) is to be successful. Since the person must (i) recreate his feelings and (ii) inspect and interpret them, the educator is required to play two roles: (i) to act as 'the other person' towards whom the man has felt in this or that way, so that he can reproduce his original feelings in the educational context, and (ii) to guide (not force) his conscious intelligence towards a correct interpretation. Both these are well known to psychotherapists, and there is a vast literature about them both, usually under the respective titles of 'the transference' and 'interpretation'. I mention them here chiefly to suggest that for education of this kind, (i) and (ii) are not merely the inventions of psychoanalytic writers, representing practices and methods which may or may not be useful in particular cases, but are rather conceptually required by any form of education which aims at increasing insight by method (b), a method which seems to have peculiar merits of its own.

By acting as 'the other person' in this way, the educator has of course the opportunity not only to develop insight in the pupil, but also to alter his actual feelings: in our language, to improve not only his EMP but also his KRAT. For he thereby provides a context in which the pupil can measure the inappropriate emotions (of which he is now aware) against the real situation. The pupil can come to see, not only that he feels that the educator is hostile to him just as (for example) he felt that his father was, but also that the educator is in fact not hostile. Because the educator remains neutral, and does not return fear or hostility with hostility, in the way that another pupil or a private person might, he gives the pupil the chance to start the relearning process on a secure basis. The pupil comes to *trust* the educator, because the educator is the only person who does not react emotionally to the pupil's fear of hostility in the way that the pupil expects (and probably unconsciously tries to produce). There is now for the pupil at least one person with whom he may form a relationship free from the pushes and pulls of inappropriate emotions; one person with whom he may communicate; one person who, whilst refusing to join with him in his neurotic game, is nevertheless on his side.

If I am right about the importance of this context both for this kind of EMP and for KRAT, then a great many practical problems arise for teachers and other educators. They will include (1) problems about how, in more precise terms than I have given above, the educator is to operate within such contexts; but also (2) problems about how schools and other institutions are to be organized so that such contexts are actually used; and (3) the way in which these particular contexts relate to other contexts of equal importance but with a different function (e.g. group cohesion or reinforcement of social solidarity). This affects all those practical issues connected with house-systems and tutor-groups, school counselling, the ability of teachers to play various roles at different times, teacher-training, and many others. We need here a much clearer account of different categories or contexts, each with its own particular function, and each shown to be related to one or more of our moral components. Only then shall we be able to escape from talking vaguely about the 'atmosphere' or 'ethos' of a school, its 'social norms', and so forth: and we shall at least begin to have some idea of what we are trying to achieve at different times, and by different features, within the school.

APPENDIX V

'Mental health', delinquency, etc.

There is the same sort of muddle, and the same sort of anxiety, about 'mental health' as there is about religion: and they operate in the world of education in particular, as well as in society generally. For it is very hard to maintain that 'mental health' is not importantly connected with education in some sense of the word. Even if we draw a sharp – perhaps too sharp – distinction between teaching and curing, and hold that the ordinary teacher or university tutor need have nothing to do with 'mental health', it is still going to be highly relevant to those who *plan* schools, universities and other educational institutions. And for this reason alone it is going to be difficult to maintain that the ordinary teachers and tutors within those institutions need know nothing about it.

Yet it is equally plain that none of us is very clear about what 'mental health' *is*. Is it, indeed, something which can be left almost entirely to doctors, like physical health? (Though this isn't really true even of physical health, as perhaps our belief in the merits of 'physical education' suggests.) Do psychiatrists cure people as doctors do? Is having a neurosis like having a tumour on the brain? How far does 'mental health' come into other things we try to do in schools under the vague titles of 'moral education', 'personal relations', 'social skills', 'learning to live', and so on? All these questions are just as baffling as those concerned with religious belief; and they may be even more pressing. More thought has perhaps been devoted by educationalists and philosophers to religion than to 'mental health'; but this may not be so in future. Many issues that have hitherto been discussed under the general topic-heading of 'religion' may very soon be discussed under the heading of 'mental health'. Changing the topic-heading will not of course help to clarify the issues: and if we do not get clear about them, we shall simply have the same muddles that we had about religion all over again, under a new heading.

The reactions to the conceptual difficulties about 'mental health' parallel the reactions to the difficulties about religion:

(a) Just as some rely upon what is currently believed in this culture, or upon a particular church or creed, to tell them what religion is, so some rely upon the norms of contemporary society or upon 'modern psychology' (or whatever is the prevailing fashion therein) to tell them what is to count as 'mental health'.

(b) By contrast, just as some wish to free religious education from the fetters of a particular religion, so others will want a specification of 'mental health' which is not culture-bound, i.e. which is not conceived in terms of adjustment or conformity to the particular standards of this society; and as the former will talk vaguely about 'ultimate reality', 'commitment', 'apprehension of the nature of things', etc., so the latter will talk vaguely of 'awareness', 'integration', 'normality', and 'self-development'.

(c) Just as, for lack of any clear view about what the aims of religious education should be, some propose to drop religious instruction altogether, so there are those who would look askance at any attempt to build the concept of 'mental health' more effectively into education, for fear that we may be indoctrinating or brain-washing our children into accepting some particular and partisan view of what is 'mentally healthy'.

I have written something on this topic elsewhere[1], and need not repeat it here. But it may be noted that the existing distinctions that we find in administration, and in our national life generally, do not at all correspond to the real distinctions noticed there or in the present work (Chapters 6 and 7). The concept of 'mental health' is a hybrid, made up partly on the analogy of physical health, but partly also including the notion of rationality and the education of the emotions. A child may be quite 'mentally healthy' in one of these senses, but not in the other. So great are the practical (as well as the conceptual) differences between these two cases that it seems grotesque for both to be subsumed under the aegis of a single administrative department or organization: it is almost as if the Classics Department at a school were also to be responsible for anything which had a linguistic connection with the word 'classics' – teaching 'classic' English authors, or training horses for 'classic'

[1] *Education and the Concept of Mental Health.*

races. The fact is that some 'mental health' cases are strictly 'medical' or 'physical', and have to be dealt with by doctors: others are strictly 'educational', and have to be dealt with by educators. Only a fool would imagine that the same person can deal with those who suffer from a thyroid deficiency and with those who (in a quite different sense) 'suffer from' false unconscious beliefs, or the misapprehension of other people's feelings.

This is not, of course, to say that we should relapse into trades-unionism or encourage demarcation disputes. We already have too many cases where individual children or adolescents, who need personal attention *as* individuals, slip easily between the gaps left by a plethora of 'experts', all of whom deal with aspects or facets of the individual's life but none of whom actually takes full responsibility for him. There is a great need for someone to take overall responsibility for such cases – indeed for each and every individual child – much as a competent housemaster will feel responsible for the lives of his charges in general, irrespective of whether their problems are concerned with law-breaking, physical illness, moral deficiency, or emotional irrationality; whether they need guidance in their careers, or the loan of a pound or two if they get into financial trouble.

The point I am making is rather that at the political and governmental level, and also at lower levels of administration, there is no critical understanding of the various ways in which those who take this responsibility – be they parents or teachers or doctors – need the support of experts whose expertise is clearly defined. There are, indeed, innumerable bodies with various titles and functions (some of which are vaguer than others) such as 'probation', 'child care', and 'mental health', and the whole apparatus for dealing with children described as 'delinquent', 'maladjusted', 'subnormal', 'backward', 'disturbed', etc. – as if anyone were at all clear about what such terms *meant*. Other organizations are responsible for 'moral welfare', 'the unmarried mother', spastics, autistic children, and so forth. How far such bodies should remain independent, and how far they need to be subsumed under a common administrative famework and a common policy, is a complex question. What I am saying here is that no such policy can be successful, and no such framework efficient, unless based on a clear conceptual understanding of the different needs involved.

In particular, there seems to be a lack of clarity about how far such organizations and the individuals who staff them intend to achieve either of the two logically different types of objectives mentioned briefly on pp. 105-11: that is, how far they intend (a) to improve their patients' or pupils' *rationality* by *education*, and/or (b) to keep them out of trouble, adjust them to society, or attain other desirable ends by methods which need have nothing to do with rationality or education at all. It would be foolish to generalize about the comparative importance of (a) and (b), though there are perhaps reasons for preferring (a) whenever possible.[1] But at least we should try to be clear about what objectives we are trying to attain by what methods. Thus a general title like 'curing drug addicts' may represent (a) an attempt to educate drug addicts so that they no longer feel compelled to take drugs, or (b) simply stopping them from taking drugs. (a) might involve a very lengthy process of education or psychotherapy: (b) might be achieved just by making sure that drugs are not available to them, or by bringing to bear the pressures of authority or peer-groups. Again, we can try (a) to redirect the aggression of a juvenile delinquent by educating him so that he no longer wants or needs to assault people, or (b) simply to check his aggression by locking him up or giving him tranquillizers.

It is not only that a satisfactory *assessment* of the practices of various institutions cannot be made without taking this distinction into account (for the two objectives are very different): it is also that a good deal of the *practical* work, and of the trial and error which inevitably goes on in such institutions, would profit from a clearer understanding of aims. Without it, we are likely to fall victims to a temptation criticized elsewhere,[2] the temptation simply to follow fashion or our own prejudices. 'Tender-minded' or 'progressive' people in charge of Borstals, prisons, or hospitals will be good at treating their patients and pupils as equals and trying to help them as in (a), but will shrink from any tough methods that are required to achieve the more down-to-earth objectives of (b). Conversely, the 'tough-minded' will be prepared to use the methods of force, conditioning or social pressure which are required for (b), but less aware of the importance of (a). Failure to observe the distinction may produce a situation where neither objective is attained because neither is properly understood. The educator, of

[1] See *I.M.E.*, pp. 155-64.
[2] *I.M.E.*, pp. 22-23.

course, is by definition concerned only with (a): but in practice it must be recognized that teachers do other things beside educate. The importance of the distinction for the teacher is the same as it is for (say) the staff of a mental hospital or a Borstal: namely, he must recognize it if he is to tailor his methods to fit the objectives.

Failure to appreciate the distinction results in doctrinaire views, swayed almost entirely by fashion rather than by fact, which do nothing to advance our theory or our practice. Just as it is obvious that in schools teachers are required to play various roles in various contexts, including the extreme 'authoritarian' in order-and-command contexts and the extreme 'liberal' in discussion-contexts or equality-contexts, so it seems equally obvious that in institutions such as prisons, Borstals, approved schools, mental hospitals and elsewhere there are a number of *different* aims, which require *different* methods; and that the idea of only *one* 'ethos', 'atmosphere', 'system' or 'set of rules' is plainly absurd. We have a violent criminal: very well, we need (a) to ensure that he is educated (reformed, improved, made more sane); (b) to ensure somehow – anyhow – that he does not repeat his violence. Quite different methods may be appropriate to these two different aims: there is nothing inconsistent in employing some effective and tough-minded conditioning-process for (b), and a lengthy 'liberal' course of non-directive psychoanalysis for (a), *on the same person*. Only those wedded to some doctrinaire view, to whom certain methods will be irrationally tabu, will find this hard to accept.

APPENDIX VI

Techniques and tools in educating the emotions

I want here to say something about the specific techniques, tools, pieces of equipment and so forth that may be found useful for the education of the emotions.

When we confront the enormous literature on this topic, we may perhaps begin to make some sense of it by distinguishing between (1) specific *activities* (mime, drama, games, impromptu acting, 'creative dance', 'music and movement', role-playing, etc.), and (2) specific *equipment* (films, tape recorders, video-tape machines, machines for programmed learning, and so on). We may judge the merits of (2) partly in terms of how far the items contribute to the activities in (1). What is not at all obvious is how we judge the merits of the activities themselves. Again, we can point out that when research workers have devised the necessary tests and done the necessary experiments, we shall be able to assess these methods in terms of PHIL, EMP, and so on, and thereby give a firm answer to the question of whether they contribute effectively to moral education. But this is still in the future: and in order to make an intelligent assessment of their own, teachers and others need some grasp of the general ways in which such techniques might be thought valuable.

The trouble with getting such a grasp is this: it is easy to say, and constantly said, that pupils enjoy such techniques, that they become less inhibited and more lively, that the techniques are a nice change from the old-style teaching-across-the-desk-tops, that the results are interesting, and that they have an important effect on the pupils' minds and character. But this tells us little or nothing about their *educational* merits. What do the pupils actually *learn* from them? Do these activities just make them enthusiastic and happy, or do they teach them something?

For lack of any really effective instruments to measure their effects, we may easily slip into one of two doctrinaire attitudes. The first would be that of a person who is anxious at all costs to break out of the old-style methods, which seem to him to teach the children nothing of personal or moral importance. The children sit there like logs absorbing, or more probably not absorbing, sets of facts presented nearly always in linguistic rather than visual form: they are lifeless, they don't *do* anything, they are not adequately motivated. So somehow, anyhow, we must get things moving – break down artificial subject-divisions, move the classroom chairs around, forget about examinations, put the children on their feet, fill the school with art and colour, and so forth. The second would be that of a person who wants to assure himself that the children are *learning* something; and since it is not clear that the new techniques produce this result, he would prefer (in default of good evidence to the contrary) that we stuck to methods whereby, at the very least, children were kept close to the notions of hard work, absorbing information, solving problems, and other activities which we are accustomed to associate with words like 'academic' or 'intellectual' – words which are often disdained by a person of the first type.

Techniques of this sort may, of course, be defended not as in themselves educational – that is, not as in themselves developing the pupils' cognitive grasp of important disciplines and ways of thinking – but as producing essential *preconditions* for education. A defender of them might say 'No, they don't themselves teach the kids much: but (1) they make them happier, or calmer, or less inhibited, and generally put them in a mental state in which learning is *possible*, and (2) by arousing their curiosity and interest, they put them in a mental state in which they *want* to learn – they provide them with motivation.' All this may (or may not) be true, but it is not enough. For though these methods may (1) permit and (2) encourage or motivate children to learn, are these the *only* ways in which we may do so, or even the most effective? Certainly they are more fashionable and 'liberal' than other ways we might think of, such as the fear of punishment, or the incentive of tangible rewards, but who is to say that they are more efficient? And even if all this be granted, we should still feel a gap: for surely there must be some techniques in the general area of moral education, or education of the emotions, which are techniques of *learning* rather than techniques which merely make learning possible or desirable.

We have also to remember that these and other techniques may produce benefits which we should not want to justify on specifically *educational* grounds. Not every good thing that can happen to a child, or that we give to him, comes under the heading of 'education'.

For instance, we may think it a good thing in itself for people simply to feel more (or less) *intense* emotion, so that they shall not be apathetic (or over-excited). There is this element, perhaps, in demands that we should help our children to be 'enthusiastic', 'idealistic', 'concerned', 'involved', 'sensitive to beauty', and so on. But there is also, in such words and phrases, something of the idea that the child's emotion should be *appropriate*: we do not want him simply to go into a state of ecstasy *when* he hears beautiful music, but also to be appreciative *of* it: we want him not just to be 'enthusiastic', but to direct his enthusiasm properly. In practice we may try to achieve both types of aim by the same method or technique: and I certainly do not wish to say that educational aims must always have priority. But I shall concentrate on them here, partly because they are more directly connected with the role of the *teacher* (rather than the psychologist or physiologist), and partly because our concern is with the education of the emotions in a fairly strict sense. Non-educational aims are important, but require to be distinguished and studied in their own right.

In considering these techniques as learning-methods, then, we may formulate one dimension that will be helpful to us. At one end of this dimension we have what might be called 'natural' expression. Pupils will talk, dance, form groups, and behave towards each other without any self-consciousness, without *thinking* very much about it. Some of these 'natural' activities may of course be rule-governed, as when children play games together, but the rules are likely to be fairly simple, and not concerned in any very sophisticated way with their own feelings or the feelings of their fellows. At the other end we have highly specialized subjects or disciplines, like science or English grammar or musicology, which are very far from 'natural', and represent the capital accumulated by many generations of human invention and scholarship. These disciplines represent ways of answering questions about things in the world (physical objects, words, musical sounds) which have been found most efficient and useful.

In education we try to get children to move from the first to the second. The difficulty with the education of the emotions is that we are ourselves not very clear about what disciplines we want to move them towards. We know that our aims are to give them awareness of their own and other people's feelings (EMP), the ability to regard others as equals (PHIL), and so on: but we cannot formulate disciplines in practical detail, in the way that we can with (say) science, because we are at a loss about how to fill in the surrounding framework. In science, we want the pupil to ask and answer such questions as 'How do the planets move?', and we are able to provide him with apparatus and procedures which have proved their worth for such questions – experiments, telescopes, some mathematics, and so on. In the education of the emotions, we can state the sort of question clearly enough – for instance, 'Why does so-and-so feel humiliated?', or 'Am I tired or depressed?', or 'Ought I to feel angry with him?': but we are not so sure about the apparatus and procedures.

However, the aims (PHIL, EMP, etc.), and the kind of questions we want pupils to answer, do give us *some* guidance: we have no excuse for just trying *anything* that interests the children and makes them more lively. Whatever particular techniques prove most efficient, it has at all cost to be remembered that they are intended as techniques of *learning*. This means that it is fatal to look with disfavour on such words as 'academic' or 'intellectual': for we have to give the children a *cognitive* grasp of their emotions – we have to get them to *know* certain things, not just to feel differently or act differently (objectives that might in principle be achieved better by drugs or behaviour-therapy than by education). We are trying to improve their *rationality* in the sphere of the emotions.

The importance of the dimension we formulated above, therefore, consists partly in the recognition that we have to get the children to move along it. But it is also important, in the context of the emotions, for another reason. The subject-matter dealt with by other disciplines – the planets and chemicals of science, the dates and events of history – remain constant for the child as he grows up: they are always available. But his own emotions, and what appear to him as the emotions of others, do not: they become masked, mutated, and distorted. I do not mean necessarily that they are changed for the worse, but they become altered and overlaid by successive adaptations to the world, so that it becomes progressively more difficult to recover their natural expression and their earlier history. Hence the particular importance of preserving or recreating the ability to feel and express feeling. For without this 'natural' subject-matter to work on, it will not be possible for the child to learn those disciplines which deal with the subject-matter.

There is thus a special educational point in what is (too vaguely) said about 'keeping the children interested' or 'lively'. It is not that the young child has a great interest in his emotions, and then loses it: that argument may apply to other topics also (e.g. it is said that young children have an initial interest in numbers and physical objects which they lose if we teach mathematics and science in old-fashioned ways). It is rather that the emotions themselves, their natural signs, and the child's awareness of them, go underground. We do not require a passionate belief in the Freudian unconscious to appreciate that our work here is largely a work of *recovery*, of making the pupil *conscious* of what he has forgotten, or repressed, or of what his fears and impulses have simply not given him time to notice. Because of this, the awakening of the emotions itself is of prime significance; and it may plausibly be argued that some of the techniques we are considering may do this job efficiently.

But once this has been said, we have immediately to turn to the quite different business of *learning* about the emotions. The difference is considerable. Thus certain types of what is supposed to be 'training' in the emotions – 'group dynamics', 'T-groups', and so on – plainly have the effect of awakening and arousing (or perhaps sometimes engendering) very vigorous emotions: and this may well be desirable, particularly for those whose consciousness is emotionally narrow and constricted. But whether such methods produce *insight* or *awareness*, let alone an actual change of feeling and behaviour, is a quite different question. The 'acting out' of emotions is one thing, and no doubt a necessary thing if the person would otherwise be quite unconscious of the emotions: but it is a far cry from a person learning to understand, come to terms with, and control himself and his feelings.

Our techniques and tools may thus be judged or assessed on very different grounds: and it is perhaps more important to be clear about these grounds than to commit ourselves too strongly to the merits of particular techniques or tools. If we are using, or thinking of using any of these techniques – drama, video-tape, films, dancing, discussion, and so forth – we must be careful to ask ourselves what it is supposed to be *for*. And now there seem to be four general sorts of answers we may give to this:

1. it achieves non-educational aims;
2. it helps to establish the *preconditions* of education or learning (relaxes the children, motivates them, etc.), and perhaps in particular

R

3. it *arouses* or *evokes* the emotions which are to be the subject-matter of this learning.

4. it is useful as part of a discipline whereby pupils *learn* about their emotions and how to control them, either (a) by putting the subject-matter of such learning before the children in a clearer form (we might say, it *objectifies*, *externalizes*, or *highlights* particular emotions, pieces of behaviour, attitudes, etc.), or (b) by helping to clarify various points about the emotions and behaviour, once they have been clearly highlighted.

How far any of these defences, as applied to any particular activity or tool, do in fact stand up is of course an open question: here (as always) it is probably better for practising teachers to get a clear grasp of these general objectives, and work out for themselves what sort of activities and tools are most likely to satisfy them, than to accept or reject particular instances without question. I want however to take a closer look at 4 above; for here at least we have a genuinely educational process which is also immediately capable of far more practical applications than are usually made. This is not to deny the importance of 1–3: it is simply that less practical sense can be talked on 1–3 without a good deal of further research.

There are three basic points I want to make:

(a) First, if we are considering the use of this 'hardware' and other devices to *learn* about one's emotions, we have to be clear just what it means to 'learn about one's emotions'. Thus we could imagine forms of teaching in which children learned

(i) in a very objective, quasi-scientific fashion, perhaps by reading text-books on psychology, that there were certain emotions common to all human beings;

(ii) to identify particular emotions in the abstract, so to speak: i.e. to be able to state what was meant by 'jealousy', 'fear', etc., and hence to be able to recognize these in principle;

(iii) to identify other people's (conscious or unconscious) emotions 'in the field', i.e. as they actually cropped up in everyday life;

(iv) to identify their own (conscious or unconscious) emotions in everyday life;

(v) the physical causes of various emotions (glands, drugs, etc.);

(vi) the psychological 'case-history' of various emotions (e.g. the

Freudian story of emotional development and change from infancy onwards).

And no doubt we could add to this list. For many of these items (perhaps all) we should need to familiarize the pupil with the *concept* of an emotion (belief, symptoms, actions and circumstances) as described in Part II of this book.

Now it is plain that particular tools or techniques will serve different items on this list more or less well. This is simply to point out that, even after we have dismissed 2 (techniques providing pre-conditions of learning) and 3 (techniques arousing or evoking emotions), and confined ourselves simply to our present interest, 4 (techniques for teaching about emotions), we still have to get clear what *kind* of 'learning about the emotions' we are interested in. No doubt all the kinds mentioned in the list above may be valuable: but they are different. For instance, (i), (ii), (v) and (vi) do not seem to lend themselves very much to 'progressive' techniques: we are concerned here with factual learning – visual aids may help, but we are here simply trying to teach the child some elementary psychology (just as, in explaining the concept of emotion, we are teaching him some elementary philosophy). On the other hand, (iii) and (iv) suggest the use of video-tape, tape-recorders and other 'objectifying' methods. It will be easier for the child to identify what he (or another) feels if he can *see* and *hear* himself evincing the symptoms and behaviour of the emotion: and he may acquire the habit of looking at himself more objectively in this way.

As moral educators, we are concerned with all the 'moral com-ponents': and the reader should be able to see how these components fit into the list above. Thus (iii) and (iv), for instance – the actual identification and awareness of emotions in everyday life – involve KRAT(1) as well as EMP: that is, the pupil must bring his knowledge of emotions to bear on actual cases as they crop up. Given a clear understanding of what we are trying to teach, it will not be too hard to imagine what sorts of methods might work. Thus we might think of tape- or video-recording a discussion, or a piece of social behaviour (say, in the playground). We show this to the pupils afterwards, playing the tape and stopping it at relevant points. We ask them questions, encourage them to comment, help them to identify what they felt at various points and why. We get them to have another discussion, or we look at another similar piece of behaviour next day. Perhaps we then act a prepared or impromptu scene relevant to some of the emotional situations or express them in mime or dance or movement: or we consider a piece of literature which includes them, or maybe even a piece of music or some other art-form. We might then try to see whether this not only made the pupils more aware (EMP), but also helped them to bring their awareness to bear in situations outside the classroom (KRAT(1)), so that perhaps they actually behaved and felt differently in the playground or in their homes.

(b) Secondly, in so far as we are concerned with 'learning' in a practical sense – that is, with the pupils' being able to identify emotions, as in (iii) and (iv), in their ordinary lives – then we are concerned ultimately with giving the child a truer picture of himself and others as subject to various emotions which he can recognize. It is not just a question of the pupil being able to say, of himself and and others at odd particular moments, 'Ah, now I feel angry, how interesting' or 'Coo, he is nervous, isn't he?' Of course this is important, but it is not the whole story. He needs also to be able to have what we might call a realistic 'profile' of himself and others, which will include such propositions as 'I am liable to feelings of irrational anger, even when I get my fair share, because I still feel that I somehow ought to get special treatment': 'John very often wrongly expects older people to be hostile to him, because his father treats him roughly and he thinks unconsciously that they will do the same', and so on.

This means that, as in most cases of learning, we are on a dimension ranging from the particular to the general. We want the pupils, indeed, to be able to identify particular instances of emotion, but also to be able to see these *as* instances of a general pattern in some individual (himself or another), and hence to use this more general knowledge to make more sense of other particular cases. We have to take the pupil to and fro, from particulars ('What is John feeling now? Yes, frightened') to the general ('John is generally frightened of authority-figures'), and back to other particulars ('What will he feel towards this boy who is in a higher form? Will he feel frightened of women?', etc.). So in using our video-tapes or our impromptu acting of our 'group therapy', we must all the time be encouraging the pupils to generalize, to put their particular bits of perception together, to make predictions about themselves and other people.

Of course this is difficult for anybody, even a skilled psychotherapist: but equally anybody can get better at it. It will do no harm for pupils to appreciate the considerable complexity, opaqueness and unpredictability of most human beings, and the different levels of emotion that underlie their conscious feelings. And it will do them a great deal of good to realize that, despite all the difficulties, sense *can* be made of oneself and other people in this area: that people do not work by magic, but for reasons which are often detectable if we put our minds to it: that even the oddest, most 'abnormal' cases are ultimately intelligible.

A further important point follows from this:

(c) Because education is to do with improving the pupil's rationality, cognition and awareness – rather than just getting him to *have* certain feelings, or *do* certain things – there is a sense in which it is necessarily connected with the use of language. If human beings were not language-using creatures, they would not be educable: if they were not able in principle to follow rules, act on reasons, and use criteria, we could not teach them to understand anything. Even in those areas of education which are concerned with art or 'creativity' or 'self-expression', we try to teach our pupils what is *appropriate*, to have *reasons* for assessing what they do. If this were not so, there would be nothing to distinguish an 'artistic' or 'creative' production from a mere mess or muddle.

Because of the connection between language and rule-following, it is likely that the pupil's ability to express himself in words is of the highest importance. By this I do not, of course, mean that he must be able to express himself according to the strict rules of grammar and syntax, or that he must have a wide and polysyllabic vocabulary: nor is it necessarily desirable that he should be able to express himself fluently and correctly on paper. The connection between language and learning is not of that kind. It is rather that, if a pupil cannot (in however halting a fashion) give some account, even to himself, of what he is doing and why he is doing it, then he is probably not acting rationally at all. The ability to give such an account (which necessarily involves some use of language) is a symptom, or a criterion, of whether he is acting as an intelligent and thinking human being, or just 'responding' or 'going through the motions' like an animal.

Hence, although all kinds of visual aids and stimuli, 'real-life'

R*

experiences, and 'creative situations' in the classroom are no doubt very useful methods of beginning the development of awareness, the acid test of such methods is whether they lead in the end to *understanding*: and understanding, as I have tried to show very briefly, necessarily involves concepts and language – not just 'responses'. It would be disastrous to identify some children as 'non-verbal' types, and to imagine that they can learn all they need to learn by purely visual means. Of course everything here depends on the type of child. As we know, there are some who have to be shown a great many practical instances and examples before they can grasp a concept properly: others may pick it up more quickly. But for both, the test of whether they know, or understand, or have learned something, must ultimately be their grasp of certain concepts. It is easy to make the mistake of supposing that a child has grasped a concept, when in fact all he can do is to repeat the teacher's words without understanding (that is, without being able to give his *own* account). But it is also easy to imagine a child has understood, when in fact he has merely been emotionally or sensorily affected by some experience.

I should guess, then, that encouragement of pupils' ability simply to *talk*, and also to use language when facing situations and solving problems, is likely to be crucial for education in the emotions, as for most other kinds of education. The ability to conduct (as it were) a kind of internal dialogue with oneself is, in effect, the ability to think. Any techniques and tools which develop this are to be greatly sought after: for otherwise we alternate between the two fashions of 'parrot-learning' on the one hand, and 'creative expression' on the other.

What emerges from these three points is that we must use our tools and techniques as aids to a serious, even in a sense an 'academic', *study*. It is utterly fatal to fall victim to a pseudo-antithesis of 'reason' and 'emotion': to treat emotion as something which either messes up our 'rational' learning or gives us a much needed holiday from it. If we do this, the way in which we deploy any methods is likely to be very superficial. The pupil has to see just *how* his emotions may assist, or militate against, his acquiring the moral components. To teach him this is not a matter of encouraging or suppressing 'good' or 'bad' emotions, but of taking his emotions as a serious *subject*, as something which he can learn about.

APPENDIX VII

The meaning of 'moral' and the planning of research

The title of this Unit's researches was given to us in the phrase 'moral education': and the area which we have allowed to fall under the heading of 'moral' is explained, and to some extent defended, in our first publication.[1] However, it is clear that alternative points of view are possible: and such points of view have been put forward recently, by very able and persuasive writers, to which some attention must be paid – not simply in order to defend our own position, but in order to make sure that the planning of other research under such titles as 'moral education' covers the right ground (and, incidentally, to justify the claim made in the Preface that the topics dealt with in this book fall within such ground).

A

1. On the one hand, there are those[2] who appear to think that an investigation of what is *meant by the word* 'moral' would settle some substantial question, perhaps the question of what sorts of considerations are relevant in moral argument. This might be true if, and only if, all those who used the word 'moral' would, after sufficient reflection and cross-questioning, come to see that they all used it in much the same way – that, for instance, they only talked of a 'moral issue' when other people's interests were either in fact involved or thought to be a relevant consideration, and never talked of a 'moral issue' when this was not the case. Even this, indeed, would hardly be sufficient: for it would give us agreement only on the use of 'moral' in the phrase 'a moral issue'. There might still be great differences when 'moral' was applied – as in fact it is applied – to the nouns 'person', 'action', 'fibre', 'behaviour', 'belief', 'knowl-

---

[1] *I.M.E.*, Chapters 1 and 2. Some of these reasons are reinforced by the more recent remarks of R. M. Hare in his review of G. J. Warnock's *Contemporary Moral Philosophy* in *Mind*, July 1968, pp. 436–7.

[2] E.g., G. J. Warnock, op. cit., p. 67 ff.

edge', 'doubt', 'problem', 'effect', 'virtue' and many others. But in any case there is no reason to suppose that such agreement could be reached, or that the use of 'moral' obeys – still less, that it *has* always obeyed – only one set of rules; indeed there is *some* reason to suppose the opposite, for most English-speakers live in a pluralistic society in which different concepts of morality, and hence different uses of 'moral', are likely to flourish.[1]

Thus let us suppose that the word 'science', as used by all or nearly all twentieth-century English-speakers, has a determinate meaning in the sense that there is agreement amongst all such speakers that only one form of enquiry counts as 'science' and other forms do not. Then to investigate the meaning of the word 'science', as used by twentieth-century speakers, would go some way towards elucidating that form of enquiry: for the rules governing the use of the word would be coextensive with the rules defining the form of enquiry. This would be true, even if (a) the 'agreement' among the speakers was (so to speak) unconscious, so that some cross-questioning and philosophical reflection was required to elicit the fact that all speakers followed the same rules when using the word – for some might *think* that they used the word according to different rules, but nevertheless *be wrong*; or (b) there were borderline or otherwise difficult cases, where the rules left it unclear whether some particular enquiry counted as 'science' or not.

Suppose however that the word 'moral' is not like the word 'science' as used by twentieth-century English-speakers, but has a variety of uses which is as wide as the variety we might find if we investigated (say) the uses of 'scientia' and 'science' from Lucretius to Einstein. Then it seems plain that we should not be able to talk about 'the' meaning of 'moral' or 'the' meaning of 'scientia/science', because the same words would be used by various groups of speakers in accordance with widely varying sets of rules, some of which might be coextensive with widely varying forms of discourse or enquiry. Investigation of the various meanings of the words might be *one way of* investigating the logic of these forms of enquiry, but certainly not the only way. As I have tried to show when dealing with 'religion',[2] the business of philosophers is to sort out and clarify the logic of different *possible* kinds of human activity and forms of

---

[1] See A. C. MacIntyre's *A Short History of Ethics* (Macmillan, N.Y. 1967), *passim*: also his review of *I.M.E.* in *New Society*, 29 February 1968.

[2] Chapter 2.

thought; and it is always an open question how much help the philosopher may get from investigating the meanings of particular words as used in particular cultures.

2. On the other hand there are those[1] who are impressed by the fact that 'just as moralities vary, so do concepts of morality, so does what counts as morality'.[2] There is no such thing as 'the' concept of morality: hence – such at least is the impression created by this line of argument – any attempt to define the scope of 'moral education' must be culture-bound, inasmuch as any concept of morality must be culture-bound; and hence, more generally, philosophy is perhaps not here very useful except in the service of historical and sociological description of various concepts of morality and moral practices.

This seems to me to run against the same rock as 1 above, but from an opposite direction. Let us suppose that the philosopher can elucidate the logic of a form of enquiry into natural phenomena which uses the methods of observation, experiment, hypothesis, quantification, prediction and all that most English-speakers today understand as 'science'. Suppose that this form of enquiry is sufficiently distinguished from other activities, to which (having duly elucidated them) we might attach labels such as 'astrology', 'sympathetic magic', 'religion' and so on. Then (a) it makes no difference to this elucidation whether or not 'science' is or was practised by particular social groups (just as clarifying the rules of a game – which one may indeed have invented oneself – does not imply that the game has actually ever been played); (b) it makes no difference what activities or enquiries various societies have applied the *word* 'science' to; (c) merely distinguishing between the various activities in this purely logical or philosophical way is plainly useful, if only because it presents people with a clearer set of possibilities; (d) the elucidation of the activities, taken in conjunction with certain human desires and purposes, may show that some activities fit these desires and purposes better than others – if we want to know how the world works and to predict events, we should do 'science' rather 'astrology'; and (e) this elucidation may show that some supposedly rational activities break rules which

[1] A. C. MacIntyre, op. cit.: see also C. C. W. Taylor's review in *Mind*, October 1968.
[2] MacIntyre, op. cit. (*New Society*).

should govern all forms of discourse – they are internally inconsistent, neglect facts, or are in other general ways irrational.

If this were not so, the introduction of 'scientific education' into
schools would appear as an arbitrary and culture-bound imposition
of *one* 'concept of science' on future generations. We might argue:
'Just as scientific practices vary, so do concepts of science, so does
what counts as science: and what right do we have to say that our
twentieth-century concept of science is *the* concept, or corresponds
to what science "really is"?' But to this we reply: 'We do not make
children learn about a form of enquiry which we call "science"
because we call it "science", or because it happens to be a popular
activity in our society: we rely ultimately neither on the use of the
word among twentieth-century English-speakers, nor on the mere
existence of a common social practice. Our defence for initiating
our children into this activity is that the activity is a rational and
a very worth-while one: and our defence for calling it "science" –
though we do not particularly mind calling it something else – is
simply that the activity bears *some* relation to what *some* people
mean by the word "science" – perhaps a close relation to what our
contemporaries mean by it.'

Despite these two views, then, I should still maintain that the
title 'moral education' can most sensibly be made to stand for the
kind of area we have suggested. This area includes a good deal of
education in the range of religious and other outlooks, and in the
sphere of the emotions, with which the present work is concerned:
and I should regard it as regrettable, both from a purely philosophical viewpoint and for the future of practical research, if it
were assumed *a priori* that the word 'moral' (1) had a determinate
meaning which covered a much smaller area, or (2) could not,
because of cultural variations in the concept of morality, be sensibly
used to determine a particularly (albeit very large) area, in which
certain abilities and skills could be shown to be necessary for
rational thought and behaviour, and could reasonably be imparted
to the children not only of this but of any other culture.

I do not imply by this that the question of how the word 'moral'
(or other words in other languages) is actually used by various
social groups is uninteresting or unimportant. But so far as twentieth-
century educators and other highly literate English-speakers are
concerned – and in so far as it is simply a question of picking a title
that is not misleading, it is this social group that interests us – I

should claim that the area as we have defined it is more in accordance with the actual usage of this group than with any other usages that may exist. This is not to say, of course, that even this group may not realize that this *is* their usage of 'moral': on the contrary, they may well feel inclined to give false accounts of how they use the word. That is why it seemed to me worth spending some time trying to correct such false accounts.[1] Such attempted correction always runs a certain risk: briefly, that whereas the philosopher wants his readers simply to *reflect* on their own usage, and end up by saying 'Oh, yes, I see now that I don't actually use "moral" in the way I thought I did, I use it in the way you describe', it may be that in fact he persuades them to *change* their own usage, so that they end up (or ought to end up if they were honest and clear-headed) by saying rather 'Yes, well, I did use "moral" in one way, but the considerations you have advanced have persuaded me to use it in another way henceforward.' But I should still guess that (in so far as people are persuaded at all) it is the former rather than the latter process, in the case of 'moral', that characteristically occurs.

The possibility of changing usage in the way just described opens up the prospect that the word 'moral' in the remote future may come to be used in a much more determinate way, at least when conjoined into terms like 'reason', 'view', and 'judgement'. Just as the impressiveness of one particular form of enquiry has persuaded people to adopt the term 'science' for this form and this alone, it may be that the importance of what I should now describe only as one *kind* of moral outlook – say, the utilitarian kind – becomes so generally accepted that the word 'moral' is used for this alone. And as long as everybody agreed, *and had good reason to agree*, that all questions like 'How ought I to live?' or 'What ought I to do?' should be settled within this particular form of discourse, this self-imposed restriction on 'moral' might be harmless. But it is obvious that the present position is very different, and that such a change (if it ever occurred) is likely to be far in the future.

To summarize these arguments briefly:

1. The fact that the word 'moral' (and corresponding words in other languages) has been used differently by different people goes no way to show that there is not an important and distinguishable human activity which may reasonably be called 'morality'.

[1] *I.M.E.*, Chapter 1.

2. The fact that different societies have given different contents to their moralities goes no way to show this either (and, incidentally, goes no way to show that these societies did not recognize or identify this human activity, nor that they did not sometimes use the word 'moral' to refer to it).

This is why we have preferred to take as a starting-point what R. M. Hare describes as 'anxiety about Plato's question "How ought we to live?"' [1] and R. S. Peters as the 'serious' asking of the question 'What ought I to do?' [2] Here it needs to be stressed (a) that we are not thereby concerned with a man's overriding principles and beliefs only in so far as they affect his deliberate *actions* (what he does), but also in so far as they affect his emotions (what he feels) and character (what he is); (b) that we are concerned not only with helping people to *answer* this question which they are supposed to be 'anxious' about or to raise 'seriously', but also with getting them to *be* anxious about the question and to *raise* it 'seriously', since it is quite evident that many people do not do this at all. Granted this, the most sensible approach seems to be in terms of a set of components or qualities, which are logically required for anybody to raise and answer this sort of question reasonably, and to act on the answer.

This is not to deny either that further questions may be asked about this area, or that alternative delimitations of the area are possible. Thus we may approach morality via the Oxford English Dictionary, and say that it is concerned with 'good and evil in relation to action, volitions or character' – with the will (heart, soul) rather than the mind or body; and we may attempt distinctions of various kinds within any delimitation of the 'moral' area. [3] We may also point out that many of the skills and abilities required by the morally educated person are not *specific* to this 'moral' area, and we may enter into the question of what types of error or deficiency we can regard as uniquely moral, or morally blameworthy. But I do not think any answers to these questions, important though they may be, would show our general approach to be thoroughly misguided.

---

[1] op. cit., p. 436.

[2] *Ethics and Education*, pp. 151–66.

[3] E.g., *I.M.E.*, pp. 72–92, where I attempt a rough break-down into 'other-people's-interests' cases, 'prudence and ideals' cases, and 'mental health' cases.

This approach produces an overall picture somewhat as follows: We use the phrase 'moral education' in the way described above. Within this very wide area, there will be certain sub-areas for which we commonly use titles like 'education of the emotions', 'education in personal relationships', 'social education', 'mental health', 'religious education', or (still more vaguely) 'learning to live', 'personal education', and so on. Wholly or in part, these sub-areas will fall within the domain of 'moral education'. According to how we define the scope and nature of these sub-areas, different components (out of the full range of components needed by the 'morally educated person') will be particularly relevant. Thus in this book I have laid stress on certain components, EMP and KRAT, and endeavoured to clarify them, in reference to the areas 'religious education' and 'education of the emotions': for the sub-area 'social education' – if I understand what is meant by this newly minted phrase – other components might be more relevant: perhaps GIG, if 'social education' is particularly concerned with knowledge about the norms and *mores* of one's society, (GIG(1)), or with developing 'social skills' (GIG(2)).

Of course this approach has its difficulties. But this brief account may help to make plain why we have adopted it. On any account of educational theory and practice, the area of 'moral education' indicates a large and important gap. Of the views criticized earlier in this Note, (1) seems to us to close only part of the gap by an unjustifiable restriction of 'moral'; and (2) makes no attempt to close it. Our approach tries to cover the whole gap. Of course it is not enough merely to weave a slender conceptual network over it: but it is our hope that, if this web is adequately strengthened by empirical findings and practical educational arrangements, it may eventually prove strong enough to keep out the forces of evil.

B

In this area, which I have argued above may fairly be called 'moral education', there is of course an enormous amount of research to be done. Certainly, the experimentation of teachers themselves, and the efforts of various other workers in such fields as curriculum development, are of the greatest importance. But the topic is so vast that I do not myself think it is much good nibbling at it, or simply trying out different things in the vague hope that they will work better: in particular, we cannot know this without adequate means of assessment, and such assessment must follow from the conceptual principles, and use a properly established taxonomy.

It implies no criticism of these workers, then, to say that a much more coherent and large-scale effort is needed. Educational subjects and topics, perhaps for the first time in history, are now beginning to come under consideration and be criticized seriously, from first principles: and if it is ridiculous to expect quick results even in areas about which we have some conceptual clarity (as for instance in the teaching of mathematics and science), it is even more absurd to expect this in such conceptually difficult areas as religious education or the education of the emotions.

Orthodox and reasonable fears, particularly in countries like the U.K. where education is highly decentralized, are:

(a) That researchers should not dictate to teachers or seem to do so;
(b) That academic research should not become 'ivory tower', instead of relating (in the short or long term) to what can actually be done in schools;
(c) That areas of research should not be *monopolized* by particular projects, lest only one point of view be put forward.

None of these fears, however, militates against the need for long-term projects of a particular kind in those areas that involve a good deal of hard thinking and conceptual clarity. Such areas are not receiving the sort of attention they deserve. Research relating to them at university level tends to become 'ivory tower', and to be done by single individuals rather than teams; short-term research by people of low academic ability fails to meet the case. Briefly: intellectually respectable and coherent projects are not related adequately to education, and projects that are so related are not adequately coherent.

Research adequate to deal with these areas should satisfy the following criteria:

(a) It must be interdisciplinary: in particular, the existence of conceptual problems must be appreciated, and those with adequate philosophical training are required as well as psychologists, sociologists, and others.
(b) It must be able to attract people of the highest academic ability, and the conditions of employment must be so arranged.

(c) Partly because of (b) above, and partly for other obvious reasons, the time-scale and resources must be ample: indeed, given that an effective team is set up, it would seem logically odd to suggest (in these areas) that the research would ever be *completed*.

(d) Conditions of communication must be excellent: this is a criterion of any serious interdisciplinary study, where much of the work involves members of the team learning each other's languages, without which the work would fragment and not be genuinely interdisciplinary at all.

(e) The team must be geared to the eventual production of results that will be of practical value.

Without such teams, it is unrealistic to hope either (i) that top-level academics will produce work that is both relevant to these areas *and* will be effectively communicated to educators and teachers (particularly the latter): or (ii) that a conceptually clear and coherent plan of research or plan of action will emerge from 'experience', 'development', 'trial and error', etc., or from short-term projects. Briefly, effective research projects in these areas are not adequately served by top-level academics on steering committees: you have to get them actually *working* on them, in conjunction with other academics on the team, and on the clear understanding that their work will be *used*.

This is not of course to say that short-term projects in these areas are necessarily useless for research purposes, but only that they will function more efficiently if they are started off by, or spring from, longer-term projects where the groundwork is adequately covered to begin with. This would bring educational research more into line with research in the natural sciences, where the position is more like that which I have argued for here.

In particular, as we have ourselves found in the area of moral education, the problems of assessment are so enormous that they necessitate a very large-scale and coherent effort. In Chapter 10 of this book I put forward a taxonomic framework, intended to summarize the various ways in which a man might fail to be emotionally educated'. The difficulties of devising assessment-methods for the components in such a framework are plainly considerable: yet it is equally plain that, without proper assessment-methods, not much valuable research work can be done. Hence, for those seriously interested in this field, the next stage must inevitably be the development of such methods. We have ourselves made some progress with this development: but there remains an enormous amount to be done by others.

It is important to realize that there are two kinds of difficulty here:

(1) The business of thinking in general about what assessment-methods would do the job is a hard one. For this is emphatically *not* a matter of simple tactics, or even strategy, in devising techniques for components which we all understand clearly, in the way in which we perhaps understand the various component-skills of (say) being educated in mathematics or Latin. There are many conceptual problems about what exactly it is that we are trying to test for. We have faced some of these problems in our first publication,[1] and in this book, but there will be others. Hence a good deal of hard interdisciplinary thinking is first needed, in which philosophers, as well as psychologists and social scientists, have a crucial part to play.

(2) The strategy of devising assessment-methods is complicated by the fact that, in this field above all others, a great many different types of method will be needed. We shall have to concern ourselves, for instance, not only with pencil-and-paper tests and questionnaires, but also with methods designed to inspect behavioural factors and the kind of reasoning that underlies overt behaviour: one thinks here naturally of simulation techniques, 'laboratory' test-situations, observation of behaviour in ordinary life, and so on.[2] All these methods have their disadvantages and advantages, and need to be used to reinforce each other. This will inevitably be expensive in money and man-power. But it will not be as expensive as doing nothing.

---

[1] *I.M.E.*, Chapter 4.
[2] See *Problems of Research in Moral Education* (Farmington Trust Research Unit).

A LIST OF THE 'MORAL COMPONENTS'

PHIL *attitude* respect/concern for others
    PHIL (1) respect for equals, justice, giving others their rights
    PHIL (2) benevolence, love, altruism

Separable into (a) *belief* that others count
             (b) *feeling* of respect/concern
             (c) appropriate *action* taken as a result of (a) and (b), at
                 least under normal circumstances.

EMP *ability* awareness of emotions
    EMP (1) (AUTEMP) awareness of one's own emotions
    EMP (2) (ALLEMP) awareness of others' emotions

Separable into (a) awareness of conscious emotions
             (b) awareness of unconscious emotions ('insight')

GIG *attainment* mastery of relevant knowledge
    GIG (1) knowledge of facts, 'knowing that'
    GIG (2) 'know-how', social and other relevant skills

KRAT (1) *attainment* 'bringing to bear' of above components
    KRAT (1a) 'noticing'
    KRAT (1b) 'thinking fully'
    KRAT (1c) 'taking responsibility'

The above, taken together, will lead to a decision about what to do or to feel. We mark this stage by the term DIK (when other people's interests are involved) or PHRON (when they are not).

KRAT (2) *attainment* translation of the decision into action

In the equation form:

$$\left. \begin{array}{l} \text{PHIL} \\ \text{EMP} \\ \text{GIG} \end{array} \right\} \text{plus KRAT (1)} \rightarrow \text{DIK/PHRON: plus KRAT (2)} \rightarrow \text{right} \left\{ \begin{array}{l} \text{action} \\ \text{emotion} \end{array} \right.$$

For purposes of assessment, i.e. of assigning some kind of 'score' to individuals or groups for each component, it is necessary to consider various dimensions and 'life-areas' for each component in which scores may differ. For instance, subjects may vary in the *range* of people for whom they have PHIL (high PHIL for gang-members, low for adults), or the *consistency* within that range: or they may have high KRAT (1) for sex but low for drug-taking: high GIG (1) for facts concerned with safe driving, low for facts concerned with laws and social norms: and so forth. These and some other assessment-problems are discussed in *Problems of Research in Moral Education* and *Testing and Assessment in Moral Education (Conceptual Notes).*[1]

[1] Pamphlets obtainable from the Farmington Trust.

Short Bibliography

The volume of literature relevant to this field is naturally immense. What follows is a 'short list' of those works that are, in my view, among the most useful and intelligible for anyone concerned with the particular problems dealt with in this book.

Philosophy of Religion
RENFORD BAMBROUGH, *Reason, Truth and God* (Methuen 1969)
KARL BRITTON, *Philosophy and the Meaning of Life* (C.U.P. 1969)
A. FLEW and A. C. MACINTYRE (eds.), *New Essays in Philosophical Theology* (S.C.M. 1963)
JOHN HICK (ed.), *Faith and the Philosophers* (Macmillan 1964)
BASIL MITCHELL (ed.), *Faith and Logic* (Allen and Unwin 1957)
D. Z. PHILLIPS (ed.), *Religion and Understanding* (Blackwell 1967)
NINIAN SMART, *Secular Education and the Logic of Religion* (Faber 1968)
JOHN WISDOM, *Paradox and Discovery* (Blackwell 1965)
L. WITTGENSTEIN, *Lectures and Conversations* (Blackwell 1966)

Philosophy of the Emotions
ARISTOTLE, *Rhetoric* (Loeb Classical Library, Heinemann 1967)
H. FINGARETTE, *Self-Deception* (Routledge 1969)
P. FOOT (ed.), *David Hume : a Symposium* (Macmillan 1966)
A. KENNY, *Action, Emotion and Will* (Routledge 1963)
A. C. MACINTYRE, *The Unconscious* (Routledge 1958)
R. S. PETERS, 'Emotions and the Category of Passivity', P.A.S. 1961–62
R. S. PETERS, *The Concept of Motivation* (Routledge 1960)
J. P. SARTRE, *Sketch for a Theory of the Emotions* (Methuen 1962)
M. WARNOCK, 'The Justification of Emotions', P.A.S. 1957
B. WILLIAMS, *Morality and the Emotions* (Bedford College, London 1966)

Philosophy of Education
R. ARCHAMBAULT (ed.), *Philosophical Analysis and Education* (Routledge 1965)
PAUL HIRST, 'Morals, Religion and the Maintained School' (British Journal of Educational Studies, November 1965)
T. H. B. HOLLINS (ed.), *Aims in Education* (Manchester University Press 1964)

R. S. PETERS, *Ethics and Education* (Allen and Unwin 1966)
R. S. PETERS (ed.), *The Concept of Education* (Routledge 1967)
I. SCHEFFLER (ed.), *Philosophy and Education* (Allen and Unwin 1966)
JOHN WILSON et al., *Introduction to Moral Education* (Penguin 1968)
JOHN WILSON, *Education and the Concept of Mental Health* (Routledge 1968)

Other philosophy
G. E. M. ANSCOMBE, *Intention* (Blackwell 1957)
ARISTOTLE, *Nicomachean Ethics* (Penguin 1955)
R. M. HARE, *Freedom and Reason* (O.U.P. 1965)
H. L. A. HART, *The Concept of Law* (O.U.P. 1961)
JOHN LUCAS, *Principles of Politics* (O.U.P. 1966)
BASIL MITCHELL, *Law, Morality and Religion* (O.U.P. 1967)
I. T. RAMSEY (ed.), *Christian Ethics and Contemporary Philosophy* (S.M.C. 1966)

Miscellaneous
E. COX, *Changing Aims in Religious Education* (Routledge 1966)
J. C. FLUGEL, *Man, Morals and Society* (Penguin 1955)
R. S. LEE, *Your Growing Child and Religion* (Penguin 1965)
H. LOUKES, *New Ground in Christian Education* (S.C.M. 1965)
NINIAN SMART, *World Religions* (Penguin 1966)
SIMON STUART, *Say* (Nelson 1969)
JOHN WILSON, *Moral Education and the Curriculum* (Pergamon 1969)

Educational methods
The reader who is anxious to learn more about methods of education in this area is advised (1) to take up the references in a forthcoming publication of the Farmington Trust, *Emotional Maturity* (Tim Beardsworth): (2) to consult the relevant educational journals, particularly *Moral Education* (Pergamon Press, Oxford): (3) to contact research units working in this field. Among the latter it may be useful to list

1. Farmington Trust Research Unit, 4 Park Town, Oxford.
2. Schools Council Research Unit in Moral Education, 15 Norham Gdns, Oxford.
3. Bloxham Research Unit (religious education), 15 Norham Gdns, Oxford.

Many other Schools Council research units also produce relevant material.

Index

Index of Topics

This is not a complete index, but the reader may find it helpful to have page references for the major topics, as listed hereunder: